LIST OF SUSPECTS

THE CIA
THE MAFIA
CASTRO
CUBAN EXILES
LYNDON BAINES JOHNSON
THE KREMLIN
RIGHT-WING EXTREMISTS
THE MILITARY-INDUSTRIAL COMPLEX
JIMMY HOFFA
LEE HARVEY OSWALD

Who masterminded the killing of JFK is a matter of debate. But one fact is not disputed by many—both in government and outside of it—who have questioned the Warren Commission findings. Too many people believe that Lee Harvey Oswald could not have been working alone—if indeed he even pulled the trigger of one of the rifles fired on that tragic November day.

In this book, you will find all the evidence to date about all the leads in the most momentous mystery of our time—

THE JFK ASSASSINATION
The Facts and the Theories

CARL OGLESBY was one of the founders and leaders of the Washington-based Assassination Information Bureau, credited with spurring the Congressional investigation that reversed the judgment of the Warren Commission. His writings include four books, hundreds of articles, and the afterword to Jim Garrison's *On the Trail of the Assassins*. Mr. Oglesby lives in Cambridge, Massachusetts.

OTHER BOOKS BY CARL OGLESBY

Containment and Change

The New Left Reader

The Yankee and Cowboy War

Who Killed JFK?

THE
JFK
ASSASSINATION

THE FACTS AND THE THEORIES

by

Carl Oglesby

Preface by Norman Mailer

A SIGNET BOOK

SIGNET
Published by the Penguin Group
Penguin Books USA Inc., 375 Hudson Street,
New York, New York 10014, U.S.A.
Penguin Books Ltd, 27 Wrights Lane,
London W8 5TZ, England
Penguin Books Australia Ltd, Ringwood,
Victoria, Australia
Penguin Books Canada Ltd, 10 Alcorn Avenue,
Toronto, Ontario, Canada M4V 3B2
Penguin Books (N.Z.) Ltd, 182–190 Wairau Road,
Auckland 10, New Zealand

Penguin Books Ltd, Registered Offices:
Harmondsworth, Middlesex, England

First published by Signet, an imprint of New American Library,
a division of Penguin Books USA Inc.

First Printing, May, 1992
10 9 8 7 6 5 4 3 2 1

Carl Oglesby, "Afterword: Is the Mafia Theory a Valid Alternative?" from
Jim Garrison, *On the Trail of the Assassins* (New York: Sheridan Square Press,
1988), pp. 297–308; copyright © 1988 by Jim Garrison.

Ⓟ REGISTERED TRADEMARK—MARCA REGISTRADA

Printed in the United States of America

For my wife, Sally, with love

Contents

Preface
Norman Mailer

Reading Carl Oglesby on the assassination of JFK offers the pleasure of following a first-rate mind through the processes of its thought. For a political writer, Oglesby's literary instincts are exceptional. He comprehends what so few authors of that genre begin to understand—which is that style is not the servant of our desire to inform others how to think, but the precise instrument by which we attempt to locate the truth.

So, his contribution to the JFK case has been not only illuminating but crucial. If we are left in intellectual limbo and learn no more about what happened in Dallas, then the President's death will remain obsessive in our history. We really cannot calculate the price of living with this unsolved crime, and Oglesby, in addition to his writing, has worked directly on the case. The Assassination Information Bureau, which Oglesby helped to found, and then co-directed, did a great deal to force the assassination question back on the agenda of the Congress.

So his efforts appeal to me greatly. He is one of the few contemporaries I read for the pleasure of clarifying my own thinking.

Introduction

If only in terms of sheer span of national attention and the persistence of controversy, the assassination of John F. Kennedy easily appears to be the political crime of the American century. All students of contemporary U.S. politics must visit its mystery, whether they come to solve it, to expose it as a chimera, or merely to reflect on its haunting persistence.

So was Kennedy killed by a lone nut or a conspiracy? The debate is long-standing and ongoing. It is intense and often nasty. The lone-nut side calls the conspiracy side naive, paranoid and alarmist. The Warren revisionists call the lone-nut side cynical, paralyzed and complicit. There is not much room for indifference, and there is no third position.

It took me a long time, ten years—that is, until 1973—to get focused well enough on the assassination to write about it and to try to act on it politically. I think this was because I was active in the anti-war movement and had the feeling that one unpopular cause was enough. But once I wandered into the case in 1973, I have never found my way back out. That same year, I linked up with a handful of other free-lance writers in Cambridge who had become equally fixated on the Dealey Plaza shooting. Since it seemed a large thing to let go of, we decided to see if there was something we could do about it.

As we (and the overwhelming majority of the American people) read the evidence of Dealey Plaza, at least two people shot at Kennedy; and the one who killed him fired from the front, not from the rear where Oswald was. We saw indications that Oswald was no loner and that he was very possibly the patsy he claimed to be. It appeared, moreover, that the Nixon administration was trying to conceal the truth of Dealey Plaza just as it was trying to conceal the truth of the Vietnam War. And if we were right about all this, then the question of JFK's assassination was the most fundamental political question of our period. It was the central act of the escalation of the Vietnam War. Why was the assassination not being treated politically?

The core group included Bob Katz, Dave Williams and Harvey Yazijian, who had been lecturing on the assassination to overflow audiences on college campuses across the country. The four of us formed a political-action collective dedicated to organizing a popular movement for a new investigation. In some distemper we called ourselves the Grassy Knoll Debating Society. We were soon joined by others—Jim Kostman, Jeff Goldberg, Marty Lee and Jeff Cohen—and in due course acquired a more usable name, the Assassination Information Bureau, and an advisory board that included David Dellinger, Allen Ginsberg, Tom Hayden, Murray Kempton, Norman Mailer, Jack Newfield, Phillip Nobile, Marcus Raskin and Peter Dale Scott.

The purpose of the AIB was to try to do for the JFK assassination what the student movement was doing for the Vietnam War. We wanted to use the weapons of mass protest to force the JFK-conspiracy question to the top of the national agenda. We wanted to make the whole culture respond to the question "Who killed JFK?", with its implicit assertion that Oswald did not. We wanted to help find the killers, see them prosecuted, and purge the government of their influence. We did not know or care to ask if our convictions were "politically correct," and we did not feel that we had to justify them in terms of some over-arching social program.

Rather, as I understood it, we started with extremely basic propositions.

1 an unknown group conspired to kill JFK;
2 we—as Americans—cannot feel good about our government again until we satisfy ourselves on this matter; and
3 all of us should feel personally involved with this issue because it reflects so directly upon the quality of our citizenship.

The AIB achieved a lot with few resources. In our best year, 1978, we raised $80,000. With this we rented offices in Washington's Dupont Circle and a house a short walk away. We supported two full-time people and occasionally a handful of others part-time. We put out a substantive newsletter every other month and filled a file drawer with occasional membership mailings and a stream of technical briefing documents for the congressional Assassinations Committee's staff. The chief counsel of the Assassinations Committee, G. Robert Blakey, at a soiree in New York in 1979, after it was all over, said to me, "Without you guys, there never would have been a new investigation to begin with."

As to what the AIB thought of the committee, despite serious failures, the Assassinations Committee did at last stumble upon proof of conspiracy in the JFK case, although the earth scarcely moved. And for whatever it was worth—let democracy pray that it was worth something—the AIB was indubitably a part of the Assassinations Committee's picture. The AIB was the Washington focal point of resistance to the Warren Commission cover-up, and it was that resistance that made the committee necessary.

How should we view this?

First we can reflect that an official voice, a congressional committee, actually affirmed, on the record, a finding of conspiracy in the JFK case. Then we can see how little difference this has made a dozen years later. These two facts are mind-boggling.

So the AIB's story is mixed. We achieved magnitudes more than we had thought possible, but we began without the least understanding of what was needed, so that what we thought possible turned out to be irrelevant.

When Arnold Dolin of New American Library/Dutton proposed that I select a book's worth of my short pieces on the assassination, naturally I was gratified the way any writer would be. And I immediately began to hope that, from all the bits written along the way, I might be able at least to cast the shadow of the story of what it meant to be in long-term opposition on the JFK issue, probably the most divisive issue of our time.

Now that the final selection is made and I am introducing an actual rather than an ideal book, I must admit that I regret my failure to report more often, through the two decades covered by these pieces, on my more strictly human feelings about the material I was dealing with every day. An important part of organizing around the JFK murder in Washington in the age of Watergate was the lifestyle that such work carried with it—a lifestyle immersed in a certain lower level of the Washington political scene with its white wine and brie and its crash houses and its safe houses.

* * *

The JFK assassination issue is by this time nearly thirty years old and has its own history. This history divides into several distinct passages, which I see as follows:

First was the period of the Kennedy administration from its election victory in November 1960 to the shooting three years later. Our foreknowledge that the New Frontier ends in Dallas in a still-unsolved crime tempts us to view this period as a prelude, and to search it for clues and prefigurings. Who had a motive to kill JFK? Who had the means to do so? Who had the opportunity? As with any fine mystery, there is an embarrassment of suspects: the Mafia, the CIA, the FBI, the Texan extremists, the domestic oil industry, the military-industrial complex, the anti-Castro Cubans, the pro-Castro Cubans. Who indeed did not have a bone to pick with JFK?

Then came the shooting, the Warren Commission investigation, and the complex public reaction to the commission's report. The early critics of the Warren report weighed in. Its defenders were potent, but the public's sympathy quickly drifted to the side of the revisionists.

Then came the Jim Garrison–Clay Shaw case in 1967–69. The New Orleans prosecutor thought he had solved the crime, and that as a result the CIA might have to fall. When he failed to prove his charges against Shaw, he went into a spin, lost his district attorney's office and retired temporarily to write a novel about the JFK assassination, *The Star Spangled Contract*.

The issue momentarily faded behind the Garrison failure, the stupendous crises of 1968—not least among them the assassination of Martin Luther King and Robert Kennedy—and the pre-Watergate years of the regime of Richard Nixon and Henry Kissinger.

But in 1972 President Nixon's private Plumbers were caught red-handed in the files of the Democratic party's national headquarters in the Watergate complex in Washington D.C., thus inaugurating the Watergate era. At this point, even the people in the bleachers could see the government cheating at its own game. From now on, there was no more scoffing at conspiracy theories—for a while.

Hard upon the forced resignation of President Nixon came two spectacular discoveries by the Senate Intelligence Committee. The first was that the CIA had hired the Mafia to murder Fidel Castro. This settled the uncertainty as to whether the CIA would (a) actually regard assassination as a permissible instrument of policy and (b) make a secret pact with organized crime. The second was the discovery that both the CIA and the FBI had withheld important information from the Warren Commission, notably about their pre-assassination relations with Oswald. In particular, the world now learned—twelve years later—that Oswald had visited the Dallas FBI office a few days before the assassination to leave a letter for FBI agent James P. Hosty, Jr., whose name was in Oswald's address book, and that the FBI inexplicably destroyed this letter a few hours after Jack Ruby murdered Oswald.

Now we all saw with our own eyes that national political life did indeed have a dimension of conspiracy to it, that there was a secret ground between the political bureaucracy and the national-security elite where the power struggle routinely went off the books.

As though all this was not enough, this amazing period in the mid-1970s also saw the murder of two key mobsters, Sam Giancana (1975) and John Roselli (1976), just before they were to testify to the Senate about their roles in the CIA-Mafia plots of the early 1960s.

What was clear enough already now became unavoidable, and public rejection of the Warren *Report* rose to 87 percent—virtual unity—finally motivating the House of Representatives to respond. On September 17, 1977, Congress passed H.R. 1540, creating the Select Committee on Assassinations. The committee's mandate was to reinvestigate the murders of JFK and Martin Luther King. Its chairman was a lame duck from Virginia, Thomas Downing, who had been trying to get a congressional JFK initiative underway since 1975.

The Assassinations Committee was continued by the 94th Congress under a new chairman, Henry Gonzalez, a Texas Democrat. The committee's rocky start-up phase was dominated by a loud and angry public feud between the new chairman, Gonzalez, and the committee's chief counsel, Richard A. Sprague of Philadelphia, whom the old chairman, Downing, had appointed. Both Gonzalez and Sprague were conspiracy buffs, but Sprague had laid the foundations of his investigation under Downing. When Gonzalez inherited the chairmanship in 1977 and tried to impose his own program, Sprague fought back.

Gonzalez was at last forced off the committee by colleagues who sided with Sprague on how to investigate the case. But then Sprague had to go too because no chief counsel can be allowed to win a congressional power struggle with a committee chairman and get away with it.

But soon the committee appointed a new chairman, Representative Louis Stokes, a Democrat of Cleveland, and hired a new chief counsel, G. Robert Blakey, an academic lawyer then at Cornell (now at Notre Dame) who had worked in the Robert Kennedy Justice Department's task force against organized crime. The committee stopped talking to the press and went behind closed doors to get its act together. By the fall of 1977, its investigative staff was up to speed and its probes of the JFK and King killings were making progress.

The most sensational chapter of the Assassinations Committee's story opened at a meeting between Chief Counsel Blakey and a group of Warren critics whom the committee had summoned to Washington for a weekend consultation. The purpose of the meeting was to ensure that serious leads developed by individual investigators were known to and understood by the committee.

At that meeting, one of the more widely respected critics, the JFK archivist Mary Farrell of Dallas, handed an audio tape over to Chief Counsel Blakey. She said it might contain a record of the actual Dealey Plaza gunfire.

This was an acoustic tape copy of a recording made on the Dictabelt system on which the Dallas police kept their daily radio log. The recording system was apparently activated by accident when a motorcycle policeman riding in the motorcade (well behind JFK's limo) got his mike button stuck in the on position.

The reason Farrell was uncertain of what the recording might prove was that its quality was so poor. Everyone could hear several bursts on the tape, but there were many more bursts than possible shots, and not even experts could be sure that a given burst was a gunshot and not a motorcycle backfire or mere static.

Not, at least, with the unaided ear. But Farrell wondered what a well-equipped acoustics laboratory could make of this tape. Perhaps a little computer science could coax out its hidden signals.

The Acoustical Society of America recommended that the committee take the gunfire tape to the Cambridge acoustics laboratory of Bolt, Beranek and Newman. BBN agreed to take on the analysis. In due course, in 1978 it reported that it had detected four shots.

This was a sensational discovery. It was one more shot than the Warren Commission had found, but much more significant was the fact that the third shot followed far too quickly after the second to have been fired by Oswald's weapon. The tape seemed to prove that at least two gunmen fired in Dealey Plaza.

Such a finding had to be confirmed by separate technical analysis. The committee hired two other ASA scientists, Professors Mark Weiss and Ernest Aschkenasy of Queens College of the City University of New York, who, like the people at BBN, had done similar high-tech detective work for the FBI and NASA.

Weiss and Aschkenasy were experts in the analysis of echo patterns. In a tour de force of scientific ratiocination, and working with an acoustical model of Dealey Plaza and echo patterns now audible on the cleaned-up tape, they could pinpoint the location of the motorcycle transmitter at the moment each shot was fired. This is how the motorcycle patrolman with the stuck microphone was discovered. And, lo, he told the committee that he had been having trouble with his switch all day.

Moreover, Weiss and Aschkenasy said they determined that the first, second and fourth shots were fired from behind JFK, while the third shot was fired from the area on JFK's right-front quarter known as the grassy knoll. Dozens of eyewitnesses had insisted to the Warren Commission that a shot had been fired from that area, so the expert finding rang true.

The acoustics tape thus appeared to prove once and for all that the attack on the President went beyond any single person. How far beyond could not be told, but at least it now appeared certain—so we supposed—that the hypothetical Dallas conspiracy did in fact exist.

The committee's time expired a few weeks after its presentation of the acoustics evidence. Much of its investigative work remained unfinished. But it had at least removed the question of conspiracy in JFK from the realm of debate. An enormous controversy seemed to have been finally resolved. Now perhaps something would happen.

But not so fast. The Carter Justice Department, to which the committee handed over its findings and its leads, became the Reagan Justice Department, which dallied, then convened another panel of scientific experts to review the fourth-shot and grassy-knoll-shot findings. Under Harvard Professor Norman Ramsey, this third panel, in 1982, rejected the BBN finding of four shots on grounds that it was based on faulty mathematical analysis. BBN and Weiss and Aschkenasy protested but had neither funds nor time with which to repeat their tests and amend their work.

Soon thereafter a devoted student of the case, Steve Barber, working with a commercially produced 45-rpm vinal copy of the gunfire tape, discovered that a voice signal was faintly audible in the background behind the four shots. Barber realized that the voice was that of Sheriff Bill Decker telling his men to search the grassy knoll: "Move all men available out of my department back into the railroad yards there . . . to try to determine just what and where it happened down there."

Clearly, these words were spoken well after the shooting. The Ramsey panel decided that the committee's four "shots" were therefore only random bursts of static.

A BBN spokesman defended the original analysis and speculated on possible causes of the overlap of the shots and the later voice signal. The original recording device, he observed, was a two-channel system in which a needle for each channel recorded signals in a certain part of a single belt. Maybe one of these needles was somehow physically displaced. Maybe the machinery got bumped and a needle jumped back to record over a previous recording, or skipped onto the wrong track.

But to prove that something like this actually happened would take money for new tests. Where would it come from with the Assassinations Committee by this time long defunct?

And there the debate foundered. The perceived ambiguity of the acoustical evidence could not be overcome. In 1982, the Justice Department closed its investigation.

In the ensuing years of the Reagan administration, I suppose I was not the only activist in this argument to think that the JFK case might at last be in the process of sinking out of sight. Until then, Dealey Plaza had been a continuing current story, but now it seemed to be slipping away into the domain of history, no less mysterious than before but no longer on anyone's political agenda.

The story might have ended there. No, not *ended*. The JFK story cannot end until the assassination riddle is either solved or otherwise dispelled. On the other hand, at some point it may well undergo a metamorphosis that carries it away from attention.

Indeed such a metamorphosis appeared to be in process throughout the Reagan and early Bush years, when there no longer seemed anything at all to do about the case but to brush one's teeth in the morning. New books continued to advance novel and powerful conspiracy arguments, and a huge public majority remained steadfast in rejecting the lone-assassin theory.

But there was no longer the former sense of purpose to the skepticism. Now I heard people saying, "So there was a conspiracy. So the government covered it up. So what else is new?"

Then in late 1991 came Oliver Stone's movie *JFK*, espousing the mother of all JFK conspiracy theories in the central pit of popular culture. To the vast consternation of orthodox pundits, the case came howling suddenly back to life, the debate soon rejoined as never before, Warren defenders angrier than ever, Warren critics more excited. The conservative columnist and TV-news pundit George Will actually accused Warren revisionists of being "worse than the people who deny the Holocaust."

But such nastiness did not stop the American people.

By early February, a CBS polled showed a 73-percent support for a conspiracy theory of some kind. Did the CIA have a hand in it? Thirty-five percent thought so.

What will come out of the current surge of enthusiasm for the case? It now seems quite possible that certain new JFK files will be published. As of early 1992, former Assassinations Committee chairman Stokes seems about to introduce legislation that will open up the files of the Assassinations Committee (maybe two million pages). Stokes also seeks to publish the remaining files of the Warren Commission, the FBI, the CIA and the military intelligence services. Former President and Warren Commissioner Gerald Ford and Senator Edward Kennedy have recently expressed support for the Stokes initiative.

The whole revisionist community is jumpily insisting that there will be no compelling, sweeping revelations in these files. For one thing, they will all be heavily censored (''redacted,'' in the term of art) before reaching the eyes of the public. This may be why the government files stand a chance of actually being ''released.'' They will be released, that is, in censored form. The mainstream media will show up in the reading room of the National Archives, shine their TV lights on hundreds of boxes containing millions of pages, and blink in their usual incomprehension. That same day the first editorials will remind us of having said all along that there would be nothing new here because (damn it) there is nothing new to know. The conspiracy people, these editorials will say, should now have the grace to shut up, sit down and leave it alone.

Without question, however, the Stokes move to open the files is good and should be fought for and passed. Even censored, the documents *will* yield clues. And in any case, the American people need the bracing experience of getting the government to do something they want it to do.

I have organized these occasional pieces on the JFK assassination generally along the historical route sketched out above.

Section I presents two pieces devoted to the question of "conspiracy theory" as such. Despite the long chain of governmental abuses of trust that might by now have convinced a less patient intelligentsia that something is rotten in Denmark, I think most literate Americans still accept the authority of the mediated surface. They suppose they must shun conspiracy speculation as a crude, even a somewhat suspect waste of time. I felt a need to confront this prejudice straight away.

Section II confronts a related prejudice: that analysis of events must choose between "broad historical forces" and conspiracy. This dichotomy is false. "Forces" and "conspiracies" are not mutually exclusive. Rather, they embody the same energy but in different quantum states. It is only broad forces that give conspiracy its context, and it is only conspiracy analysis that reveals the innermost destructive potential—the dialectic—of broad forces.

Section III is an edited and updated chapter from my 1976 book, *The Yankee and Cowboy War,* laying out the basic details of the Dealey Plaza conspiracy arguments. This section goes hand-to-hand against the lone-assassin fantasy.

Section IV deals with the congressional reinvestigation of the case in the late 1970s. This is the longest and most concrete part of the book for two basic reasons. First, the technical work done by the Assassinations Committee remains the most sophisticated and complete attempt made to date by an official body to determine precisely what happened in Dallas. Second, this was also the period of my most total absorption in the issue. When the House created the Assassinations Committee in 1976, the AIB moved its office from Cambridge to Washington, and Jeff Goldberg and I went to Washington to be its co-directors.

This is the place for me to say that those two years with Goldberg gave me the most rewarding partnership of my life. Each of us was solid in some respect in which the other was soft. Goldberg and I co-authored two of the pieces reprinted here, one for the AIB's bi-monthly magazine, *Clandestine America,* and one for the *Washington Post*'s Sunday "Focus" section. Goldberg was also my first reader of choice of everything I wrote on the case in the Assassinations Committee period.

Section V reprints three pieces, two of which bear directly and one indirectly on the explosive arrival of Oliver Stone's *JFK,* which immediately put the debate about the JFK assassination on a whole new footing.

Section VI presents a table with several leading answers to the question "If Oswald (alone) did not do it, who did?" This is not a question that can be answered today, but that does not mean that it can be ignored. Some sacrifice of detail is involved, but I think the tabular display used in this section helps reveal the key differences and similarities between the several theories that compete for appreciation.

Finally, a piece written for this book takes up the question of what we must do to get closer to truth and justice in the JFK assassination, how to lay the ghost to rest and be set free from this haunting case.

I

On Conspiracy

Mainstream political thinking rescues itself from the need to confront evidence of conspiracy in JFK's murder primarily by invoking a deep-seated faith that the world is really made of much trickier stuff. The writer of one all too typical work attacking conspiracy speculation about the assassination quoted a passage from Sigmund Freud asserting that "it takes a high degree of sophistication to believe in chance; primitive fears are allayed more easily by a devil theory of politics."

This is argument *ad hominem* with a vengeance. One does not quite know how to approach an adversary consoled in advance by Freud, no less, in the self-flattering unction that the real subject in the JFK assassination dispute is the "primitive" character of certain sensibilities, a lack of "sophistication" that exposes them to irrational fears. Forget Iran-Contra, forget Watergate, just get analyzed.

Following are two attempts to speak reason to the happy face. By coincidence, both are from papers delivered before an audience. The first passage, "Paranoia As a Way of Knowing,'' is from a paper I read at a joint MIT-Harvard seminar in 1973 when I was teaching part-time at MIT, and I must confess I still like the way it puts the shoe on the other foot. The second, ''On Seeing the Invisible State,'' is updated from a speech I delivered at the Massachusetts Libertarian Party's meeting in Boston on December 15, 1991, to celebrate the two-hundredth anniversary of the Bill of Rights. Thus, for whatever it might be worth, the first of the following two pieces was written at the outset and the second at the end of the two-decade period covered by this book. The first one seems to me much the more confident. But as to what an ''internal coup'' might look like and how it might transpire in detail, the second one is much more informative.

1

Paranoia As a Way of Knowing*

A word about paranoia as a political concept.

This is, yes, an odd subject, but it comes up because, as we all notice, the defenders of received ideas so often challenge the conspiracy critic's sanity. It seems one can take comfort in the notion that conspiracy theories arise not in the facts surrounding us but in a kind of madness.

Our liberal heritage teaches us to imagine that the world operates in accordance with natural laws, and that these laws can be understood. This is the underlying faith of contemporary political science and sociology, which are loosely called "sciences" less because of anything they do or produce than because they have learned how to adopt a certain tone of voice.

This is why, so it seems, the liberal imagination does not want to read a history made by acts as random-seeming as assassinations and as "ahistorical" or "apolitical" as conspiracies of fanatics. To concede the power of such modes of activity—of assassinations as such, of conspiracies as such—is somehow, for the orthodox political mind, to concede that the lawfulness

*Notes for a lecture at MIT, 1973.

of social nature can be disrupted by a fool or two and thus that the human world cannot finally be understood. And if it cannot be understood, how can it be controlled? And if it cannot be controlled, how can there be progress?

A part of the abiding power in our lives of the political murders of the 1960s is their awful affront to our sense of living in a reasonably well-known and predictable world. The gunplay is a challenge and a blow, concrete, bloody and of immense practical consequence in the world of daily political life. That affront can be rebuffed with spirit and good police work but only if reason's partisans are willing to enter into the struggle against the political madness of the conspirator, of Cassius's "honest Brutus" and "honest Casca" and the like, *as well as* against the madness of the state, that shop where madness does its really serious work.

This means we ought not be too paranoid about paranoia, ought not be too afraid of ambiguity and irreducible doubt, too afraid of confronting worst-case scenarios and outer-limit possibilities on the grounds merely that they disarm, dehumanize and defeat us. We ought not be too afraid of opening the closet door in a dark room in the middle of a bad dream—at least in theory.

I am trying to say that liberal political criticism, even in its mightiest East Coast redoubts, must at some point be willing to meet madness on its own terms, must stare it in the eye and not melt in hysteria or freeze in paralysis. Reason must come down from its castle and greet madness like a friend.

For ten rather awful years—we see how the war grinds on—the castle has declined to respond except in hysteria and paralysis to the events of that weekend in Dallas when Kennedy and Tippit and Oswald were murdered one upon the other. I am willing to assume this is because the castle is busy trying to figure out what in the world to do about Vietnam.

But I am afraid that JFK's murder might have been the first step to the fully escalated Vietnam War we see today, that JFK's murder and the great escalations of the Johnson-Nixon period were one. I think we must be willing to contemplate this possibility. If the assassination of Kennedy turns out to be the true beginning of the escalation to full-out conventional force, if revving up the Vietnam War was the underlying objective of the JFK assassination, then the humanities' disdain for "paranoid conspiracy theories" only intensifies the madness.

The madness, I mean, in which the same intellectual elite that is so put off by what it disdains as "conspiracism," as though it were an optical disorder, tries to fill the void with a pallid academic dress-up discipline it self-pamperingly calls "psychohistory."

Mainstream liberalism now stands with ten years of silence on the problem of the Dallas murder and conspiracy from the right. Perhaps this silence is in memory of its former struggle against the Red Scare politics of the 1930s, '40s and '50s, when the issue was conspiracy from the left and liberalism was on the defensive. Liberalism's contempt for "the paranoid style," in any case, keeps it from facing what may after all prove to be its real enemies, the assassins of JFK.

The question about the JFK assassination for serious thinkers to face is simple but very hard: Does the liberal tradition—does liberal education—have the resources to survive the collapse of the illusion of progress? Can it entertain the conspiracy thesis about its current real situation? Can it grasp its growing imprisonment within an infrastructure of secret knowledge? Can traditional liberalism understand the real events that brought Johnson and Nixon to power, the forces for whom the Vietnam War is now being fought? And can liberalism entertain the thought of conspiracy when it implies a fait accompli and a coup d'etat?

2

Seeing the
Invisible State*

The occasion of the two-hundredth anniversary of the Bill of Rights reminds us to be very worried about the growth since World War II of a national-security oligarchy, a secret and invisible state within the public state.

The national-security state has come upon us not all at once but bit by bit over a span of several decades. It is useful to review the episodes—the ones that are now known to us—through which the current situation evolved.

1. 1945: The Gehlen Deal

Wild Bill Donovan of the wartime Office of Strategic Services, the OSS, proposed to President Roosevelt before the war was over that the United States should set up a permanent civilian intelligence agency, but military foes of Donovan leaked his plan to a conservative journalist, Walter Trohan, who exposed the idea in the Chicago *Tribune* and denounced it as "an American Gestapo."[1]

---

*Speech, Massachusetts Libertarian Party: 200th Birthday of the Bill of Rights, December 19, 1991.

But only a few weeks after this, after Roosevelt's death and the inauguration of Harry Truman, in the utmost secrecy, the Army was taking its own much more dangerous steps toward a quite literal American Gestapo.

Days after the Nazi surrender in May 1945, a U.S. Army command center in southern Germany was approached by Nazi Brigadier General Reinhard Gehlen. Gehlen was the chief of the Nazi intelligence apparatus known as the FHO, Foreign Armies East. The FHO ran spy operations throughout East Europe and the Soviet Union during the war, and it remained intact during the late-war period when the rest of the Wehrmacht was crumbling. In fact, the FHO was the one part of the Nazi war machine that continued to recruit new members right through the end of the war. SS men at risk of war crimes charges in particular were told to join with Gehlen, go to ground, and await further orders.

Gehlen presented himself for surrender to the American forces with an arrogant, take-me-to-your-leader attitude and was for a few weeks shunted aside by GIs who were unimpressed by his demand for red-carpet treatment. But he had an interesting proposal to make and was soon brought before high-level officers of the Army's G-2 intelligence command.

Gehlen's proposal in brief: Now that Germany has been defeated, he told his captors, everyone knows that the pre-war antagonism between the Soviet Union and the United States will reappear. Who emerges with the upper hand in Europe may well depend on the quality of either side's intelligence. The Soviets are well known to have many spies placed in the United States and the American government, but the Americans have almost no intelligence capability in East Europe and the Soviet Union. Therefore, Gehlen proposes that the United States Army adopt the FHO in its entirety, including its central staff as well as its underground intelligence units, several thousand men strong, throughout East Europe and the U.S.S.R. Thus, the FHO will continue doing what it was doing for Hitler—that is, fighting Bolshevism—but will now do it for the United States.

The OSS was formally dismantled in the fall of 1945 at the very moment at which General Gehlen and six of his top aides were settling into comfortable quarters at the army's Fort Hunt in Virginia, not far from the Pentagon. For the next several months, in highly secret conversations, Gehlen and the U.S. Army hammered out the terms of their agreement. By February 1946, Gehlen and his staff were back in Europe, installed in a new village-sized compound in Pullach, from which they set about the business of reactivating their wartime intelligence network, estimated at between 6,000 and 20,000 men, all of them former Nazis and SS members, many of them wanted for war crimes but now (like the famous Klaus Barbie) protected through Gehlen's deal with the United States both from the Nuremberg Tribunal and the de-Nazification program.

Thus it was that the superstructure of the United States' post-war intelligence system was laid on the foundation of an international Nazi spy ring that had come to be the last refuge of SS war criminals who had no other means of escaping judgment. The Gehlen Org, as it came to be called by the few Americans who knew about it—and needless to say, the United States Congress knew nothing of the Gehlen deal, and the evidence is strong that Truman knew very little about it—continued to serve the United States as its eyes and ears on Europe and the U.S.S.R. until 1955. At that time, fulfilling one of the terms of the secret treaty of Fort Hunt in 1945, the entire Gehlen Org was transferred to the new West German government, which gave it the name of the Federal Intelligence Service, or BND, and which the descendants of General Gehlen serve to this day. The BND continued to serve as the backbone of NATO intelligence and is said to have supplied well into the 1960s something in the order of seventy percent of the NATO intelligence take.

This is the base upon which the U.S. intelligence system was founded. The National Security Act of 1947 reorganized the military and created the CIA, but the Gehlen Org was the base from which U.S. intelligence developed throughout the decades of the Cold War. I am not trying to imply here that Stalin was not a villain or that Soviet communism was not a threat to Europe. I am saying rather that everything American policymakers believed they knew about Europe and the U.S.S.R. on most reliable report well into the 1960s was sent to them by an intelligence network made up completely of Hitler's most dedicated Nazis. I believe this fact helps to explain how the American national-security community evolved the quasi-fascistic credo we can observe developing in the following incidents.

2. 1945: Operation Shamrock

This program, set up by the Pentagon and turned over to the National Security Agency after 1947, was discovered and shut down by Congress in 1975. As a House committee explained in a 1979 report, Shamrock intercepted "virtually all telegraphic traffic sent to, from, or transitting the United States." Said the House report, "Operation Shamrock was the largest government interception program affecting Americans" ever carried out. In a suit brought by the ACLU in the 1970s to declassify

Shamrock files, the Defense Department claimed that either admitting or denying that the Shamrock surveillance took place, never mind revealing actual files, would disclose "state secrets." A judicial panel decided in the Pentagon's favor despite the ACLU's argument that to do so was "dangerously close to an open-ended warrant to intrude on liberties guaranteed by the Fourth Amendment."[2]

3. 1945: Project Paperclip

This is perhaps the most famous of such programs but it is still not well understood. The U.S. Army wanted German rocket scientists both for its own interest in rocketry and to keep them out of the hands of the Soviets, who had the same ambitions. United States law forbade these scientists' entry into the U.S., however, because they were all Nazis and members of the SS, including the prize among them, Dr. Werner von Braun. The Army acted unilaterally, therefore, in bringing the rocket scientists to the United States as prisoners of war and defining the Redstone rocket laboratory in Huntsville as a POW compound. Later the Paperclip scientists were de-Nazified by various bureaucratic means and emplaced at the center of the military space program. What is not well understood is that hundreds of additional Nazi SS members who had nothing at all to contribute to a scientific program were also admitted. This included the SS bureaucrat who oversaw the slave labor efforts in digging the underground facilities at the Nazi rocket base on Peenemunde.[3]

4. 1947: Project Chatter

The U.S. Navy initiated this program to continue Nazi experiments in extracting truth from unwilling subjects by chemical means, especially mind-altering drugs such as mescalin. This was at the same time that U.S. investigative elements detailed to the Nuremberg Tribunal were rounding up Nazis suspected of having experimented with "truth serums" during World War II. Such experiments are banned by the laws of war.[4]

5. 1948: Election Theft

New to the world and eager to learn, the CIA immediately began spending secret money to influence election results in France and Italy. Straight from the womb, it thus established a habit of intervention which, despite being rationalized in terms of the Red menace abroad, would ultimately find expression within the domestic interior.[5]

6. 1953: MK/Ultra

The CIA picked up the Navy's Project Chatter and throughout the 1950s and '60s ran tests on involuntary and unwitting subjects using truth drugs and electromagnetic fields to see if it could indeed control a subject's mind without the subject's being aware. This research continued despite the fact that the United States signed the Nuremberg Code in 1953 stipulating that subjects must be aware, must volunteer, must have the aid of a supervising doctor, and must be allowed to quit the experiment at any moment.

7. 1953: HT/Lingual

The CIA began opening all mail traveling between the United States and the U.S.S.R. and China. HT/Lingual ran until 1973 before it was stopped. We found out about it in 1975.[6]

8. 1953: Operation Ajax

The CIA overthrew Premier Mohammed Mossadegh in Iran, complaining of his neutralism in the Cold War, and installed in his place General Fazlollah Zahedi, a wartime Nazi collaborator. Zahedi showed his gratitude by giving 25-year leases on forty percent of Iran's oil to three American firms. One of these firms, Gulf Oil, was fortunate enough a few years later to hire as a vice president the CIA agent Kermit Roosevelt, who had run Operation Ajax. Did this coup set the clock ticking on the Iranian hostage crisis of 1979–80?[7]

9. 1954: Operation Success

The CIA spent $20 million to overthrow the democratically elected Jacabo Arbenz in Guatemala for daring to introduce an agrarian reform program that the United Fruit Company found threatening. General Walter Bedell Smith, CIA director at the time, later joined the board of United Fruit.[8]

10. 1954: News Control

The CIA began a program of infiltration of domestic and foreign institutions, concentrating on journalists and labor unions. Among the targeted U.S. organizations was the National Student Association, which the CIA secretly supported to the tune of some $200,000 a year. This meddling with an American and thus presumably off-limits organization remained secret until *Ramparts* magazine exposed it in 1967. It was at this point that mainstream media first became curious about the CIA and began unearthing other cases involving corporations, research centers, religious groups and universities.[9]

11. 1960–61: Operation Zapata

Castro warned that the United States was preparing an invasion of Cuba, but this was 1960 and we all laughed. We knew in those days the United States did not do such things. Then came the Bay of Pigs, and we were left to wonder how such an impossible thing could happen.

12. 1960–63: Task Force W

Only because someone still anonymous inside the CIA decided to talk about it to the Senate Intelligence Committee in 1975, we discovered that the CIA's operations directorate decided in September 1960: (a) that it would be a good thing to murder Fidel Castro and other Cuban leaders, (b) that it would be appropriate to hire the Mafia to carry these assassinations out, and (c) that there would be no need to tell the President that such an arrangement was being made. After all, was killing not the Mafia's area of expertise?

It hardly seemed to trouble the CIA that the Kennedy administration was at the very same time trying to mount a war on organized crime focusing on precisely the Mafia leaders that the CIA was recruiting as hired assassins.

13. 1964: Brazil

Two weeks after the Johnson administration announced the end of the JFK Alliance for Progress with its commitment to the principle of not aiding tyrants, the CIA staged and the U.S. Navy supported a coup d'etat in Brazil overthrowing the democratically elected Joao Goulart. Within twenty-four hours a new right-wing government was installed, congratulated and recognized by the United States.

14. 1965: The DR

An uprising in the Dominican Republic was put down with the help of 20,000 U.S. Marines. Ellsworth Bunker, the U.S. ambassador, Abe Fortas, a new Supreme Court justice and a crony of LBJ's, presidential advisors Adolf Berle, Averill Harriman and Joseph Farland were all on the payroll of organizations such as the National Sugar Refining Company, the Sucrest Company, the National Sugar Company, and the South Puerto Rico Sugar Company—all of which had holdings in the Dominican Republic that were threatened by the revolution.

15. 1967: The Phoenix Program

A terror and assassination program conceived by the CIA but implemented by the military command targeted Viet Cong cadres by name—a crime of war. At least twenty thousand were killed, according to the CIA's William Colby, of whom some 3,000 were assassinated. A CIA analyst later observed: "They assassinated a lot of the wrong damn people."[10]

16. August 1967: COINTELPRO

Faced with mounting public protest against the Vietnam War, the FBI formally inaugurated its so-called COINTELPRO operations, a rationalized and extended form of operations under way for at least a year. A House committee reported in 1979 that "the FBI Chicago Field Office files . . . [in] 1966 alone contained the identities of a small army of 837 informers, all of whom reported on [antiwar activists'] . . . political activities, views or beliefs, and none of whom reported on any unlawful activities by [these activists]."[11]

17. October 1967: MH/Chaos

Two months after the FBI started up COINTELPRO, the CIA followed suit with MH/Chaos, set up in the counterintelligence section run by a certifiable paranoid named James Jesus Angleton. Even though the illegal Chaos infiltration showed that there was no foreign financing or manipulation of the antiwar movement, Johnson refused to accept this, and the operation continued into the Nixon administration. By 1971, CIA agents were operating everywhere there were students inside America, infiltrating protest groups not only to spy on them but to provide authentic cover stories they could use while traveling abroad and joining foreign antiwar groups.[12] Chaos was refocused on international terrorism in 1972, but another operation, Project Resistance, conducted out of the CIA Office of Security, continued surveillance of American domestic dissent until it was ended in June 1973.

18. April 1968: The King Plot

The assassination of Martin Luther King, Jr. led at once to massive urban riots, the breakup of the nonviolent civil rights movement and in ten years to a congressional investigation that found evidence of conspiracy, despite the initial finding that, as in the JFK case, the assassin was a lone nut. The conspiracy evidence included proof that the FBI had directly threatened King and that, in the certain knowledge that King was a target of violent hate groups, the Memphis Police Department had withdrawn its protective surveillance and let this fact be known.[13]

19. June 1968: The RFK Hit

The assassination of Robert Kennedy came on the heels of his victory in the California presidential primary. This victory had virtually guaranteed his nomination as an antiwar presidential candidate at the Democratic convention in August. The assassinations of King and the second Kennedy were body blows to the civil rights and antiwar movements and drove nails in the coffins of those who were still committed to the principles of democratic, nonviolent struggle.

From now on there would be virtually nothing left of the organized movement except the Black Panthers and the Weathermen, both committed to violence and thus both of them doomed. The official verdict in Robert Kennedy's murder was, predictably enough, that it was the work of another lone nut. This conclusion was reached by a still-secret Los Angeles Police Department investigation despite the fact that L.A. coroner Thomas Noguchi found that RFK's wounds were fired point-blank behind him whereas the alleged assassin, Sirhan Sirhan, by unanimous testimony of many eyewitnesses, never got his pistol closer to Kennedy than six feet and was always in front of him. It was true, nevertheless, that Sirhan fired. It was also true that he was, and apparently remains, insane. Was Sirhan the offspring of Project Chatter and MK Ultra?

20. 1969: Operation Minaret

This was a CIA program chartered to intercept (according to a House report) ''the international communications of selected American citizens and groups on the basis of lists of names, 'watchlists,' supplied by other government agencies. . . . The program applied not only to alleged foreign influence on domestic dissent, but also to American groups and individuals whose activities 'may result in civil disturbances. . . .' ''[14]

21. April 1971: Helms Protests

In a rare public speech to the American Society of Newspaper Editors, CIA Director Richard Helms asked the nation to "take it on faith that we too are honorable men devoted to her service." He went on to say, "We do not target on American citizens."[15]

22. 1972: Watergate

As though to give body to Helms' touching promise, seven CIA operatives detailed to the Nixon White House played the same political game the CIA learned abroad in all its clandestine manipulations from France to Brazil, from Italy to Guatemala, but now in the context of U.S. presidential politics. Whether through sheer fluke or a subtle counter-conspiracy, Nixon's CIA burglars were caught in the act, and two years later Nixon was therefore forced to resign. For a moment, a window opened into the heart of darkness.

23. 1973: Allende Murdered

Frustrated in its 1970 effort to control the Chilean election, the CIA resorted to murder once again in the elimination of Salvador Allende. Allende government official Orlando Letelier along with an American supporter, Ronnie Moffit, were soon also killed, not far away in Chile but in Dupont Circle in our nation's capital.

24. Late 1970s: "Defenders of Democracy"

As death squads raged through Latin America, FBI agents and U.S. marshals in Puerto Rico secretly created, trained and armed a super-secret police unit named ''Defenders of Democracy'' and dedicated to the assassination of leaders of the Puerto Rican independence movement.[16] This was in the Jimmy Carter period. Did Carter know?

25. 1980: October Surprise

The facts in this strange first act of the Iran-contra episode are still in dispute, but the charge made by Barbara Honegger, activist in the Reagan 1980 campaign, and by Carter national security aide Gary Sick, is of mega-scandal dimensions.*

Honegger and Sick claim in outline that in 1980 William Casey, long-time U.S. super-spy but at that point without the least portfolio, led a secret Reagan campaign delegation to Europe to strike a secret deal with Iran, a nation with which the United States was virtually at war because of the 42 hostages Iran had seized from the U.S. embassy.

In the alleged deal, Iran agreed not to release the hostages until the U.S. presidential race was over, thus denying President Carter the political benefit of getting the hostages back. Reagan agreed that, if elected, he would help Iran acquire certain weapons. Well, for a few bucks here and there, too, of course, and something for Israel,

*The House of Representatives opened up an official inquiry into the Honneger-Sick charges as we went to press.

but the basic deal was U.S. arms for U.S. hostages held by Iran.

The basic deal was also so deeply criminal as to go beyond all statutes but those that deal with treason.

26. 1970s and 1980s: The Noriega Connection

The CIA was exposed time and again throughout these decades in big-time international dope trafficking. This was not altogether new. Already in the late '60s we had discovered that this was happening in Southeast Asia, where the CIA's regional airline, Air America, was found deeply involved in the opium trade being run out of the so-called Golden Triangle centered in Laos and involving Chinese drug lords associated with the anti-Communist Kuomintang.[17] The CIA's support in moving large amounts of opium was valuable, it seemed, in maintaining good relations with our anti-Communist friends. In the 1970s and '80s, CIA drug operations appeared in this hemisphere for a related but even better reason: they were a convenient way to finance anti-Communist operations that the Congress would not fund.

The rash of drug cases around former Panamanian strongman Manuel Noriega—once a darling of the CIA until he dared oppose U.S. policy in Nicaragua—provides a glimpse into the true heart of the contemporary CIA. Noriega received as much as $10 million a month from the Medellin Cartel (whose profits were $3 million a day) plus $200,000 a year from the CIA for the use of Panamanian runways in transhipment of cocaine to the north.

Noriega is only in trouble today because he turned against the Reaganauts. The real attitude of Reagan and

Bush toward drug trafficking is indicated much less in Noriega's trial itself than in the kind of deals the Justice Department is willing to make to convict him. According to a recent *Boston Globe* news story, federal prosecutors have paid at least $1.5 million in "fees" for testimony against Noriega. In addition, some government witnesses have received freedom from life sentences, tax-free recovery of stashed drug profits and confiscated property, and permanent U.S. residency and work permits for themselves and family members.

The best deals go to the biggest offenders, such as Carlos Lehder. Leader of the Medellin Cartel, Lehder was sentenced to 145 years in prison, but is probably facing a real sentence of less than five years on account of his collaboration against Noriega. He is said to have made a $10-million contribution to the contra cause.

The case of Floyd Carlton is also instructive. Carlton was a drug pilot whose testimony led to Noriega's indictment in 1988. He was allowed by Bush's prosecutors to transfer his cocaine profits into the U.S. tax-free. Bush also promised not to seize his various homes and ranches and agreed to pay $210,000 to support his wife, three children, and a nanny and to furnish them with permanent residence in the U.S. and work permits.[18]

27. October 1986: The Enterprise

A contra supply plane was shot down in Nicaragua. A low-level CIA agent named Eugene Hassenfus was captured alive. Hassenfus chose not to make a martyr of himself, and thus was born the Iran-contra scandal, a continuation of the politics of the October Surprise but on a far grander scale. The CIA and the NSC were learning how to operate beyond the reach of American law. With the "free-standing, off-the-books" organization they called "the Enterprise," capable of financing its operations from drug profits and thus independent of the exchequer, the likes of Oliver North and John Poindexter and Theodore Shackley and Thomas Clines and Rafael Quintero and William Casey had it made. They could form U.S. policy pretty much by themselves, especially since the super-patriot Ronald Reagan seemed content to blink and doze. Who cared what Congress might think or say? As Admiral Poindexter put it so eloquently, "I never believed . . . that the Boland Amendment ever applied to the National Security Council staff."[19]

28. 1991: BCCI

The main difference between the CIA's early Cold War scandals and the ones we are seeing today is that the more recent ones are immeasurably more complex. This is sharply true of our last two examples, one of which is that of the still-emerging scandal around the Bank of Credit and Commerce International. The BCCI scandal appears to involve the CIA in a far-flung international financial network created for the primary purpose of laundering vast amounts of drug money and with the secondary purpose of ripping off the unsuspecting smaller banks that BCCI acquired in pursuit of its primary objective.

One fascinating aspect of the BCCI scandal is that it may at last supply us with the final solution of one of the outstanding riddles of the last decades—namely, why does the government insist on keeping drugs illegal since any fool can see that the only result of this is to keep the price of drugs high? Could this be because it is the secret elements of the government—the CIA, the NSC, the Enterprise—that is actually selling them?

29. 1991: Casolaro

Finally, consider just briefly another case of astounding complexity, still not at all exposed, still writhing in the twilight—the case of Inslaw, Inc., involving the George Bush Justice Department and the death of Danny Casolaro, a free-lance investigative journalist with whom I happen to identify most closely, even though I never met him.

The story in brief: Inslaw, Inc. in the early 1980s was an enterprising computer software company whose most important product was a software program called Promis. Promis' appeal lay in the fact that it made it possible for Justice Department attorneys to keep track of an extremely large number of cases. The Justice Department bought Promis from Inslaw in 1982 and began installing it in its various offices.

Inslaw had completed nineteen installations of Promis within a year, and all seemed to be going well. But suddenly the Justice Department began to complain about Promis and soon was refusing to pay Inslaw, which therefore careened into bankruptcy.

The fact, however, was that nothing at all was wrong with Promis. Rather, the Justice Department—so it is alleged—had made a deal with Dr. Earl Brian, California health secretary under Governor Ronald Reagan. In this alleged deal—which Dr. Brian denies—the Justice Department would simply steal Inslaw's Promis software and give it to Dr. Brian, who would then be in a position to sell it back to the Justice Department for an estimated $250 million.

Part of the reason the Justice Department was willing to do this for Dr. Brian, as the allegation continues, is that Brian had helped persuade Iranian leaders to cooperate with Reagan in the October Surprise operation of 1980.

But there's more to the allegation. The attempt to get Promis out of Inslaw's hands and into Dr. Brian's had two other purposes, according to Inslaw's attorney, Elliot L. Richardson. The first was "to generate revenue for covert operations not authorized by Congress. The second was to supply foreign intelligence agencies with a software system that would make it easier for U.S. eavesdroppers to read intercepted signals." That is, a back-door access was built into the Promis software. Anyone who bought Promis was buying a Trojan Horse.

Danny Casolaro had talked to many of the informants in this case. Telling friends he was on his way to contact an informant who would put the last piece in the picture, he left his home in Washington in August 1991 to travel to Martinsburg, West Virginia, where he took a hotel room and waited for the informant to contact him. Before leaving he had told his friends not to believe it if he died in a car accident.

He was found dead in his room, in the bathtub, with both arms slashed a total of twelve times. The Martinsburg police quickly ruled his death a suicide and allowed his body to be embalmed immediately, even before notifying his family of his death. His hotel room was cleaned of the least indication that he had been in it. His briefcase and his notes were never found.

In his *New York Times* op-ed piece about this last October, Elliot Richardson ended by reminding his readers that he had called for a special prosecutor once before.

Richardson was the nominated Attorney General in 1973 and resigned in disagreement with Nixon, calling for a special prosecutor to investigate Watergate.

Now Richardson wants another special prosecutor to probe the Inslaw case. He believes Casolaro was murdered and that evidence points to ''a widespread conspiracy implicating lesser government officials in the theft of Inslaw's technology.'' These same officials, of course, would also be involved in the apparent attempt to generate funding for illegal covert operations and to sneak Trojan Horse software into the systems by which other governments monitor their litigation caseloads.

We can be sure at least that the events we have briefly reviewed here are not isolated and separate. In the painful story that begins with General of the Third Reich Reinhard Gehlen and continues down to the death of Danny Casolaro, we face a stream of systemically connected abuses.

A secret state has set itself up within the darkest corners of the American government. It is what Nixon adviser John Dean called a cancer on the presidency, but it has metastasized well beyond the White House.

It is not paranoia to call attention to this, but a simple act of realism.

NOTES

1. John Ranalegh, *The Agency: The Rise and Decline of the CIA* (New York: Simon and Schuster, 1987), p. 80.
2. *House Select Committee on Assassinations: Report,* vol. VIII, pp. 506–08.
3. Linda Hunt, *Secret Agenda* (New York: St. Martins Press, 1990).
4. Martin Lee and Bruce Shlain, *Acid Dreams* (New York: Grove Press, 1985).
5. Ranalegh, p. 131.
6. Ibid., p. 270.
7. Ibid., p. 261–64.
8. Ibid., p. 268.
9. Ibid., p. 246, p. 471.
10. Ibid., p. 440, p. 553.
11. *HSCA,* vol. VIII, p. 524.
12. Ranalegh, p. 534.
13. *The HSCA Report: Findings and Recommendations* (Washington: U.S. Government Printing Office, 1979). See p. 407 re the FBI and p. 418 re the MPD.
14. *HSCA,* vol. VIII, p. 507.
15. Ranalegh, p. 281.
16. See *Boston Globe* and *New York Times* stories of January 29, 1992.
17. See Alfred McCoy, *The Politics of Heroin in Southeast Asia* (New York: Harper Colophon, 1973).
18. *Boston Globe,* Dec. 13, 1991.
19. Iran-Contra Trading Cards #35.

II

New Frontier Camelot

JFK was not the first or the last candidate to enter office behind two faces—the champion of a purely electoral coalition whose partners were in deep disagreement on all questions of substance. The two pieces in this section attempt to account for this phenomenon at a macro level first and then more in terms of the concrete problems JFK faced in the New Frontier Camelot coalition upon which he had come to power.

"Presidential Assassinations and the Closing of the Frontier" is excerpted from a lecture I gave at the AIB's Politics of Conspiracy Conference at Boston University in 1975 and has been revised and updated. "JFK and Vietnam" is an updated fragment from my 1976 book, *The Yankee and Cowboy War*.

A few words on the Yankee-Cowboy imagery and the JFK administration:

"New Frontier" naturally evoked the Wild West and

space exploration, while JFK's preoccupation with "Camelot" looked back across the Atlantic to the point of origin; origin and horizon are in harmony in the JFK symbolism, but this harmony was shallow and tenuous in the world of real interests. The two pieces in this section try to work out at least a stylized sense of how certain large historical forces in American history may have blindly come together to create the conscious conspiracy of Dealey Plaza.

3

Presidential Assassinations and the Closing of the Frontier*

The assassinations of the past twelve years have been variously explained as symptomatic of American violence, the handiwork of psychotics seeking celebrity, an inevitable tragedy and an indication of disrespect for authority. If the shootings are not viewed as anomalies occurring in an essentially sound system, they are presented as part of a general malaise afflicting the whole society. Even the Rolling Stones say that "it was you and me" who killed the Kennedys. But if everybody killed the Kennedys, no one can be singled out for blame. The notion that responsibility for the death of certain leaders is national is moralistic rather than political.

The assassinations are supremely political events that cannot be adequately analyzed as psychological melodrama or national ennui.

I argue here that the two Kennedy assassinations may somehow be rooted in the historical antagonism between the Eastern Establishment and southwestern entrepre-

*From a taped lecture at the AIB "Conference on Conspiracy" at Boston University, February 1975.

neurs. The intensity of conflict between these wings of the American ruling elite may explain the 1960s.

The facts surrounding the assassination conspiracies behind Dallas, Memphis and Los Angeles are like a storm of incomprehensible lightning. The storm changes everything, it changes colors, familiar components of the political landscape, it turns political parties that once we thought were strong and forceful into pawns and manipulated counters on a stage controlled by hidden forces. And the act of government itself is turned most fundamentally into an act of murder.

The facts, above all, call for a new comprehension, a new conception of the political world that we live in. The Yankee/Cowboy theory is an effort to provide an overarching framework within which it will be possible to understand the fundamental logic that's been worked out in Dallas and the other sites of major conspiracy over the past ten or so years. In other words, what we are trying to do is confront the diffuse, pervasive American illusion that the events at Dallas happened because there were a few oddballs like Oswald.

An alternative theory doesn't deny accident, crossover, complexity, or ambiguity, and, in certain respects, it even demands at least a moment of ambivalence, of indecision before confronting certain basic questions. The Yankee/Cowboy theory asks us not to go completely to the end of a certain line of analysis or interpretation, notably in respect to the question ''Who did it?'' It's always necessary to divide speculation from fact and not to assert as factual what is only reconstructed, what is hypothetical. Nevertheless, it's still necessary to hypothesize. It's necessary in a sense not to be intimidated by the fear of paranoia. That is where the Yankee/Cowboy theory comes in. It is an attempt to reconstruct the general shape of the forces in play. The theory by itself is very simple.

Let me start by trying to characterize the mentalities and the general power bases of "Yankee" and "Cowboy."

By "Yankee" I'm trying to indicate the Eastern Establishment multinational monopoly capitalist formation, personified in the person, or the empire, of the Rockefellers. David Rockefeller is from this standpoint the archetypal Yankee. The perspective of the Yankee is complex and tortured and constantly in the process of reformation. I think it may be fair to produce the following kind of generalization: the Yankee stands on the East Coast and relates to Europe as to the opposite side of a lake, which exists as a medium for communication and transportation. The Yankee worldview is anglophilic and rooted in the belief that there is a special relationship between the United States and Britain, imagining that the center of the world is the North American industrial community that roughly came into being in this century and has been traumatized and molded in world wars. That world center, at least from the standpoint of itself, is historically, traditionally, the domain of current interest of the Yankee sensibility and the multinational corporation, which moves through this as the primary mode of economic organization of this class.

The monopoly capitalist class has several characteristics differentiating it from the class of modern Cowboy entrepreneurs. Entrepreneurial capitalism—Cowboy capitalism—is the capitalism that developed in the United States particularly because the United States happened to develop with a frontier that was constantly in motion. When Marx analyzed nineteenth-century societies and derived the basic conceptions of class that Marxists today still employ, he was dealing with countries that basically had finished boundaries. That was, of course, not true in detail; there were plenty of boundary altercations in that period and there remain plenty of boundary altercations in contemporary European affairs.

What was distinctive about the United States was that it had a boundary that no one else in Western Europe shared. It had a boundary that went beyond Western civilization itself, a boundary on some outside world, which the white man conqueror, moving across the Atlantic in the period of exploration and colonization, saw as his without question to dominate, exploit, and own. The movement of the frontier throughout the whole history of the United States meant that there was always an escape hatch, so to speak. There was always a way to avoid coming to conflict in the big cities over the issues that were therefore constantly suspended. The social adversaries that normally would be in sharp conflict with one another, as in Europe, in this country turned to the West.

All kinds of people went to the West, not just Cowboys. Frontier democrats and populists are as important in this country's history as the Cowboy strain that I am identifying in my particular use of the term today. But the Cowboy is a figure that emerges in the West in the wake of the Civil War and Reconstruction period when the Yankees established for the first time their leadership over federal institutions. Those who had owned the slaves, who had lost the war and who now did not run the government anymore, moved to the other side of the Mississippi. They took fortunes with them as they were able to save them; it wasn't all just gone with the wind. A whole milieu began to reconstruct itself in the 70s, 80s, and 90s. And an argument can be made for the view that the Confederacy actually began to make a comeback at the expense of Reconstruction. The great Yankees who had come into power as a result of the Civil War, in pushing their program of national industrialization, decided they needed to reconstitute some kind of southern military establishment to beat the Indians in the West. Southern power began to reestablish its hold over military institutions in the wars that followed the closing of the Reconstruction period and the dismantling of the reforms instituted by the Abolitionists.

I agree it would be a mistake for me to try to tell the whole story of the United States in such simple terms. But the Civil War is an important point, at the moment, for us to think about if only because we might be at the early threshold of another one. It seems, in any case, that the issues are somewhat similar. We know that the country in the beginning was ruled by a southern power establishment, an elite centered in Virginia. The business of this elite was basically to supply the kind of things that a colony supplies to a mother country; in return it got back from England the kind of things that a rich colonial elite is accustomed to getting back from a mother country. Raw materials went over and what came back was the fruit of the British Industrial Revolution. In spite of the southern gentry's power, forces of industrialism were doomed to prevail, and finally by the 1840s or 1850s the rule of the southern elite was challenged by emerging northern industrial interests, which wanted the tariffs to go higher against British industrial goods so that American industry would have a chance to protect itself. The southerners didn't want that to happen and the dispute got very sharp. It was expressed finally as the Civil War.

In the Civil War, Lincoln not only maintained the integrity of the Union, he also asserted over the Union the hegemony of the federal government: there is to be one United States of America; it is to be run from one central federal government; there is not to be a Confederacy; there is not to be secession; there is not to be what we might now call a Balkanization of the North American continent. The casual and ordinary opinion of the Civil War is that it was fought to free the slaves and bring about social equality. But we would have to say looking at the consequences that the dynamic that brought the Civil War about was the emergence of forces of industrial power in the North and their need to fragment the leadership of the slave-agrarian South, but then to yoke that leadership into a new national coalition. The southern Confederate power defeated in the Civil War and held down for a couple of decades when the Abolitionists tried to accomplish a genuine Reconstruction in the South in very trying circumstances finally became necessary again to the northern industrialists—Harriman of the Union Pacific, for example—who needed land, freedom, and security for moving the railroads across the continent. And it was in that task that southern Confederate-style militarism began to be reconstituted as a sub-group, a smaller power group within the overall constellation of power groups shaping American policy.

My argument is that the coalition formed between Yankee and Cowboy, with Yankee in the senior position and Cowboy in the junior position, began to change from the inside out as a result of World War II and the Cold War. World War II projected enormous energy into the Cowboy military defense sphere. The Cold War projected the same kind of energy into the national security establishment. Operating in militaristic, authoritarian, secretive ways, both Yankee and Cowboy found it easily possible to establish a clandestine sector of government that not many of us knew existed and that seems, in fact, to have been the major policy force of that period.

The President is like a president of a big company; he has the same kind of problems that the president of a big company would have. There are problems of internal factions, of coordinating the various parts of the bureaucracy, of keeping the party together. All these problems visit the head of a corporation and the chief executive of the corporate state. If we understand the president as a corporate executive subject to pressures—violent pressures—on his office, then the presidency begins to be clarified. It's not just the unrolling of a policy duel between the presidency and the legislative branches, it's the unrolling of a duel within the presidency itself for the power to stipulate policy, for the power to give definition to national energies, for the power to generate a sense of movement and program.

An internal struggle around the powers of the presidency is the definitive struggle of the '60s.

Kennedy had an instinct that American foreign policy somehow needed to make an important new departure. Specifically, there had to be some kind of change in the Cold War, because if its logic kept on rolling there would be nuclear confrontation soon. Therefore, the logic of disarmament and the SALT talks. Kennedy wasn't so much a partisan of the dispossessed as someone trying to lead the world system into rationality, coherence, and durability. Kennedy moved as a monopoly capitalist with an Atlantic outlook to produce the kind of world that Woodrow Wilson wanted, a world where the industrial powers were concertedly making world policy among themselves.

That Wilsonian view of world order essentially guided the New Deal and guided the New Frontier. Kennedy was in pursuit of that kind of order, that Camelot vision of world happiness, a frontier Camelot. Kennedy tried to effect that old Roosevelt-style synthesis between North and South, new and old, industrial and agricultural, Yankee and Cowboy. He was able to do so to the extent of getting the leading Cowboy on the ticket with him, but then seemed catapulted immediately into a situation where his least demand, where his least independence in the use of his office's powers, led him into a confrontation that he couldn't possibly win.

That confrontation speeded up during the year 1962. He got into a big fight with the steel industry and began to isolate some of his Yankee help; the steel industry is a big part of the banking industry and the banking industry is mainly what the Yankees are all about. Indira Gandhi pointed out at a certain point after the assassination that Kennedy "died because he lost the support of his peers."* The whole episode in '62 around the steel price rise was an important moment in that process of the loss of consensus, the loss of the base.

Kennedy was pushed more and more into private conversations with his brother as the New Frontier worked on toward the tragic denouement. Probably the American University speech in 1963 calling for an end to the Cold War was another big blow against Kennedy in the eyes of the Cowboys, and so was Kennedy's attack on the oil depletion allowance.

But the big push was Vietnam. Kennedy, as he is held responsible for the Cuban invasion, is also accused by basic historic texts of starting the Vietnam War. I think that if we try to move in closer and look at the divisions within the corporate Kennedy presidency, the split and enfevered presidency, we'll find a picture that resembles the Cuban situation.

A Cowboy force moves to define the national interest in a particular theater and employs military and/or clandestine means to pursue that interest. The Yankee force,

---

* Her remark is ironic since she herself was assassinated in a palace coup in 1984.

It wants to draw lines, making the commitment to maintain the open frontier in the Orient while putting a limit to the commitment.

In other words, an Atlanticist like Kennedy would ask of any Vietnam policy how it affected European-American relations. And if it were good in itself but adversely affected those relations, that might be grounds for not following that policy. That is the heart and the essence of the Yankee perspective—it sees America linked to Western Europe and fights above all to preserve its European interests. If those interests are impeached by some definition of national objectives requiring the United States to invest inordinate amounts of energy in other theaters and crusades, then America is in fundamental trouble, even if she is able to win a position in Southeast Asia. So the criticism that began to develop in the Yankee elite about the war in Vietnam began as a consciousness of frustration with what the war was doing to the privileged Atlantic relationship and how persistence in the war was producing internal social dislocation.

Kennedy, nevertheless, was a Cold Warrior and he had some responsibility to his own right wing, to the right wing of the Yankee Establishment, not to go too far. He thought maybe a little investment of clandestinism would do, coupled with some nation-building. He sent the first 16,000 so-called advisers to Vietnam and, in that respect, from a technical as well as a political standpoint, started the flow that resulted in the incredible Johnson escalations and the Nixon secret air war. But the interesting thing about those 16,000 is that they seem to have been sent with return-trip tickets, unlike the others. In other words, there were preconditions set on their commitment to the area. Just as Kennedy seems to have been saying in Cuba, "If the victory could be achieved with-other words, there were preconditions set on their commitment to the area. Just as Kennedy seems to have been saying in Cuba, "If the victory could be achieved without the B-26's and the assassination, well, I can't stop you from trying," he says in Vietnam, "if South Vietnam can be preserved in the Free World by the investment of a lot of technical and military aid and a few advisers, all right, I'm not strong enough to keep you from doing it." In any case, the whole issue had to be bartered in the context of the emerging power struggle between Kennedy and his enemies.

In September of 1963, Kennedy is saying at press conferences that it's their war, American boys can't be expected to fight it, there're limits to what we're going to spend. In October, he says: All right, we're going to bring the first thousand troops back. The reports coming from McNamara and the others are that we've almost won, it'll be just a minute.

But the big barrier to a peace in Vietnam, the Diem family, badly did not want to make any kind of peace with communists. Madame Diem tried to correct that impression later, saying that the Diem family would have negotiated with the Viet Cong. But until we get that straight, we must assume that they were a barrier and that that must have had something to do with the removal of the Diem family on November 1, 1963.

Out of a Bangkok exile, groomed for just this role of interim leader, came General Big Minh. And the distinctive thing about Big Minh was that he wasn't afraid of negotiating with the National Liberation Front. So he was coming into power on a specific program of trying to negotiate some kind of new relationship with the Viet Cong. The Vietnam War for one little moment was not going to take place. Then there was Dallas.

4

JFK and Vietnam*

How strong is the evidence that Kennedy intended a Vietnam pullback? We have a few fragments, a chronology.

1. In the summer of 1961, as an outgrowth of the bitter experience of the Bay of Pigs, the Kennedy circle promulgated two key National Security Agency memos, NSAM 263 and 273. The first, a "red-striped" memo on which Air Force Colonel L. Fletcher Prouty was the JCS briefing officer, directed the Chiefs to take the command of the Vietnam operation away from the CIA and commence a policy of disengagement. The second, not yet released, emerges in Prouty's description as a vast philosophical document of comprehensive scope propounding a doctrine of nonintervention in Third World revolutions and a concept of severe limitation in future clandestine operations.[1]†

2. (Ret.) General James M. Gavin in 1968: "There has been much speculation about what President Kennedy would or would not have done in Vietnam had he lived. Having discussed military affairs with him often and in

*Updated and excerpted from *The Yankee and Cowboy War*, New York: Berkley, 1976.
†This, recall, was in 1976. By 1992, several complete drafts of NSAM 273 had come to light, differing radically from one another.

detail for 15 years, I know he was totally opposed to the introduction of combat troops in Southeast Asia. His public statements just before his murder support this view. Let us not lay on the dead the blame for our own failures."[2]

3. Paul B. Fay, Jr., Navy Undersecretary under JFK: "If John F. Kennedy had lived, our military involvement in Vietnam would have been over by the end of 1964."[3]

4. Kennedy remarked to his aide Kenneth O'Donnell in 1963: "In 1965, I'll become one of the most unpopular presidents in history. I'll be damned everywhere as a Communist appeaser. But now I don't care. If I tried to pull out completely now from Vietnam, we would have another Joe McCarthy red scare on our hands, but I can do it after I'm reelected. So we had better make damned sure I'm reelected."[4]

5. Wayne Morse, however, maintained that Kennedy was changing his Vietnam policy at the very hour of Dallas: "There's a weak defense for John Kennedy," he told the *Boston Globe* in mid-1973. "He'd seen the error of his ways. I'm satisfied if he'd lived another year we'd have been out of Vietnam. Ten days before his assassination, I went down to the White House and handed him his education bills, which I was handling on the Senate floor. I'd been making two to five speeches a week against Kennedy on Vietnam. . . . I'd gone into President Kennedy's office to discuss education bills, but he said, 'Wayne, I want you to know you're absolutely right in your criticism of my Vietnam policy. Keep this in mind. I'm in the midst of an intensive study which substantiates your position on Vietnam.' "[5]

6. We come to know this study through the Ellsberg Papers as the McNamara study (see especially volume 8, detailing, in Arthur Schlesinger Jr.'s phrase, "Kennedy's plans to extricate the United States from the Vietnam

War'').[6] In an interview in late 1973, Ellsberg said, "A very surprising discovery to me in the fall of '67, as I began to study the documents of '61 in connection with the McNamara study project, was that the major decision Kennedy had made was to *reject* the recommendation made to him by virtually everyone that he send combat units to Vietnam. Kennedy realized that most of the people in the country, whatever their politics, would have said, 'If it takes combat troops, or if it takes heavy bombing or nuclear weapons, it's obviously not worth it for us. We won't succeed.'"[7] Prouty supports this view also from personal Pentagon and intelligence-community experience and believes that Kennedy "gave a hint of his plans for disengagement when he said [in September 1963], speaking of the Vietnamese, 'In the final analysis it is their war. They have to win it or lose it.' "[8]

7. September 1963: The Kennedy administration launches a general program for disengagement while trying to make it appear that we have won the war without having actually fought it. Taylor and McNamara go to Saigon and come back saying they have seen the light at the end of the tunnel. It is announced that the American mission is beginning to draw to a successful end. It is a foreshadowing of the Senator Aiken Plan of 1967: announce a victory at a press conference and march home as in triumph. General Paul Harkins, commander of the Military Assistance Command in Saigon, tells the troops: "Victory in the sense it would apply to this kind of war is just months away and the reduction of American advisers can begin any time now."[9] At that point U.S. "advisers" stood at 16,732.

8. October 2, 1963: McNamara takes to the steps of the White House to tell the press of plans to withdraw one thousand U.S. troops from Vietnam before the year is out.[10]

9. November 1–2: The Diem regime, hopelessly tied to a policy of no negotiations with the Viet Cong, is overthrown, then Diem and his brother Nhu are mysteriously assassinated. General "Big" Minh's regime, incubated in Bangkok exile for exactly this purpose, takes over shortly and proclaims its intention of negotiating a settlement and a coalition government with the Viet Cong. It is no secret that Kennedy was behind the coup and the coming of Big Minh, although there is a question as to whether he was also behind the assassinations of Diem and Nhu. Kennedy had professed public disfavor with their rule and had declared Diem "out of touch with the people." He sanctioned the Minh takeover and approved of its pro-negotiations policy. But what do we make out of Howard Hunt's furtive work in the files of the State Department, busy with scissors and paste to create his own little "Pentagon Papers" convicting Kennedy of the murders of Diem and Nhu? Was he helping the truth or plying his disinformation trade?

10. November 15: In spite of confusion in Saigon resulting from the coup, "a U.S. military spokesman carried on the McNamara-Taylor-Harkins line," as recorded in the GOP's 1967 Vietnam study, "and promised 1,000 American military men would be withdrawn from Vietnam beginning on December 3."[11]

11. November 22: Dallas. Within days of taking over, Johnson issued National Security Agency Memorandum 273, reversing the Kennedy policy of withdrawal and inaugurating the period of build-up leading toward conventional war.[12]

12. Early December: The first of the one thousand U.S. troops ordered home begin withdrawal from Vietnam.[13] Johnson's new orders have not reached the field.

13. March–April 1964: Joint Chiefs draw up and sub-

mit to Johnson a list of ninety-four potential targets for bombing in Vietnam.[14]

14. May: The new government in Saigon calls on the United States to bomb the North. Johnson declines to rule it out.

15. June: There is a big war powwow of LBJ and JCS in Honolulu. Johnson resists pressure for a congressional resolution and decides to step up the war effort. General William Westmoreland takes command of U.S. forces in Vietnam. Ambassador Lodge resigns and is replaced by Taylor.[15]

16. July: South Vietnamese commandos, i.e., CIA/Special Forces units, raid two North Vietnamese islands in the Gulf of Tonkin.[16]

17. August: On intelligence patrol in the Gulf of Tonkin, U.S. destroyers *Maddox* and *Turner Joy* report being attacked by North Vietnamese torpedo boats. Circumstances of the attack remain unclear. Doubt remains as to whether the incidents were real or staged. In the posturing at which he was so adept, in his imitations of passion, Johnson terrified all but Morse and Gruening of the Pacific Northwest and got the Senate to give him the Tonkin Gulf resolution, opening the way for major escalation.

18. November: The Viet Cong hit Bien Hoa air base in the South and the Joint Chiefs grow heated in their demand for heavy U.S. retaliation. Johnson wins the 1964 election on a "peace" platform vs. Goldwater's (and later Nixon's) air-war line. Johnson's was the biggest "peace mandate" ever until Nixon's of 1972.

19. December: Johnson approves a plan for air attacks on North Vietnam, "reprisal air strikes for 30 days, then graduated air warfare against North backed by possible deployment of ground combat troops."[17]

20. February 1965: The Viet Cong attack a U.S. mil-

itary advisers' compound at Pleiku. In "retaliation" Johnson orders the first air strikes against the North. The air war is on.

21. April 1965: The First March on Washington to Protest the War in Vietnam is held by Students for a Democratic Society; twenty to twenty-five thousand hear SDS and SNCC* speakers call for a mass antiwar movement.

Double-faulting on the invasions of Cuba and Vietnam was not Kennedy's only failure in the eyes of chauvinism, but that was without doubt the major problem. Cuba and Vietnam bracket Frontier Camelot as the ends of a coffin. But in between, there was much more for the Cowboy conscience to find deplorable in Kennedy's administration. Making no attempt to be inclusive, and leaving aside the much observed differences of style and manners between the Kennedy group and the Johnson group, I cite the following examples as making the case that from the Cowboy standpoint Kennedy was as bad as he could be.

1. Kennedy's 1962 Geneva Accords on Laos made concessions to the Communists and led to the pullout of eight hundred U.S. military advisers.

2. Kennedy intervened through the UN and, with direct U.S. assistance, supported Congolese nationalism against Belgian-backed secessionists.

3. Kennedy cut off foreign and military aid to seven Latin American countries, most sensationally Haiti, on grounds that repressive strongman government was incompatible with the aims of hemispheric reform.

4. He struggled with Big Steel and Detroit Iron to hold down prices. Faced with an inflation rate of four percent, Kennedy actually wanted to impose a provisional price

---

*SNCC: The Student Nonviolent Coordinating Committee, chief arm of the black youth movement of the 1960s.

freeze. He won labor's agreement to the most limited settlements since World War II on the promise that industry would hold the line on prices. When Big Steel took it all back, Kennedy fought (unsuccessfully) for a court-ordered price rollback. It brings to mind the observation of Indira Gandhi that Kennedy "died because he lost the support of his peers"—i.e., the support of the Yankee financial powers animating the vast reaches of the iron and steel industry. For contrast, when steel raised its prices five dollars a ton in 1967, Johnson merely said that steel executives "knew his feelings" and that price controls "could not be ruled out" in the future. Johnson allowed another steel price rise to pass without comment in 1968.

5. JFK proposed elimination of the oil-depletion allowance in January 1963. This by itself could easily have screwed to the sticking point the courage of the American oil cartel as a whole, and most particularly its mainly Southwestern components, the so-called Independents (distinct from the mainly Yankee "Majors"). The oil-depletion allowance was and remains the whole basis of Southwestern oil's special power and glory. Kennedy had already aroused Texan ire in 1961 by attempting to collect a federal tax on the state business transactions, a tax no Texan could remember having ever seen collected. Now came the attack on the depletion allowance. Oil industry spokesmen angrily predicted a thirty percent drop in earnings if Kennedy's proposed tax reforms won out.[18]

6. JFK encouraged the civil rights movement openly. He introduced his civil rights bill in June 1963 in concert with Martin Luther King's giant march on Washington. The temperature of Congress rose ten degrees and the whole Camelot legislative program was blocked by the civil rights debate.

7. The New Frontiersman attack on Johnson as a per-

sonality began in 1961 and intensified toward Dallas focusing in the Kennedy brothers' pressure on Johnson's Bobby Baker soft spot. The feud between Johnson and Robert Kennedy was unrivaled. What was at stake was not simply Johnson's political career but the whole question of Texas power and its political relationship to Eastern power. When Johnson's man Connally was dispatched in October 1963 to convince Kennedy that he must come politicking soon in Texas, Connally's argument was that the Texas Democratic party was in a growing state of disaffection from the national party under the reign of the Kennedys and that fences had to be mended or Texas might bolt the party in 1964.

8. Robert Kennedy's Justice Department campaign against Jimmy Hoffa, within a wider Frontier Camelot campaign to bust the larger Teamster-Syndicate connection, threatened to expose and destroy a major and basic sphere of Syndicate activity, the Teamster Pension Fund complex.

9. On the first of April, 1963, Kennedy announced that all U.S. raids on Cuba would stop. On April 4, Detective Sgt. C. H. Sapp of the Miami Police Intelligence Unit reported to Assistant Chief of Police A. W. Anderson the following:

> For the past three days the Intelligence Unit has been receiving information concerning the feelings and proposed actions of the Cuban refugee colony in Miami. Since President Kennedy made the news release that the United States government would stop all raiding parties going against Castro's government, the Cuban people feel that the United States Government has turned against them. . . . All violence hitherto directed toward Castro's Cuba will now be directed toward various governmental agencies in the United States.[19]

10. In September 1963, even as he was taking the first perceptible steps toward a Vietnam pullback, Kennedy ordered the FBI to raid secret CIA guerrilla training camps and staging bases in Florida and Louisiana. Dave Ferrie, linked by New Orleans District Attorney James Garrison to Clay Shaw and the CIA, was involved in the operation of the Louisiana camps. The camps were situated on land owned by a gambling associate of Jack Ruby's, Bill McLaney. The McLaney brothers, cogs in the Lansky Syndicate,[20] were among the big losers when the Cuban revolution ejected the Syndicate and its casinos from the island. Frank Fiorini (aka Sturgis) of the Watergate burglary was also connected to the base Kennedy closed at No Name Key. Sturgis was visible at Dallas two months later and was actually questioned by the FBI in connection with the assassination.

The mystery which Nixon resigned to protect, and which the Ford pardon sought to "shut and seal," appears to center on some as-yet-unknown intertwining of Nixon's and Kennedy's fates as adversaries in the great misadventure of the Bay of Pigs. To get at what this mystery might be, we find we have to go beyond the conventional Cold War picture of the Bay of Pigs operation. Instead of seeing the invasion simply as a U.S. vs. Cuba conflict and "the policy of the Kennedy administration," we see it as the product of a conflict internal to the policy apparatus pitting a liberal-minded Yankee president against conservative-minded stalwarts of the defense and security bureaucracies.

The motive of the Cowboy-Nixon side in this conflict was its desire to push through with Cuban plans laid lovingly in the last days of Eisenhower. (Vice-President Johnson also supported the Bay of Pigs "activists.") The motive of the Yankee-Kennedy side was its desire to avoid being drawn into a war against Castro's Cuba. The pro-invasion side was strong enough to break out, to overcome, and be satisfied, just as the anti-invasion side was strong enough only to take the sting out of the invasion, not to stop it.

The result, the Cuban Fiasco, set the model for the Vietnam Quagmire, which followed exactly the same logical course, except in giant steps.

The period before Kennedy's assassination is thus a period of accumulating polarizations throughout the universe of the White House policy apparatus. The Massachusetts-Texas electoral coalition that squeaked into the White House in 1960 had by 1963 proved itself nonfunctional and self-destructive as a governing coalition. It is one measure of the power relativities of this coalition's crisis that the assassination of the President seemed to resolve it.

NOTES

1. Prouty, *Secret Team*, pp. 114–21.
2. James M. Gavin, "We Can Get Out of Vietnam," *Saturday Evening Post*, February 24, 1968.
3. *Santa Barbara News-Press*, February 11, 1975.
4. Kenneth O'Donnell, *Johnny We Hardly Knew Ye* (Boston: Little Brown & Co., 1972), p. 16.
5. *Boston Globe*, June 24, 1973.
6. *Boston Globe*, March 13, 1973.
7. *Rolling Stone*, December 6, 1973.
8. Prouty, *Secret Team*, p. 415.
9. *Stars and Stripes*, November 1, 1963.
10. *New York Times*, October 3, 1963.
11. "GOP Vietnam Study," *Congressional Record*, May 9, 1967 (the "Hickenlooper Study").
12. Peter Dale Scott, "The Death of Kennedy and the Vietnam War," *Government by Gunplay*, ed. Sid Blumenthal and Harvey Yazijian (New York: New American Library, 1976), pp. 152–87. NSAM 273, says Scott, is still unpublished and known only from various passing references to it. Scott's impressive reconstruction is printed in the cited article on pp. 170 ff.
13. *New York Times*, "Vietnam Chronology," January 28, 1973.
14. Ibid.
15. Ibid.
16. Ibid.
17. Ibid.
18. James Hepburn, *Farewell America* (Canada and Belgium: Frontiers Publishing, 1968), p. 244.

19. This memo is from the files of the James Garrison investigation of the JFK assassination. A copy is on file with the Assassination Information Bureau, 63 Inman St., Cambridge, Mass: 02139.

20. William Turner, ''The Garrison Commission on the Assassination of President Kennedy,'' *Ramparts,* January 1968, p. 52; Paris Flammonde, *The Kennedy Conspiracy* (New York: Meredith, 1969), p. 112.

III

The Shooting in Dallas

This section excerpts other passages from *The Yankee and Cowboy War* to spread out a basic sense of the several technical issues (e.g., the direction of the fatal head-shot, the "single-bullet" or "magic-bullet" theory). The subject is the actual gunplay in Dealey Plaza, and how the technical questions stand today.

The text and line of argument are from 1975–76. I have freely updated figures and texts where that was necessary. This review of the classical second-gunman arguments is factually current as of 1992, but the original subtext remains unchanged: how well do we really think we know what happened in Dealey Plaza?

5

Dealey Plaza*

According to the Warren Commission, Lee Harvey Oswald was a chronic malcontent and loner who in 1959 broke off his career in the U.S. Marines with an irregular discharge in order to defect to the Soviet Union, to which he may have supplied valuable military secrets. He married in Russia, tried to settle down to a Communist domesticity with a job in an electronics factory in Minsk, but reconsidered after two years and decided to come home. He returned in mid-1962 with his wife, Marina, and child, stayed briefly in Fort Worth, Dallas and New Orleans, then settled in Dallas–Fort Worth.

He clung to his Marxist beliefs in spite of his evidently unhappy experience in Russia and became indeed an activist, setting up the New Orleans chapter of a pro-Castro group called the Fair Play for Cuba Committee—a chapter of which he remained, however, the only member. Early in 1963, he may have fired a shot at retired General Edwin Walker, a hardline right-winger. Strangely enough for one of his apparent views, he tried later to join up with Carlos Prio Socarras' Cuban Revolutionary Council, the major anti-Castro grouping among the militant Cuban exiles camped those days in Miami and New Or-

*From *The Yankee and Cowboy War*, 1976.

leans and still seething over the Bay of Pigs. But then Earl Warren found him back in character a few days later passing out pro-Castro leaflets (a courageous act in the New Orleans of that period), then going to Mexico City in September in an (unsuccessful) effort to get a visa to visit Cuba. On November 22, in Dallas, at 12:31 P.M. at Dealey Plaza, according to Warren, he shot and killed the president and shot and severely wounded Texas Governor John Connally in the presidential limousine. Then less than an hour later, in another part of town, desperate to escape, he shot and killed Dallas patrolman J. D. Tippit.

He was captured soon after by a police squadron alerted to a gate-crasher at the Texas Theater. He was interrogated for six hours off the record by Dallas officers, who charged him early with the murder of Tippit, then later with the Dealey Plaza shootings. Unlike the standard political assassin qua lone nut, who characteristically boasts of his deed and claims it before history, Oswald took an unashamedly frightened stance, begged someone to come forward to help him, and said from the beginning that he was being made a patsy and could prove it.

On the Sunday morning after that Friday, Oswald was to be transferred from the city jail to the county jail, where it was said he would be more secure. The millions absorbed in television scenes of the funeral procession were switched to Dallas for the on-camera murder of Oswald by Jack Ruby in the very basement of the Dallas jail. Ruby was a Dallas nightclub operator who said he was motivated by sorrow for the plight of the widow, who would have to come to Dallas for the trial of Oswald, a further ordeal he wished to spare her. As a result of Ruby's act, the case against Oswald was effectively closed. Ruby's extensive ties to the Dallas police, organized crime, and the Dallas oligarchy were briefly noted by Warren, but not explored. Like Oswald, Ruby was painted as another lone nut.

Ruby died of cancer in prison in 1967, protesting in a voice constantly breaking into hysteria that the real truth about Dallas was still not known.

As will emerge from point to point in the following critique of the Warren theory of Dealey Plaza, the early objections to his theory have only been fortified over the years of debate by new discoveries and insights. More than a dozen years later, the classic critique of Warren retains its original form and power. The first-generation critics, notably Sylvia Meagher, Harold Weisberg, Josiah Thompson, Mark Lane, Edward Epstein, and Penn Jones, have not been surpassed.

This attests to their good sense, but it also points out the *magnitude* of the Warren theory's main faults. There they stand for all who look to see—the problems of the bullet and the rifle, the medical indications, the sloppy not to say prejudiced character of the deliberation over the evidence, the concealment of doubts, etc.

The newcomer to the detailed evidence is often surprised to find the Warren *Report*'s flaws so apparent. For example, Connally never gave up his conviction that he was hit by a different bullet from the one that went through Kennedy's neck. If that is true, then (as we see in detail below) any lone-gunman theory tied to Oswald is ruled out absolutely, no subtlety to it. Yet Connally is today, as he always has been, a *supporter* of the Warren theory. Asked to reconcile the two beliefs, he answers that he knows he was not hit by the first Kennedy shot, but that the Warren commissioners were "good patriots" whose word could not be doubted. The main support for the Warren no-conspiracy theory was Warren's reputation.

Contemporary critique is not so dazzled by Warren's moral genius. We do not for a moment doubt his passionate desire to do the right thing. We insist, however, that in the complex moral predicament into which the assassination of Kennedy plunged Warren (and Warren liberalism), it was entirely possible that Warren lost his way and did not know what the right thing was. Then he could not resist taking the path others were expecting him to take, the path of the lone-assassin pretense.

The Shootings

Oswald had been a stock handler at the depository since October. At lunchtime on Friday, November 22—according to Warren—he was alone in the southeast corner window of the sixth floor with a 6.5-mm bolt-action Mannlicher-Carcano rifle in his hands, an early World War II weapon which, according to Warren, he had purchased only a few months before from Klein's Mail-Order Sporting Goods for $12.79, and which he had brought to work that morning wrapped as curtain rods.

At 12:30 the lead cars in the motorcade from Love Field appeared below him at the corner of Main and Houston (see map), turned up Houston directly toward him, then turned again to pass in front of him down Elm toward the triple underpass. Then the presidential limousine followed. J. Edgar Hoover once observed that Oswald's easiest shot came as his target was approaching him up Houston. He waited until the car had made the turn and was several hundred feet down Elm. According to Warren, he then fired three shots at the president's back within a period not longer than 5.6 seconds.

Of the first two shots, according to Warren, one or the

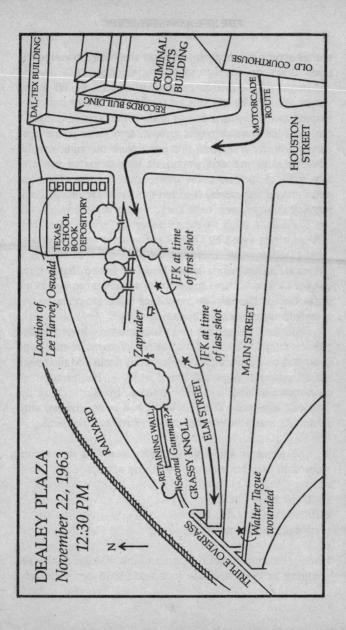

DEALEY PLAZA
November 22, 1963
12:30 PM

N

RAILYARD

*Location of
Lee Harvey Oswald*

TEXAS
SCHOOL
BOOK
DEPOSITORY

DAL-TEX BUILDING

RECORDS BUILDING

CRIMINAL
COURTS
BUILDING

OLD COURTHOUSE

MOTORCADE
ROUTE

HOUSTON
STREET

Zapruder

RETAINING WALL

Second Gunman?

GRASSY KNOLL

ELM STREET

*JFK at time
of first shot*

*JFK at time
of last shot*

MAIN STREET

TRIPLE OVERPASS

*Walter Tague
wounded*

other struck Kennedy high up on the back, deviated the first of several times from its original flight path, ranged upwards and leftwards through his body, exited at his neck, nicked the left side of the knot in the necktie, deviated again downwards and to the right, struck Connally in the back over the right armpit, tore through the governor's body, and came out just inside the right nipple, leaving a gaping exit wound. It then deviated again to strike his right hand at the wrist, smashing the wrist bone into several fragments. It exited the wrist and plunged into the left thigh just above the knee. Then it worked its way out of Connally's thigh to the stretcher at Parkland Hospital, where it was found by a hospital attendant and turned over to the Dallas police. This bullet found on the stretcher, Commission Exhibit 399, is the totality of the hard evidence tying Oswald's Mannlicher-Carcano rifle to the crime, just as the rifle itself is the only hard evidence tying the crime to Oswald. Everything else is circumstantial.

The other of the first two shots missed altogether and hit the curb far ahead of the car. A fragment of curbstone chipped off by the bullet superficially wounded the cheek of a bystander, James Tague.

Oswald's third shot, said Warren, hit Kennedy in the back of his head. The limousine had been slowing until then. At that point it sped off for Parkland Hospital.

The physical and logical inadequacies of this reconstruction may be grouped into three areas:

1 the magic bullet;
2 the magic rifle; and
3 indications of a front shot.

1. *The magic bullet* (Commission Exhibit 399), according to Warren, made four wounds in two men, then

turned up on a stretcher in the hospital in what ballistics experts call a "pristine" condition. There are several reasons for thinking this bullet did not do what it is said to have done.

Its relatively undamaged condition is the simplest of these reasons and in any other situation would easily be conclusive all by itself. One can simply see from the Warren photos that the bullet is all but undamaged.[1]

As if indeed to force us to see this, Warren prints the photograph of CE399 alongside an identical bullet fired by the FBI through the wrist of a cadaver.[2] As all can see, the test bullet came through severely distorted; the whole upper body of the bullet was flattened by impact with the wristbone, one of the denser bones in the body. The explanation offered by Warren for CE399's condition was that it must have tumbled upon smashing through Connally's ribs and hit his wrist flying backwards, that is, with the blunt end to the fore—as though a blunt-end impact would not lead to a still more radical shape deformation and still greater weight loss.

Second, as we have noted, Connally was convinced that the bullet that hit him and the bullet that hit Kennedy in the neck were two separate bullets, not the same CE399. Warren Commission Attorney Arlen Specter, the author of the single-bullet theory, examined Connally before the commission on April 21, 1964. The exchange on this point went as follows:

MR. SPECTER: In your view, which bullet caused the injury to your chest, Governor Connally?

GOVERNOR CONNALLY: The second one.

MR. SPECTER: And what is your reason for that conclusion, sir?

GOVERNOR CONNALLY: Well, in my judgment, it just couldn't conceivably have been the first one because I heard the sound of the shot. In the first place, I don't know anything about the velocity of this particular bullet [2000 fps], but any rifle has a velocity that exceeds the speed of sound [6-700 fps], and when I heard the sound of that first shot, that bullet had already reached where I was, or it had reached that far, and after I heard that shot, I had time to turn to my right, and start to turn to my left before I felt anything.

It is not conceivable to me that I could have been hit by the first bullet, and then I felt the blow from something which was obviously a bullet, which I assumed was a bullet, and I never heard the second shot, didn't hear it. I didn't hear but two shots. I think I heard the first shot and the third shot.

MR. SPECTER: Do you have any idea as to why you did not hear the second shot?

GOVERNOR CONNALLY: Well, first, again I assume the bullet was travelling faster than sound. I was hit by the bullet prior to the time the sound reached me, and I was in either a state of shock or the impact was such that the sound didn't even register on me, but I was never conscious of hearing the second shot at all.

Obviously, at least the major wound that I took in the shoulder through the chest couldn't have been anything but the second shot. Obviously, it couldn't have been the third, because when the third shot was fired I was in a reclining position, and heard it, saw it and the effects of it, rather—I didn't see it, I saw the effects of it—so it obviously could not have been the third, and couldn't have been the first, in my judgment.[3]

Third, the famous Zapruder film shows that as much as a full second after Kennedy was shot in the neck, Connally remained apparently unwounded. When he did react, there was nothing ambiguous about it. His hair shot up. His mouth dropped. Then he seemed to be hit a second time. He slumped immediately to his left into his wife's lap.

The Warren lawyers explain away the time lapse as a

"delayed reaction," even though the specific pathology of Connally's wounds, notably the breaking of the ribs and the wrist, make such a theory implausible on its face, and even though the commission had heard expert medical testimony against the delayed-reaction explanation. (Connally is visibly holding his Stetson in the hand with the shattered wrist many Z-frames after Kennedy had first been hit.)

Fourth, the commission produced out of its own inquiries the most technically conclusive evidence against the magic-bullet theory, although the significance of this evidence may have been concealed from the commission by the FBI, which arranged for the test to be conducted for the commission by the Atomic Energy Commission. This test, neutron-activation analysis, or NAA, involves the same technique that two Swedish scientists used in 1961 to prove that Napoleon had actually been murdered by gradual arsenic poisoning. The method is to bombard the specimen material with neutrons and then measure the emissions thus produced. The operating premise is that any difference in atomic structure of two materials, however slight, will be observable in these emissions. This is why Allegheny County coroner Cyril Wecht described NAA as "one of the most powerful and sophisticated forensic science methods ever developed."[4]

In the current case, NAA was used to compare fragments of a bullet taken from Connally's wrist (and elsewhere) with material taken from the nose of CE399. If the fragments and the slivers were from the same bullet, they would give off *precisely* the same emissions under neutron activation.

Until the success of Harold Weisberg's Freedom-of-Information Act suit in 1974, it was not known for a fact that NAA had been performed. Hoover reported that it had been, but knowingly or not, he concealed the significance of it in a letter to Warren's chief counsel Rankin dated July 8, 1964. By that time, Specter's draft of chapter 3 of the *Report*, setting forth the single-bullet theory, had already been submitted to Rankin. As Wecht observes, Hoover's language "has to be read in its entirety to be appreciated," so I follow him in repeating the letter in full:

> As previously reported to the Commission, certain small lead metal fragments uncovered in connection with this matter were analyzed spectrographically to determine whether they could be associated with one or more of the lead bullet fragments and no significant differences were found within the sensitivity of the spectrographic method.
>
> Because of the higher sensitivity of the neutron activation analysis, certain of the small lead fragments were then subjected to neutron activation analyses and comparisons with larger bullet fragments. The items analyzed included the following: C1—bullet from stretcher; C2—fragment from front seat cushion; C4 and C5—metal fragments from President Kennedy's head; C9—metal fragment from the arm of Governor Connally; C16—metal fragments from rear floor board carpet of the car.
>
> While minor variations in composition were found by this method, these were not considered sufficient to permit positively differentiating among the larger bullet fragments and thus positively determining from which of the larger bullet fragments any given small lead fragment may have come.
>
> Sincerely yours,
>
> > [s] J. Edgar Hoover[5]

The boiling obfuscations of that last paragraph show us Hoover at his best. There is no way for the technically uninformed to know that in the NAA test *any* difference is "sufficient." If one could strip down Hoover's subordinate clause to its grammatical essentials, one would

have the heart of the matter right enough: "Variations
. . . were found." Therefore the fragments from Connally's wrist and CE399 were not of the same bullet.
Which should have been obvious to grown men to start
with from looking at bullet CE399 with their two eyes
open.

2. *The magic rifle* is Oswald's 6.5-mm Mannlicher-
Carcano. Like its companion bullet CE399, it rates the
status of magic because it too shows so little sign of
having been able to do what, for the Warren theory purposes, it must have done.

The weapon Oswald is supposed to have selected for
his great moment was a bolt-action Italian army rifle
mass-produced in the early 1940s. It was not a serious
sharpshooting weapon when it was made and two decades of aging could not have improved it.

The telescopic sight was fitted for a left-handed marksman. Oswald was right-handed.

The scope was misaligned so badly that the FBI had
to adjust the mounting apparatus before it could test-fire
the rifle.

But the deeper problem would still exist even if the
rifle had been straight-shooting and fitted with a properly
mounted and adjusted scope, because the deeper problem
is that the maximum number of shots Oswald could have
taken with that rifle in five and a half seconds was three,
and three shots are too few to explain all the damage that
was done that moment to people and things in Dealey
Plaza.

Add to this the fact that Oswald was rated only a poor
marksman in the Marines and that, in one expert's words,
"The feat attributed to Oswald at Dallas was impossible
for anyone but a world champion marksman using a high-
precision semiautomatic rifle mounted on a carriage and

equipped with an aim corrector, and who had practiced at moving targets in similar set-ups.''[6]

The most impressive defense of the Mannlicher and Oswald's ability to use it in the way claimed by Warren that anyone has seen so far was produced by CBS News in the first of its four-part special called *The American Assassins*, aired in most cities around Thanksgiving 1975. The first part was devoted to the physical analysis of the JFK case. Setting out to settle the dispute about the rifle's capabilities once and for all, CBS erected in the countryside a target-sled and platform arrangement simulating the geometry and distances of the shot from the southeast corner of the sixth floor of the Book Depository, then brought 11 expert riflemen—from the military, from the police, from the firearms industry—to give it a crack. Here goes the sled at the speed and along the path of the limousine. You have 5.6 seconds to squeeze off three shots and score with two of them. After practice, two of the eleven experts were able to do what Oswald is said to have done, two hits out of three shots in 5.6 seconds. CBS does not pause to say how many total series were fired by these eleven, or how many times the two who did it once could do it again. They were impatient to state their interpretation of this result. The reasoning now goes: since a small percentage of expert riflemen could do it, it was possible. Since it was possible, it was possible for Oswald. Therefore he must have done it. CBS knew that Oswald had never practiced from that position or elevation, that he had not even been on a target range for at least two months, and that all his ex-Marine comrades regarded him as a poor shot. CBS is forced to make the argument, read from the teleprompter by an unblinking Dan Rather, that Oswald had scored, "after all, in the second highest category of marksmen in an outfit, the United States Marines, that prides itself on its marksmanship.'' Whoever wrote that had to know that when Oswald was in the Marines, there were only three categories, that you were already in the third of these if you could heft the rifle to your shoulder, that the minimum score required to enter "the second highest category" was 190, and that Oswald's score was 191. CBS knew this. It is all in the Warren hearings. It is all nicely accessible in Sylvia Meagher's work, which CBS says it consulted (see her *Accessories After the Fact*, pp. 108–109). Misunderstanding or differences of interpretation can always be understood, but does this treatment of the rifle's capabilities, the demands of the shot, and Oswald's skill with the weapon fall within that dispensation? Do these look like honest mistakes?

But the worst problem is that for all its testing and proving, CBS did not even address the real issue with the rifle. The problem that leads people to doubt that Oswald did what Warren said he did with that rifle is that the shot that first hit Kennedy and the shot that first hit Connally came only 1.8 seconds apart, as is easily determined by analysis of the Zapruder film, and not even the fastest of the CBS team of experts was able to reload and refire the Mannlicher anywhere near that fast.

3. Among several *indications of a front shot,* the backward snap of Kennedy's head and body visible in the Zapruder film at frame 313 is without doubt the most gruesome and most convincing piece of evidence against the lone-Oswald theory. Indeed, not taking Zapruder into advance account may ultimately prove the big mistake the assassination cabal made.

With his brand-new 8-mm Bell and Howell camera, Abraham Zapruder was standing partway up the grassy knoll that borders Elm on the north and runs up to the railroad tracks (see map). He looked to his left (east) to pick up the motorcade as it turned from Houston left onto Elm, and panned with the Kennedy limousine as it passed in front of him. Kennedy disappeared momentarily behind the Stemmons Freeway sign. He was shot first at precisely that one moment offstage to Zapruder's camera. When he reappeared a fraction of a second later, his hands were already going to his throat. Then in about a second and a half Connally was going over too.

Just when the episode seems finished comes that endless-seeming moment before the fatal headshot. Zapruder had steadied his camera again. The limousine is actually slowing down. Four-one-thousand, five-one-thousand. Kennedy is straight in front of us. Then his head explodes in a plume of pink mist and he is driven violently into the back of the carseat.

Members of the Assassination Information Bureau, including myself, presented the Zapruder film and other photographic evidence to the editorial board of the *Boston Globe* at the meeting at the *Globe* offices on April 23, 1975. Two days later *Globe* Executive Editor Robert Healey published a long editorial in which he summed up the board's general reaction to the Zapruder film as follows:

> It is this particular piece of film, with stop action and with individual still frames, that is being shown around the nation and which has convinced some, at least, that Oswald could not have fired all the shots that killed President Kennedy. . . . This visual presentation is far more convincing than all the books and all the magazine articles that have ever been advanced. They make a simple and convincing case that President Kennedy had to be killed by bullets fired from two directions and thus by more than one person. And no words can make the case better than the Zapruder film. It is as simple as that.[7]

It was not as simple as that to CBS, of course, or its carefully selected array of medical and ballistics experts.

Warren defenders, among them CBS prominently, have searched over the years for a plausible explanation of the backward movement of Kennedy's head. How could a shot fired from behind the President have driven him backward?

An early theory was that the car lurched forward at just that moment, but that was abandoned when it was pointed out (from Zapruder) that the limousine continued to slow down until Secret Service agent Clint Hill got to the back of the car and climbed on. It did not speed up until Jackie Kennedy had crawled out on the rear deck to pick up a piece of her husband's skull.

Then it was explained that "a neuromuscular spasm" was to blame, but that lost favor when resort to Zapruder's film showed Kennedy's body not stiffened but rather hitting the back seat (in Robert Groden's phrase) "like a rag doll." Then came the theory that the bullet hit the back of the head with such force that it caused the brain to explode, that in exploding, the brain blew out the front of the head, and that, as a "jet effect" of this explosion, the head was driven backwards. This novel explanation suffers unfairly from the painfulness of explaining it, but its main problem is that the technical premise has never been demonstrated outside its creator's backyard.

CBS was satisfied with none of these explanations and preferred, again through an unblinking Rather, to offer an altogether new explanation for the backward motion. "Jackie pushed him!" (??) Yes, in her shock, she pushed him away. Again we turn to the film. Can we see it? Does she push? Is there the least sign of a pushing motion on her part? We go frame by frame again and again through the horrible sequence of images from Z-300 or so through 313 and on to 330. What could be clearer? He is knocked backwards out of her hands by a violent force. She is like a statue as he moves. CBS people can see that as readily as you and I. Then why do they say Jackie pushed him?

There are other indications that shots were fired from the front. Here are a few of these.

Another film of the assassination moment, this one taken by Orville Nix from the south side of Elm. He was on the inner mall of the plaza panning with the limousine from right to left (see map). In much poorer quality exposures and with eye-level crowd interference, we nevertheless see everything in the Nix film we see in the Zapruder film, except from the other side—the president thrown backwards. We see Zapruder filming this. We also see the whole crowd on that side of the street reacting spontaneously as though they hear gunfire from the area of the grassy knoll and the railroad bridge.

Two thirds of the ninety witnesses whom Warren asked said the firing came from the grassy knoll area.

Two Parkland Hospital doctors, the first to reach and examine Kennedy upon his arrival at emergency, thought the hole in Kennedy's neck was a wound of entrance, not exit. A complete autopsy might have determined this one way or another, but the throat wound was never explored by the autopsy surgeons.

A Dallas policeman named Joe Smith, one of several policemen who hurried to the grassy knoll area and the shoulder of the railroad bridge in the belief that the gunfire had come from there, said he was summoned by a woman crying: "They are shooting the President from the bushes." When he got to the knoll he found a man. He told the FBI, "I pulled my gun from my holster and I thought, 'This is silly, I don't know who I am looking for,' and I put it back. Just as I did, he showed me he was a Secret Service agent." Secret Service records, which in this respect are careful, show that no Secret Serviceman was assigned that area. No Secret Service agent afterward identified himself as the person confronted by Smith.[8]

Oswald

First we examine the evidence linking Oswald with the crimes he was accused of. This will lead us to a reconsideration of his identity—the Warren story that he was pro-communist and pro-Castro—and to a challenge of this story based on his discernible background with U.S. intelligence.

The Case Against Oswald

Here is the chain of evidence that convicts Oswald. The wounds to Kennedy and Connally are caused by CE399. The bullet CE399 was fired from the Mannlicher-Carcano found in the depository at the sixth-floor window. The Mannlicher-Carcano had been purchased from a mail-order gun supplier a few weeks before in the name of one A. Hidell. Oswald was carrying papers identifying him as Hidell at the time of his arrest.

The astonishing thing is that this is the entirety of the case against Oswald. Besides that chain of associations, the rest of the evidence comes down to an eyewitness who could not repeat his identification of Oswald at a police line-up and a photograph of the alleged assassin published to the whole world on the cover of *Life* which contained as plain as the nose on Oswald's face the ocular proof of its totally bogus character.

First take up the links of this chain one by one.

1. The bullet's link to the wounds: We have already seen how conjectural this link is. It simply does not appear that CE399 was fired into anything harder than a bale of cotton.

2. The bullet's link to the rifle: This is the Warren theory's strong point. There is no doubt that CE399 was fired from a 6.5-mm Mannlicher-Carcano.

3. The rifle's link to Oswald: As we have noted, Oswald did not own this rifle in his own name. He used the name A. Hidell to buy it through the mail, said the Dallas police, who claimed they found papers on him identifying him as that person. The Alek Hidell whom Oswald supposedly pretended to be is reckoned by Warren to be the same A. Hidell who left off the Mannlicher-Carcano at a Dallas gunshop several weeks before the shooting to have the sight mounted.

The problems with this link are several. First, the gunshop tag showing that the weapon had been scopesighted was discounted by the commission itself as unverifiable and suspect because at the time Oswald brought it into the gunshop, he was supposed to be in Mexico City.[9] Second and most important, Warren's only source for this Hidell information was the Dallas police, and the Dallas police cannot be relied on in this matter. Even one of the Commission's members, Assistant Council (now Judge) Burt W. Griffin, has discredited the role of the Dallas police in the investigation, telling reporter Robert Kaiser in 1975, "I don't think some agencies were candid with us. I never thought the Dallas police were telling us the entire truth. Neither was the FBI."[10]

This is not to say that the rifle could not be Oswald's. The Dallas police are not reliable in this case, but one may still not claim that they always lied in it, or presume that since it was the police who found the Hidell papers on Oswald, then the Hidell papers must be attributed to them as part of the frame-up; or that since it was the police who discovered the rifle at the depository window with its three spent shells neatly in a row against the wall and the cartridge jammed in the firing chamber, it must be the police who set the scene.[11] It would be playing games to deny that there is a certain temptation toward saying the cops did it because who else could get away with it. But there may be other answers to our questions going beyond current anticipations and fantasies. It would be better to wait for a real investigation, if only because of the likelihood that there are *several* cover stories hiding the truth of Dallas, of which the lone-Oswald cover story is only the most thinly transparent. Once the necessity for *some* conspiracy hypothesis is clearly and widely acknowledged, only then will the real arguments erupt. What *kind* of conspiracy? Left or right? Foreign or domestic? Private or public?

We are already seeing the Castro-plot theory recirculated. On the CBS News for April 24, 1975, Walter Cronkite screened for the first time some footage from his September 1969 interview with Lyndon Johnson which had formerly been suppressed to comply with a government request based on the usual standard of national security. CBS now revealed this footage, said Cronkite, because a columnist had lately given the secret away. Actually, it had been out of the bag since Leo Janos's reminiscence of Johnson's final days published in the *Atlantic Monthly* of July 1973, in which Janos quotes Johnson as saying that while he could "accept that Oswald pulled the trigger" he could not be sure the commission had gotten to the bottom of it, and his hunch was that Oswald might have been linked to pro-Castro Cubans out for revenge for the Bay of Pigs.

So we have the first-degree cover story that Oswald was alone; now we have the second-degree cover story that Oswald was Castro's agent. There are likely to be other stories increasingly difficult to challenge and explore from afar: The CIA did it. The FBI did it. The Secret Service did it. The Pentagon did it. The Dallas cops did it. The White Citizens Council did it. The Syndicate did it. The Texas oligarchy did it.

We have every citizenly need and right to voice our intuitions in this matter; we also have a citizenly right to force the question politically on the basis of the flimsiness of the official case against Oswald, not on the basis of a necessarily speculative interpretation. No new interpretation could possibly be elaborated and defended in the absence of subpoena powers and a strong national commitment to find the truth. The issue is not whether I or someone else can tell you who killed JFK. The issue at the moment is whether or not the government has been telling or concealing the truth.

Oswald's Identity

Oswald joined the Marines in 1957 and after basic training was sent to Atsugi, Japan, where one of the CIA's larger outfront bases was located, a staging area at that time for covert operations into the Chinese mainland and for U-2 overflights.

In September 1959, two months before normal mustering out, Oswald suddenly applied for a hardship discharge to take care of his mother, who had been slightly injured at work ten months before. Mother Oswald was supported by her regular doctor and an Industrial Accident Board when she denied that this or any other accident cost her any wage-earning capacity or that it was the real motive of her son's hasty discharge. According to researcher Peter Dale Scott, ''. . . the swift handling of Oswald's release suggests that it was a cover: Oswald was being 'sheep dipped' [prior to] assignment to a covert intelligence role.''[12] Scott points out that his immediate application for a passport to travel to Europe suggests that the role concerned his "defection" to the Soviet Union.

The commission was of course not interested in such speculation and decided to take the word of two CIA and five FBI officials that, in the *Report*'s words (p. 327), "there was no, absolutely no type of informant or undercover relationship between an agency of the U.S. Government and Lee Harvey Oswald," even though in its secret session of January 27, 1964, the commission heard its own member say that the CIA and the FBI both would deny a connection with Oswald even if one existed.

From the moment of Oswald's arrest, the story circulated to the effect that he indeed did enjoy such an FBI relationship. This story was finally passed on to the Warren Commission as a formal charge by Texas Attorney General Waggoner Carr. Carr said he had learned from reliable informants (who turned out to be on the Dallas district attorney's staff) that Oswald got two hundred dollars every month from the FBI as an informer and that his FBI number was 179. On January 27, 1964, the commission went into a secret session to deliberate on this. The record of that meeting would not be released for ten years. The transcript shows Chief Counsel J. Lee Rankin defining the problem and the task: "We do have a dirty rumor that is very bad for the Commission . . . and it is very damaging for the agencies that are involved in it and it must be wiped out insofar as it is possible to do so by this Commission."

But as spy-wise Commissioner Allen Dulles was quick to point out, even if Oswald was an agent for Hoover, it would never be possible to prove it because Hoover would deny it and there would be no way to prove him wrong. "I think under any circumstances," said Dulles, ". . . Mr. Hoover would certainly say he didn't have anything to do with this fellow. . . . If he says no, I didn't have anything to do with it, you can't prove what the facts are.'' Would Dulles lie in the same situation, asked the commissioners. Yes, said Dulles, and so would any other officer of the CIA. Whereupon the commission went on to ask two CIA and five FBI officers if Oswald was secretly connected with their outfits, and recorded their answer that he was not as the basis of their official conclusion on the matter.

Discharged in record time from a CIA-related detachment of the Marines on a seemingly fabricated need to take care of a mother who was not infirm, Oswald stayed home a total of three days, then set off for the Soviet Union by way of France, England and Finland with a $1500 ticket purchased out of a $203 bank balance (never explained).

By 1960 he was in Moscow to stage a scene at the U.S. Embassy. First he renounced his American citizenship, then declared that he was about to give the Russians valuable military secrets. He was then shipped off by the Russians to a factory job in Minsk. There he met and married Marina Pruskova, the niece of a top Soviet intelligence official in the Ministry of the Interior.

He decided in 1962 that he now wanted to come back to the States. In spite of his former scene at the embassy and the radar secrets and failure to recant, the State Department speedily gave him a new passport and an allotment of several hundred dollars for the expenses of the return trip with Marina and their child.

The Oswalds were met in the United States by Spas T. Raikin, whom Warren identifies as an official of Travellers Aid. Warren knew, of course, but decided not to add that Raikin was also the former secretary general of the American Friends of the Anti-Bolshevik Bloc of Nations, a group with extensive ties to intelligence agencies in the

Far East and Europe, including the Gehlen-Vlassov operation and the CIA.

The presumed left-winger Oswald and his Red wife Marina immediately were taken into the bosom of the two most militantly anti-Communist communities in the United States, the White Russians of Dallas and the Cuban exiles of New Orleans and Miami. They were befriended by George de Mohrenschildt, an officer of the World War II Gehlen-Vlassov operation.

In April 1963, the Oswalds moved to New Orleans. According to former CIA official Victor Marchetti, Oswald at that time came into contact with Clay Shaw, now identified positively (by Marchetti) as a CIA officer. Shaw was also close to David Ferrie, an instructor at the guerrilla training camps at which, at this point, militant anti-Castro exiles and possibly breakaway elements of the CIA were preparing raids if not new invasions of Cuba. This was the month in which Kennedy for the first time publicly acknowledged the existence of these bases and ordered them closed. The world does not now know what Oswald's relationship to the CIA's Shaw was, only that it existed (this by the testimony of nine witnesses). It was while this intimate association with the CIA was alight, however, that Oswald became the one-man New Orleans chapter of the Fair Play for Cuba Committee, supposedly a pro-Castro organization.

The pro-Castro leaflets Oswald once distributed for this committee were stamped with the address, "544 Camp Street." The commission found no evidence that Oswald kept an office there, but it did find the office of an anti-Castro group, the Cuban Revolutionary Council. We now know the Cuban Revolutionary Council was a CIA creation put together by Howard Hunt, and the 544 Camp Street was a major headquarters of anti-Castro activity throughout that period.

In August 1963, while passing out his pro-Castro leaflets (something he did twice), Oswald got into a scuffle with some anti-Castro Cubans and was arrested by the New Orleans police. The first and only thing he said at the police department was that he wanted to speak to the FBI, a novel request for a left-winger of that place, period, and predicament. The agent appeared and Oswald got off quickly with a ten-dollar fine.

In September 1963 Oswald supposedly took a bus from New Orleans to Mexico City. His purpose is said to have been to obtain a Cuban travel visa. On October 1, the CIA cabled the State Department and the Office of Naval Intelligence to tell of information from "a reliable and sensitive source" that one Lee *Henry* Oswald had entered the Soviet Embassy. When the National Archives released a previously classified memo from Helms to the commission dated March 24, 1964, another piece fell into the puzzle: "On 22 and 23 November," said Helms "immediately following the assassination of President Kennedy, three cabled reports were received from [deleted] in Mexico City relative to photographs of an unidentified man who visited the Cuban and Soviet Embassies in that city during October and November 1963" (Commission Document 674, National Archives).

The original description of this Oswald in the CIA report ran like this: "The American was described as approximately 35 years old, with an athletic build, about six feet tall, with a receding hairline." Oswald was 24, about 5′8″ and 160 pounds. Who was pretending to be Oswald at the Russian and Cuban embassies in Mexico City a month before this same Oswald allegedly was to shoot the President?

There is evidence actually of several Oswalds in circulation at this time. There is in the first place the presumptive original himself installed since late October in the depository. There is the thirty-five-year-old Oswald in Mexico City freshening up the Red spoor at the Cuban and Soviet missions. There is the Oswald or Oswalds who move around Dallas just before the hit, planting unforgettable memories of a man about to become an assassin: the Oswald of the firing range who fires cross-range into another person's targets and then belligerently starts a loud argument in which he carefully and loudly repeats his name; the Oswald of the used-car lot who sneers at Texas and the American flag and drives reck-lessly, though Oswald had no driver's license and did not know how to drive; the Oswald who visited exile Sylvia Odio a few weeks before the assassination in the com-pany of two anti-Castro militants at a time when the *real* Oswald (or is it the other way around?) is supposed to be in Mexico City. Who are all these Oswalds?

In another crucial Freedom of Information suit, Harold Weisberg forced the government to make and release the transcript of a theretofore untranscribed stenographer's tape of another secret meeting of the Warren Commis-sion on January 22, 1964. The transcript indicates that Congressman Gerald Ford suspected Oswald of being an informant for the FBI. Ford participated in a discussion concerning Oswald's repeated use of post office boxes, an operating method characteristic of undercover FBI in-formants, and remarked on Oswald's informer-like be-havior in playing both sides of the wrangle between the Communists who identify with Stalin and the Commu-nists who identify with Trotsky. "He was playing ball," said Ford of Oswald, "writing letters, to both elements of the Communist Party. I mean, he's playing ball with the Trotskyites and the others. This was a strange cir-cumstance to me."

In that same meeting, Chief Counsel Rankin told the commissioners the FBI was behaving in an unusual way in the Oswald investigation and seemed to be attempting to close the case without checking out numerous leads into Oswald's activities. On the final page of the thirteen-page transcript, Allen Dulles summed up his reaction to the idea of an Oswald connection to the FBI by saying, "I think this record ought to be destroyed."[13]

Ruby

The Warren *Report* tells us that "Ruby was unquestionably familiar, if not friendly, with some Chicago criminals" (p. 790). A partial list of Ruby's organized-crime connections, *as they were known to the Warren Commission*, would include:

Lewis McWillie, a "gambler and murderer" who had managed the Lansky Syndicate's Tropicana in Havana before 1959 and by 1963 was an executive at the Thunderbird in Las Vegas, another prime Lansky holding. Ruby traveled to Cuba with McWillie, received two phone calls from him from Cuba, and shipped him a pistol, all in 1959.[14]

Dave Yaras, an intimate of Ruby's from Chicago childhood days, a Syndicate mobster operating out of Chicago and Miami.[15] Yaras told the Warren Commission that Ruby was also close to:

Lenny Patrick, another Chicago-based hood also known to Ruby's sister Eva as a friend of her brother's. Yaras and Patrick are both prominently identified in congressional crime hearings as important figures in the Chicago Syndicate.[16]

Paul Roland Jones, Paul "Needlenose" Labriola, Marcus Lipsky, Jimmy Wienberg, Danny Lardino, and *Jack Knappi,* the Chicago Syndicate group that moved into Dallas in 1947 (the year Ruby moved to Dallas).[17] Jones, an opium smuggler in the forties, told the Warren

Commission that "if Ruby killed Lee Harvey Oswald on orders, the man to talk to would be Joe Savella [properly *Civello*]," then head of Syndicate operations in Dallas. *Chicago Daily News* crime reporter Jack Wilner also told the commission that Ruby was involved in 1947 in the Chicago Syndicate takeover of Dallas gambling. "The Commission finds it difficult to accept this report," said Warren.[18]

Robert "Barney" Baker, a Teamster hood convicted by RFK. His phone number was in Ruby's address book.[19]

Milt Jaffe, also in Ruby's address book, a point holder in the Stardust of Las Vegas with Cleveland Syndicate heavy Moe Dalitz.[20]

At the age of fifteen Ruby already belonged to a gang of Chicago youths who ran messages for *Al Capone.* This gang produced such other notables as Frank "The Enforcer" Nitti, Capone's successor as head of the Chicago Syndicate, and his associate, Charles "Cherry Nose" Gioe, busted in 1943 with John Roselli, who is later associated with the CIA-Syndicate scheme to assassinate Castro.[21]

Peter Dale Scott (whose citations I gratefully borrow here) has identified three independent reports to the Warren Commission strongly suggesting that Ruby was "in fact a pay-off or liaison man between organized crime and the Dallas police department (over half of whose policemen Ruby knew personally)."

1. In 1956, the Los Angeles FBI advised the Dallas FBI that Mr. and Mrs. James Breen, "acting . . . as informants for the Federal Narcotics Bureau," had become involved with "a large narcotics setup operating between Mexico, Texas and the East. . . . In some fashion, James [Breen] got the okay to operate through Jack Ruby of

Dallas.''[22] In 1964, reinterviewed by the Chicago FBI, Mrs. Breen confirmed her 1956 story.[23]

2. After the assassination, a prisoner in an Alabama jail told the FBI that a year previous to the assassination, when he had tried to set up a numbers game in Dallas, he was advised ''that in order to operate in Dallas it was necessary to have the clearance of Jack Ruby . . . who had the fix with the county authorities.''[24]

3. Again after the assassination, another prisoner in Los Angeles, Harry Hall, contacted the Secret Service (who vouched for his reliability) with the information that in his days as a Dallas gambler he had turned over 40 percent of his profits to Ruby, who ''was supposed to have influence with the police.''[25]

The Warren Commission's conclusion was that ''the evidence does not establish a significant link between Ruby and organized crime.''[26]

The commission also failed to investigate a communication received on June 9, 1964, only two days after Ruby's testimony, from J. Edgar Hoover, in which Hoover disclosed that Ruby may have been an FBI informant for several months in 1959.[27] Nor did it seek to reconcile its picture of Ruby as a small-time psychotic with evidence that Ruby was on good terms with such powerful Texas millionaires as H. L. Hunt, his son Lamar (whose office Ruby visited the day before the assassination),[28] Billy Byars, and Clint Murchison, a power behind Johnson and involved heavily in the Bobby Baker scandal.[29]

Ruby's story is a long way yet from reconstruction, but he gives us leads and fragments, the most spectacular of which is a whole rich set of suggestions tying him variously into high-level Syndicate figures operating in pre-revolutionary Cuba, and as we know today, involved later in attempts against the Castro government in covert operations connected with elements of the CIA and stemming from the Bay of Pigs, operations which Kennedy used force to extirpate two months before his death. This makes the Ruby case totally of a piece with the over-all affair of the Bay of Pigs/Dallas reactions. The world of Ruby, of the Carousel, and of the Dallas cops was also the world of the Bay of Pigs and of the secret staging bases outside Miami and New Orleans.

Ruby asks us as directly as he can to entertain the hypothesis that he was a member of the JFK assassination cabal, that his purpose in liquidating Oswald was to satisfy the cabal's need to keep the patsy from standing trial, and that something happened to him in the Dallas jail between the time he killed Oswald and the time he began demanding to come before Warren, something to change his mind. Of course I do not press this speculation, but I do say that it better fits the few facts we have than the Warren theory that Ruby too was just another lone nut of Dallas. Thanks to the providential bust at Watergate, we are now too ferociously educated about our government to dismiss as inherently crazy Ruby's fear of covert reprisals from the police or his warnings that "a whole new form of government" was being installed as a result of Dallas.

For this is indeed the direction in which our current discoveries and insights about the assassination and its cover-up are propelling us—namely, that what happened in Dealey Plaza was a coup d'etat. The motive of this coup no one could have grasped at the time without access to the innermost closets of the group that engineered it. As Johnson began shouldering Yankee advisers aside (see the Pentagon Papers), meanwhile mystifying his relationship to Kennedy to make himself seem merely the continuation of Kennedy by other means, it was hard for many to see the coming of a radically new war policy in

Vietnam, though the big war was very soon upon us (two hundred thousand troops by the time of the first national March on Washington against the war in April 1965). Johnson also set in motion plans to carry out a for-good invasion of Cuba, the so-called Second Naval Guerrilla, abandoned only because of the outbreak of the Dominican revolt in early 1965 and Johnson's decision to suppress it with the invasion forces assembled originally for Cuba. Now we see these under-the-table moves quite clearly and see them as radical *departures* from Frontier Camelot policy lines, not as the *continuations* which Johnson and Nixon and all the other chauvinists found it convenient to pretend they were. The Johnson administration was not the fulfillment of Kennedy policy; it was its defeat and reversal.

Among the witnesses who testified to Warren, few more than Ruby make us feel the presence of these momentous themes. He is garbled, murky, incomplete, and as his friend and roommate George Senator says, apolitical in any conventional sense. Yet something about what happened to him after killing Oswald makes him more fully in touch with the situation's underlying realities than anyone else who testified—or who listened from the bench.

In November 1965, nationally syndicated columnist Dorothy Kilgallen advised a few close friends, including Mark Lane, that she was developing a lead that would "blow the JFK assassination case wide open." Twice before, Kilgallen had achieved major scoops on this case, both times in connection with Jack Ruby. First, she published Jack Ruby's secret testimony to the Warren Commission months before the Warren *Report* came out. Second, she interviewed Ruby privately in the judge's chamber during Ruby's murder trial. Before she could make good on her promise, she died of an overdose of alcohol and barbiturates, ruled an accidental death. Her JFK-case notes never turned up.

Sick with cancer (he claimed he was being poisoned), Ruby died in his hospital room in 1967.

So who was Oswald? Even Ford admitted he doesn't know. The campaign to reopen the investigation of Dealey Plaza succeeded at least to that extent. The likes of Time, Inc., and CBS and Ford clung to the theory that Oswald killed Kennedy, but by the time of the CBS special of Thanksgiving 1975, even they had been compelled to admit that the loner theory of Oswald had not withstood a decade of criticism. But then they wanted to say that Oswald must have been a Castro agent.

This move was anticipated by the Assassination Information Bureau in its January 1975 conference at Boston University, "The Politics of Conspiracy," when it called for a larger effort to understand Oswald from the standpoint of his bureaucratic and personal associations. The no-conspiracy position is going to collapse, we predicted, and when that happens, and suddenly everyone is an assassination buff or a conspiracy freak, then the great claim of the cover-up artists will be that Oswald was part of a left-wing conspiracy answering to Cuban or Russian discipline.

This repeats completely the bias of the Warren Commission in its original work. Always for them the word "conspiracy" actually meant "international Communist conspiracy," such that the alternative to the lone-assassin concept was axiomatically the next thing to war. The idea that a conspiracy to murder Kennedy might as well be domestic as foreign and as well right-wing as left-wing certainly occurred, but if it was given any serious thought, we have yet to see the record of it. Now again, still in the time of Ford, the same bias is imposed: probably there was no conspiracy, and if there was a conspiracy, probably it was the work of the Castroites or the KGB.[31]

After the Thanksgiving 1975 CBS specials on JFK and Ford's positive reaction to them, the AIB at once raised its tiny voice to say that the questions of the assassination itself had by no means been resolved by CBS's self-commissioned board of inquiry (as if CBS had a mandate to resolve this dispute!), and that nobody was going to get anywhere at all with the question, "Who was Oswald?" by starting out convinced that Oswald killed Kennedy. That was where Warren had started. Any new investigation starting from the same assumption will come to the same or worse confusion. As it always was, and as it will remain until an open investigation is carried out by some group (such as a federal grand jury?) capable of commanding the public trust, the key question is still, "Who killed JFK?" Oswald is not yet proved guilty.

But at the same time, the question of Oswald's identity obviously remains one of the outstanding submysteries of the larger drama and contains within it many of the decisive threads. If it is explored without a presupposition of Oswald's guilt, it can prove a rewarding—a startling, an astonishing—area of study. For my part, I would have no desire to try to anticipate the outcome of such a study were it not for the insistence with which Warren defenders press the unfounded picture of Oswald as the lone assassin upon the public consciousness. Be reminded that it is a *theory* that Oswald did it, not a fact—a minority theory, to boot. However speculative it must be, then, the presentation of a different theory of Oswald seems justified if only to counter the impression that Oswald, whatever else, must have been a left-winger.

* * *

From his involvement in top-secret CIA intelligence work (the U-2 flights) at a big CIA base (Atsugi), we surmise that Oswald became a CIA workman while he was still a Marine. From the peculiarities of his defection in 1959 and his turnaround and return in 1962—how precipitous the going, how smooth the coming back—we surmise that he was in the Soviet Union on CIA business for which the role of Marxist defector was only a cover. When he came back to the United States, he was met by one CIA operative (Raikin), taken under the wing of another CIA operative (de Mohrenschildt), and accepted in the two most militantly reactionary communities in the United States at the time (the White Russians and the exile Cubans).

Assuming Oswald might have been a CIA man, what possible mission could have brought him to this scene?

Think back to the Bay of Pigs Fiasco and recall the anger of Cuban exile reaction to Kennedy's last-minute shortening of the invasion effort and his refusal at the crisis of the beachhead to stand by implied promises of support. We know now that a group around Howard Hunt and Richard Nixon was sentimentally and politically at one with the anti-Castro Cubans in their sense of outrage with Kennedy and their desire to force the issue.

A militant faction of this group broke regular discipline in the period after the Fiasco, the period in which Kennedy fired Warren commissioner-to-be Allen Dulles, installed John McCone in his place, and threatened "to smash the CIA into a thousand pieces and scatter it to the winds." This breakaway component operated independently of official control and carried out, with the exile Cubans, its own program of "pinprick" raids along the Cuban coast. These attacks were staged from bases inside the United States.

This group existed. It was organized. It was being

funded. It was getting large supplies of weapons. It was mounting illegal operations from within the continental interior. Yet Kennedy could not find it. And particularly after the October 1962 Missile Crisis, he *had* to find it, because he had to shut it down; for now he had promised the Russians that the United States would respect the integrity of the Castro government. How do you look for such a group?

You get a trusted agent with the right background and capabilities. You dress up your agent to look like one of the other side's agents. You get your agent circulating in the flight patterns of the suspect communities.

Obviously we are still far from being able to say for sure what Oswald's identity and role really were. But to my mind, the hypothesis that best fits the available facts about him is that he was a loyal CIA man sent out to help locate the renegade Bay of Pigs group, contact it, penetrate it, and determine its organization, backing and plans. The now-famous Oswald letter to the Dallas FBI of November 19, 1963, which the FBI first destroyed and then lied about, and which it now says contained a threat to blow up its Dallas office, was just as likely a warning from Oswald that he had discovered a plot against the President's life set to be sprung that Friday in Dallas. Oswald and his control could not guess the FBI communications were not secure, or that Oswald himself was all the while being groomed for the role of patsy.

NOTES

1. *Hearings before the President's Commission on the Assassination of President John F. Kennedy*, vol. 17. (Hereafter cited as *Hearings*.)
2. Ibid.
3. *Hearings*, vol. 4, pp. 136.
4. Cyril Wecht, "A Pathologist's View of the JFK Autopsy: An Unsolved Case," *Modern Medicine*, November 27, 1972.
5. Cyril Wecht, "JFK Assassination: A Prolonged and Willful Cover-Up," *Modern Medicine*, October 28, 1974.
6. Hepburn, *Farewell America*, p. 57. See also Sylvia Meagher, *Accessories After the Fact* (New York: Bobbs-Merrill, 1967), pp. 94–133.
7. Robert Healey, "Time to Reopen the Dallas Files," *Boston Globe*, April 25, 1975.
8. *Hearings*, vol. 7, p. 535.
9. *Report of the President's Commission on the Assassination of President John F. Kennedy*, pp. 553–55. (Hereafter cited as *Report*.) Warren discounted the gunshop owner's testimony because the official reconstruction had already placed Oswald in Mexico at the time the contact was supposedly made.
10. Kaiser, "The JFK Assassination: Why Congress Should Reopen the Investigation," *Rolling Stone*, April 24, 1975.
11. But note that former CIA officer George O'Toole implies that Oswald had no papers on him at all and that the Hidell-Oswald link was another of the preforged components of the cover-up. See O'Toole, *The Assassination Tapes* (New York: Penthouse Press, 1975).

12. Scott, "From Dallas to Watergate," in Blumenthal and Yazipan, *Government by Gunplay*, p. 122.
13. Zodiac News Service release, April 30, 1975. We are in galleys as the final volume of the Church Committee's probe of the intelligence agencies is released. This volume bears on the role of the intelligence agencies in the JFK assassination and concludes, as we have argued above, that the FBI and the CIA obstructed the investigation. What the Church Committee totally failed to do, however, was investigate the relation of Oswald to the FBI, the CIA and military intelligence. Likewise, it ignored late-developing information that Jack Ruby was also an FBI informant. *The Investigation of the Assassination of President John F. Kennedy:* Performance of the Intelligence Agencies, Final Report, Book V, published July 23, 1976, Senate Select Committee to Study Governmental Operations with respect to Intelligence Activities. (See note 31 below.)
14. *Hearings*, vol. 23, p. 166. See also Ed Reid and Ovid Demaris, *The Green Felt Jungle* (New York: Simon & Schuster, Pocket Books, 1963).
15. *Hearings*, vol. 14, p. 444. See also Scott, "The Longest Cover-up," in Weissman, *Big Brother.*
16. Senate Committee on Government Operations, "Organized Crime and Illicit Traffic in Narcotics," *Hearings*, 88th Congress, Second Session, p. 508, chart 11.
17. Warren *Hearings*, vol. 22, pp. 300, 360, and 478. I am indebted to Peter Dale Scott for pointing out the following passages in the Warren *Hearings*.
18. *Report*, p. 793.
19. *Hearings*, vol. 25, p. 244, Commission Exhibit 1268.
20. Ibid.
21. Ibid., vol. 22, p. 423.
22. Ibid., vol. 23, p. 369.
23. Ibid., vol. 23, p. 371.
24. Ibid., vol. 23, p. 372.
25. Ibid., vol. 23, p. 363.
26. *Report*, p. 801. But from the much-later-released transcript of the Warren Commission's meeting of January 27, 1964 (its second emergency secret meeting within five days), we

know for a fact that the commissioners were not always so confident of this interpretation. Chief Counsel Rankin said at that meeting: "He [Ruby] has apparently all kinds of connections with the underworld. . . . There isn't any question but what he planned to go down to Cuba, and he did, and the story was that it was in regard to armaments. . . . My recollection is that one of the stories was that he was to try to sell guns and ammunition to Castro. . . . That is all denied, and that he was going down there to make money on other kinds of sales but not anything that was munitions or armaments. There is no explanation of where he was there, what he did, or who his connections were. He had all kinds of connections with the minor underworld, I think you would call it, in Dallas and Chicago. . . ." *(New Republic,* September 27, 1975).

27. Tad Szulc, "The Warren Commission in its Own Words," *New Republic,* September 27, 1975.
28. Warren *Report,* p. 368.
29. Warren *Hearings,* vol. 22, p. 426 and vol. 23, p. 362.
30. "Murdered—For Having Too Much on JFK's Killers," *Midnight,* January 18, 1977.
31. The Church Committee's review of the intelligence community's relationship to the JFK assassination and its cover-up (Book V of the Church report, published in July 1976), might easily have begun correcting this remarkable distortion. The committee knew, for example, as the Warren Commission evidently did not, that Ruby had at some point enjoyed some form of cooperative relationship with the Dallas FBI, but this fact did not even find its way into a footnote. Yet at the same time, the committee devoted pages of repetitious detail to the story of a would-be assassin of Castro, Rolando Cubela (CIA code name, AM-LASH), whose attempt on Castro it imagines *may* have motivated a Castro-Oswald attempt on JFK.

IV

The Congress Finds a Conspiracy: Is It the Right One?

The eleven pieces grouped in this section are all from or about the period in which the House of Representatives had its Select Committee on Assassinations up and running—late 1976 to early 1979.

For the last two of those years, I was in Washington as a co-director of the Assassination Information Bureau and in constant contact with the investigative staff of the Assassinations Committee as well as the community of Warren revisionists, called "the critics," whose work had brought the need and the demand for this new investigation into focus.

Those were heady days in the great conspiracy hunt.

The Watergate scandal, which arrived as a bolt from the blue in 1972, had suddenly preempted Nixon's plans for his second term. The Vietnam War was almost over at last. Immense intelligence scandals were roaring through the CIA and the FBI. J. Edgar Hoover was gone and the new leadership at the FBI was a little penitent and rueful about past episodes of FBI trampling on the rights of citizens. Maybe we were going to find out who killed JFK.

The atmosphere around the Assassinations Committee in Carter-era Washington was, frankly, often exciting, the more so no doubt for the occasional pinch of dread in the air. My memo-to-files item, "Three More Dead Men," tells of such a moment when, within just a few days of one another, three key individuals, all selected to testify before the Assassinations Committee, died suddenly and violently. These were George de Mohrenschildt, Oswald's perceptive and intriguing older friend in Dallas; Charles Nicoletti, a ranking Chicago hood who knew something about the CIA-Mafia plot; and Carlos Prio Socarras, leader of anti-Castro Cubans in the United States during the years of the JFK administration. De Mohrenschildt's and Prio's gunshot deaths were ruled suicidal. Nicoletti was clearly murdered gangland style.

No Tom Wicker rose to note that these men had been of great interest to the new JFK investigation. No Morley Safer went on camera to say how odd that they all should die with a foot in the same witness box. The Assassinations Committee might have shown a little more alarm itself. Those were its witnesses, after all, who were dropping dead. I wrote "The Behavior of the Media" about just this lack of notice.

The next two pieces, "Legend, Counter-Legend," and "The Man Who Came In From the Cold, Maybe," treat the strange story of James Jesus Angleton, chief of the

CIA's counterintelligence office during the New Frontier, and his long, bitter and destructive duel with a KGB imponderable named Yuri Nosenko.

Of the remaining seven pieces in this section, three were written for the AIB newsletter, *Clandestine America*. "Did the Mob Kill John Kennedy?" was written with my AIB co-director and close friend, Jeff Goldberg, for the "Focus" section of the Sunday *Washington Post*. By the time of the next two pieces, "Conspiracy Found" and "Media Reactions" (the latter also co-written with Goldberg), the AIB and its friends had more deeply considered the question of likely suspects. The Soviet scenario was worse than the Castro scenario, and the Mafia scenario was the best the Assassinations Committee could deliver.

But was it good enough? Was it the truth? What did it leave out or exaggerate?

Several years later I returned to the question of organized crime's putative role in the JFK assassination in a piece called "Is the Mafia Theory a Valid Alternative?" This was written and published as an "Afterword" to Jim Garrison's 1988 memoir, *On the Trail of the Assassins*. I have reprinted it here next to the three preceding pieces, out of chronological order, because it speaks to the same subject and because it is specifically critical of the Assassinations Committee's idea that two or three Mafia leaders alone, out of their own resources, could carry out and cover up such a crime.

Sharp readers will notice that these four pieces on the question of suspects do not stand in a perfectly straight line. I can only admit that and make sure to point it out. The *Post* piece was written with Goldberg at a moment early in 1979 when it seemed to both of us, well, *correct* to help the Assassinations Committee. The committee was at that point out of business, its term having just run out, but it might live on in a pro-conspiracy final report if it could find a constituency.

So the AIB's somewhat Machiavellian thought was that we should all get together, sort of, behind the committee's Mafia-conspiracy theory because it was, after all, at least a conspiracy theory, and it was probably the one that most Americans would find least threatening—a ''starter'' theory, so to speak. The idea was to first get the Justice Department to reopen the case on the basis of the Mafia evidence, then see where else a new investigation might lead. My Garrison ''Afterword'' was written almost ten years later at a moment when the Mafia-theory strategy had pretty much dead-ended.

Rereading these pieces early in 1992, I decide to stand firmly by my ambivalence. The Mafia scenario is the right thing to be ambivalent about in this case. I can see many problems with it but cannot quite bring myself to throw it away.

Of the last two pieces in this section, ''Growing Doubts'' attempts to weigh the Assassinations Committee's contribution to our understanding of Dealey Plaza. It is a tour of the battlefield as of 1980. ''A Farewell to Dealey Plaza'' was a somewhat later attempt to draw a line, come to a reckoning, and at last put this case out of my life.

6

Three More Dead Men*

What did Count George de Mohrenschildt, Charles Nicoletti, and Carlos Prio Socarras not live to tell the world about the assassination of John Kennedy?

On March 29, 1977, in a friend's sprawling Palm Beach mansion, a White Russian emigré of Dallas, Count George de Mohrenschildt, 65, pulled the trigger of a loaded 20 gauge shotgun while holding its muzzle in his mouth. Less than two hours before, he had heard that an investigator from the House Select Committee on Assassinations was in town to question him about the killing of JFK.

Near midnight the next day, in the parking lot of the Golden Horns restaurant in a suburban Chicago shopping center, 61-year-old crime lord Charles Nicoletti was pulled dead from his burning car, shot three times point-blank in the back of the neck by a small-calibre handgun. He was being sought by Assassinations Committee investigators, who had learned his whereabouts only two days before.

Six days after de Mohrenschildt's suicide, at 8:00 A.M. Tuesday, April 5, in residential Miami Beach, Carlos Prio

*AIB briefing paper, 1977.

Socarras, 74, deposed president of pre-Batista Cuba and the leader of the anti-Castro Cuban exile community in the United States, was found dying, shot through the chest, a black revolver fallen at his side—another suicide. Prio's name was also on the Assassinations Committee's list of witnesses.

Who were these people? What are we to make of their deaths coming in such a cluster at such an important moment in the new JFK investigation? What knowledge of the killing did they take to their graves? Who was threatened by this knowledge? Who is comforted by their silence?

"I'm a Patsy!"

Back in 1962, a casual friend in the Dallas Russian-speaking community asked George and Jeanne de Mohrenschildt to help look after a needy young couple fresh from the U.S.S.R., Lee and Marina Oswald. Marina had a mouthful of rotten teeth, an infant in arms, no English, no work skills, no friends, and a husband who could or would not love her.

And Lee seemed an even worse loser. Born into Dallas's lower working class in 1940, he had joined the Marines at seventeen only to defect to the U.S.S.R., give away his U.S. military secrets to the Russians, take a Russian wife, get her with child, then decide after two years in Minsk that life would be better back home after all. Now that he was back, he couldn't find a job.

So from then until the de Mohrenschildts left for Haiti in the spring of 1963, a bit less than a year later, they were the hapless Oswalds' closest thing to friends—"a case of sheer pity on their part," as a neighbor put it.

George and Jeanne had themselves come a long way to be in Dallas and might easily sympathize with the Oswalds' sense of homelessness. George was the child of an aristocratic oil-rich family that was destroyed by the Bolshevik expropriations of 1920. He was born in White Russia, raised in Poland, schooled in France. He arrived in the United States in 1938 with little cash but good family contacts in the American oil industry and began building a career as an oil geologist that would bring him in touch with many of the leading figures of the Texas oil world. He was accused by some of having been a Nazi spy during World War II, but his claim (and the more likely truth) is that he was working then with a Free-French espionage group aimed at countering Nazi activities in the United States and Mexico, especially involving oil purchases. In the mid 1950s he carried out in-country geological field surveys of Yugoslavia and Ghana for the State Department's International Cooperation Agency, now known to have been used often as a CIA cover. He had a long and close relationship with the chief of the CIA office in Dallas, who issued more than ten intelligence reports based on de Mohrenschildt's ''debriefings.''

Jeanne, who was also a White Russian exile, was his fourth wife, but they had been married for twenty years. She and her family had fled before the Bolsheviks into China, first to Harbin where she grew up, then to Shanghai, where she became an apache dancer. She came to New York the same time as George, but they did not meet until 1956 in Dallas, where they kept the company of other White Russians. Their co-exiles knew them as a bohemian, iconoclastic pair, disdainful of Dallas opinion, he a womanizer of some local fame, she a deposed but still passionate Russian princess.

An FBI hearsay report had it that George's first reaction to word of JFK's death was to exclaim that ''that lunatic Oswald'' had something to do with it, but he denied this to the Warren Commission and everyone else, rather loudly. For example, the U.S. ambassador to Haiti notified the State Department early in 1965 that Jeanne de Mohrenschildt, "during a large and noisy cocktail buffet, made some interesting remarks . . . about the president's assassination. . . . She stated that the Warren report had not been complete and that certain facts and depositions made by her had not been disclosed. She also insinuated that a sinister plot could have triggered the assassination, as Oswald had no personal grudge against the president."

The Dutch journalist Willem Oltmans originally interviewed George and Jeanne in 1964. He cultivated the relationship. In 1969 he taped a long interview in which George reportedly disputed the lone-Oswald theory in detail and named people he thought were involved in a much wider conspiracy. But he did not give Oltmans permission to release the interview without explicit instructions from him to do so. It was something he wanted in reserve.

At the beginning of 1976 he began a book, finished in manuscript that summer, setting down everything he wanted to say about the assassination. The book's title, *"I'm a Patsy, I'm a Patsy!"*, specifically recalls Oswald's cry in the Dallas jail that Friday midnight when an over-credulous press corps confronted him with this accusation. And that in fact seems to be the theme of George's still-secret book—that Oswald was framed.

This view, of course, was wholly shared with him by Jeanne. But as soon as the manuscript of *"Patsy!"* was finished, the question of what he intended to do with it brought him into a towering and finally crippling conflict with Jeanne. The book seems only to tell the same story as the Oltmans interview of 1969. But the difference was that he had never agreed to let Oltmans release that story.

Did he intend to handle the book the same way? Had writing it been a pastime? Or did he mean to look for a publisher and at long last tell all he knew?

Jeanne was soon joined by Alexandra, daughter of his first marriage, in passionate opposition to such a step. She argued that those who spoke died. George answered that this was all very well, but he was broke. He could make a lot of money with his book and his interviews. She answered that it was suicidal to do something that would certainly get him destroyed—forget the side benefits.

Even as they thrashed away at this first unresolvable problem in their twenty years of marriage, the House Assassinations Committee was taking form and enduring its early crises. This may have made it easier for George to believe he could now tell what he knew, make legitimate money for it, and be a moment's TV hero and still survive.

Then in August 1976 Oltmans appeared once again to turn the pressure up. American journalists mostly dismissed Oltmans as the kind of gorgeous TV personality it is better not to listen to seriously. It is beside the point whether he is or is not. Oltmans' function in the drama was to transform a widespread but diffuse public demand for a new understanding of the JFK case into a specific pressure on de Mohrenschildt to release the interviews, to publish the book, to tell everything he knows. The real point about him is that he was backed by major media (Dutch NOS-TV) and was a pipeline to a major world audience.

The situation thus spread itself before George in the form of Oltmans' concrete temptations and Jeanne's demands for resistance. As if this did not make his life easy enough, the next moment Edward Epstein of *Readers Digest* arrived to offer thousands of dollars for new interviews. How could such a tide be resisted? Oltmans flew back to Amsterdam with a tentative go-ahead to firm up the terms and plans.

Jeanne now drew the line. Since she knew essentially the same things about the assassination that he knew, she could herself be put in danger for things he might say. She could not allow him to be suicidal for them both. That would be a madness as great as his. She would have to help him deal better with his madness.

On October 28, according to Jeanne, George tried to drown himself in the bathtub, having before tried drug overdoses and razors. On the 29th, wife, daughter and lawyer urged him in unison to see a psychiatrist. The psychiatrist gave tests and arranged for George's admittance to Parkland Memorial (where JFK died) on November 9. George remained there as a patient of the psychiatric clinic until December 30. He was treated for "delusions" and "paranoia," having the form of fears of plotters and sinister forces in the JFK killing, and "memory problems," having the form of a stubborn false recollection of Oswald as a patsy. The mode of treatment was electric shock therapy.

While he was strapped into the electrodes, Jeanne filed for divorce and took off for California. Their marriage had lasted twenty years and had not been altogether bad.

On February 3 George met again with Oltmans in Dallas at the library of Bishop College. Oltmans said George was "a totally different guy": vacillating, depressed, ashen—changed.

George's story of Oswald and Kennedy too had changed, utterly. Now for the first time George said that Oswald killed JFK. He said that he himself had been Oswald's control in the assassination and that the overall force behind it was that of H.L. Hunt and Lester Logue, the Texas oilmen. But then later, in March 1977 in Holland, George took this new story back. "I'll be discharged at Bishop College in June. I'm sixty-five. My wife ran away. I'm at the end of the line. Let's face it. I only made up the story about Oswald because everyone else has made a million dollars out of the assassination and I haven't made anything."

Perhaps honestly confused or ignorant of George's earlier and later stories, the mass media took this "I-made-it-all-up-for-a-buck" statement as discrediting all of his statements on the assassination from 1964 on. On the contrary, the recantation referred only to the story he first told Oltmans on February 3, after two months of electroshock-boosted reconsideration in the Parkland headshop. He recanted the story that Oswald did it, that he was Oswald's boss, that Hunt was the top boss. But nothing else.

The pressure built up again. For a moment again he wavered, but then, on the first of March, he seized the time. Dragging Oltmans along, he dashed around Dallas clearing out his accounts at several banks. He drove with Oltmans to Houston and left his car with his lawyer's brother. He and Oltmans emplaned for Holland.

They reached the NOS-TV cameras in Amsterdam on March 4 and spent a day taping. On the 5th, Oltmans drove George to Brussels for a lunch meeting with one Kuznetzov, identified by Oltmans only as "a Soviet diplomat." Could George have been seeking asylum? Protection? A big buyer? Did this reflect the magnitude of what he had to tell? Or of his delirium?

The three chatted at the newsstand of the Hotel Metropole. George said he wanted to take a brief walk alone before they ate. Oltmans and Kuznetzov awaited him at the table but he did not return. He had left all his things behind except for the brown briefcase that never left his side. (It would be found in the suicide room with a few papers in it.)

For twelve days George was out of touch. Then on March 17 he arrived in West Palm Beach on a flight from Brussels, either accompanied by his daughter or joined by her right away. They went together to the mansion home of Nancy Tilton, cousin of Alexandra's mother. On the 29th, about noon, Assassinations Committee investigator Gaeton Fonzi called and found him out. An hour later Alexandra saw him and relayed Fonzi's promise to return. She thought it did not seem to bother him. She left on an errand. A housemaid happened to be tape-recording an afternoon TV soap in an adjacent room, so we know that about 2:30 George came into the upstairs room where the shotgun was kept. The shot was fired at 2:32. At 3:45 Alexandra returned home, called for her father, entered the room, then screamed. All this is audible over the gentle drone of daytime TV.

Mobster and Exile

Nicoletti and Prio represent for us the impact of organized crime and exile-Cuban reaction, allied together, upon the shaping of U.S. intelligence operations and foreign policy. They played basic roles in the whole drama of the Kennedy administration, possibly also in the assassination itself. What led to this? Here we trace the path.

Meyer Lansky is often promoted as the chief founding father of the modern Syndicate. It is said that one of the first strokes of his criminal genius was to see in the mid-1930s that U.S. organized crime could use an offshore redoubt and that Cuba could well fill the bill. The grand alliance that Lansky forged with newly arrived Cuban dictator Fulgencio Batista in 1934 was the basis of a special and large Syndicate privilege in Cuba that was respected through several changes of Cuban government until the coming of Castro in 1959.

Batista's concessions to Lansky and the corruption that raged throughout the government provoked opposition from various Cuban groups. One of these was a political party calling itself the *Autenticos*. Their sainted hero was the 19th century revolutionist Jose Marti; their chief was Ramon Grau San Martin. Their number two man: Carlos Prio Socarras.

For reasons of state, FDR desired in 1944 that Batista vacate power and permit elections. The courier whom FDR handpicked to carry this news to Batista was Lansky. How had the general manager of the organized crime Syndicate contrived to grow so cozy with the President as to be entrusted with such a sensitive and confidential mission?

The secret alliance between organized crime and American government began to develop around 1940 when two things were happening that anyone could see but only Lansky could put together. One was that Lansky's boss, Lucky Luciano, was pining away in prison. The other was that all along the East Coast docks, saboteurs were rather freely blowing up freighters burdened with supplies that would otherwise have gotten to Britain, where they were needed desperately. Speaking in a Syndicate whisper to the Brooklyn ear of the Office of Naval Intelligence, Lansky proposed the following: if FDR could lighten Luciano's discomforts now and deport/liberate him later, then in gratitude the Syndicate would guarantee the physical security of the docks.

The larger arrangement thus initiated, called "Operation Underworld," enabled the Syndicate to secure itself absolutely in Cuba, Florida and Nevada in the post-war world, three giant "properties" that the more and more corporate-style Syndicate would now help "develop." So when Roosevelt wanted to communicate privily to Batista, yet at a distance, and persuade him to somewhat open up the Cuban political scene, Lansky seemed to be the ideal messenger. Besides, Lansky could soften the blow, as he did, by offering Batista a sweet little rent-free mansion in Miami in which to while away his exile years.

So Batista left for Florida in 1944 and the *Autenticos* took power in Cuba. Grau was a prosperous survivor of his four years as president, and in 1948 happily passed the job on to his minister of labor, Carlos Prio, the former student radical who had since distinguished himself by the ferocity of his attacks on the Red unions.

Prio's somewhat shortened term saw the familiar posing and ranting about reform and justice while corruption flourished and criminal and business interests from the mainland continued to determine the overall character of Cuban development. Grau was accused of misappropriating $174 million in national funds, but the charges had to be dropped when an armed band held up the courthouse for the records the case against him was based on. Grau's minister of education withdrew his department's entire budget for diversion into Florida real estate ventures as partners with the Syndicate and the Teamsters. Prio himself is said to have absconded with some $30 million in Cuban funds when Batista reassumed command in 1952 in a bloodless coup, Prio not resisting but merely taking Batista's place in Lansky's Miami bosom.

In 1956 Castro came secretly to Reymosa, Mexico, on the Rio Grande. He disguised himself as a worker and slipped across the river for a meeting at the Las Palmas Hotel in McAllen, Texas, with Prio, who had arrived quietly from Miami. Castro had been denouncing Prio at the moment Batista toppled him, but now Castro and Prio were together in opposition to Batista.

Castro had assembled a small army in Mexico, fewer than a hundred but handpicked and well-armed. He proposed to install a long-term guerrilla struggle in the mountains of Oriente province far from Havana, where popular dislike of Batista was greatest. But to do this from Mexico he needed a boat. That was the business of the meeting in McAllen. Would Prio with his storied millions and his presumed hatred for his own usurper contribute toward the purchase of the *Granma?*

Castro said nothing came of this meeting and that *Granma* was financed by a multitude of small donations collected mainly in Havana. Prio said he put up the whole cost of the yacht, about $50,000—an act of which he later said, "It was the greatest mistake of my life."

Prio financed similar anti-Batista invasions later on. There was the expedition of the yacht *Corinthia*, which set up a base in the west of Cuba that survived only a few weeks before Batista's warplanes found and exterminated it. There was the expedition of the yacht *Blue Chip*, which was intercepted by Mexican coastal police.

Prio's view of the "Castro revolution" that finally conquered Batista was that he, Prio, was himself a part of it and deserved to profit from its victory. Certainly he too had suffered for his acts against Batista. He had been twice indicted under U.S. neutrality laws, once fined $9000 and jailed for smuggling weapons to Castro's forces.

Strangely, Prio's partners in this gun-running to the Cuban revolution were organized crime figures such as Santos Trafficante, Frank Fiorini/Sturgis, Lewis McWillie and Oswald-killer Jack Ruby. One can see why Prio might support Castro out of common opposition to

Batista. But why would the Syndicate want to help arm the revolutionaries?

Good question. Maybe the Syndicate was playing all the angles. Maybe it was following the lead of a section of the CIA that supported the early Castro as "a non-Communist alternative" to Batista. Maybe it was drawn in through its prior happy relationship with Prio. Maybe it was *not* supporting the revolution, just selling weapons to another buyer.

The mistake was in any case soon recognized by both sides and corrected. Castro threw the last casino off the island, and the Syndicate started conspiring with the CIA to bump Castro off.

To imagine the creation of this anti-Castro cabal, we may visualize a great shadowy space shading into darkness, which we call "the CIA." Half inside and half outside this darkness stands the person of Robert Maheu, known widely as a key CIA contract agent, a big Howard Hughes man, formerly of the FBI, intimately familiar with the super-secret projects (e.g., the *Glomar Explorer*) being engineered by Hughes for the CIA, as well as with the forces and figures of organized crime. A voice from the inner CIA darkness addresses Maheu then to this effect: "The Company agrees that Castro must be terminated with extreme prejudice. It prefers not to involve its own people directly." Maheu will answer that he knows just how to handle the problem. He will talk to his friend Santos Trafficante. Trafficante will bring in Chicago's Sam Giancana. Giancana will turn to John Roselli for counsel and to Charles Nicoletti for technical management. They will all be eager.

As the boss of a nest of professional hit men, Nicoletti's task in the group was to prepare detailed proposals for killing Castro. He presented these to the three others, who would send approved proposals on to Maheu. Then the proposals would be regurgitated into the CIA black hole, meditated upon by various acids, then spat back forth through Maheu in such exotic forms as a poison fountain pen to stab Castro with, or something to put in his toothpaste that would make his beard fall out.

Before October 1962 and the Missile Crisis, the Castro assassination group was almost certainly active without JFK's knowledge. Afterwards, of course, JFK tried to destroy it because it would not follow his orders to stop raiding Cuba and trying to kill Castro, orders necessitated by his Missile Crisis promise to Khrushchev to respect thenceforth the territorial integrity of the Cuban revolution.

It is usual—still—to think of Kennedy as less favoring to Castro than this seems to imply. Bill Moyers, for example, holds JFK responsible for the CIA's program of Cuban harassment and sees this as support for a Castro-did-it theory of the JFK assassination. True it is, Kennedy promised the Bay of Pigs vets at the Orange Bowl in December 1962 that he would return the flag they had just given him "in a free Havana." But this was probably Kennedy's lowest moment. The insiders to the Bay of Pigs Fiasco knew he did not mean what he was saying. The consensus of the intelligence services, the Syndicate, and the exiled Cubans had hardened by this time into the belief that JFK was their own Cuba's worst enemy and Castro's best friend, and that he had actually betrayed the invasion forces at the eleventh hour.

Such a view of Kennedy was widely held at the time of his death. The whole of the American right wing believed (and still does) that Kennedy was coddling Castro and soft on communism. The military believed this, the CIA hardnoses believed it, and the mobsters who missed their Havana casinos believed it.

The CIA network originally assembled to get weapons

to Castro in the mountains thus grew through several phases as Castro's columns neared Havana, finally turning violently against him after he took power, could not be bought off, closed the casinos, stamped out prostitution, emerged as a socialist, filled the jails with native vice lords and banished the Syndicate heavies to Miami. Castro then became target number one. When Kennedy turned against CIA efforts to rid Cuba of Castro, the shock within the cabal was great. When he deployed a special FBI squad to close the anti-Castro commando training bases in Florida and Louisiana in 1963, the treachery of it sizzled on the anti-Castro mind like a hot wire. It must have seemed irresistibly natural, logical, for this group to take in hand the gun first sold to Castro and later turned against him, and now turn it against the one who intervened to give Castro protection.

Our three dead witnesses lived their last days in the kind of fierce disappointment that comes to old passionate warriors who see everything denied them at the end.

De Mohrenschildt lost wife and sanity in his struggle. The secret information about JFK that he thought might give him power in the end only made him vulnerable. He might have told us—his book and his taped interviews might tell us still—that Oswald was involved only as the patsy and that we must look for the real killers in a different place.

Nicoletti too died in a welter of bitterness. His old boss Giancana, comrade in the anti-Castro cabal, had returned from voluntary exile in Mexico and begun to talk about JFK's death to Senator Frank Church's Committee on Intelligence when he was gunned down in his home in Chicago on June 6, 1975. Fourteen months later, on August 7, 1976, another of Nicoletti's co-conspirators, Roselli, washed ashore near Miami in a chain-draped 55-

gallon oil drum, dismembered. Roselli, like Giancana, had also started talking to Church committee investigators when he was killed. Nicoletti began complaining that things had gone all wrong with the old outfit. ''The CIA is taking over the operation,'' he snarled.

Prio died watching the once great strength of the exiled Cubans in the United States starting to fail. He saw how badly Watergate hurt the exiles' image. He saw his whole community plunged into terroristic and bloody internal fighting in Miami. Now President Carter wanted a return to the old JFK policy of detente with Castro. And when Prio went to Washington in February 1977 to talk against this move with Secretary of State Cyrus Vance, his words no longer carried the old clout. Had he lived and chosen to talk to the committee, he might have told us on whose authority the President's death warrant had been written.

As it is, we have lost all but the echoes. These echoes can tell us much, as we have seen. But the truth of the President's assassination still lies far before us, beyond these graves.

7

The Behavior of
the Media*

It is an ancient truth that the mass media have a hard
time reporting developments in the JFK assassination
case, but we have just had new opportunity to observe it
again.

The occasion was the FBI's recent release of 98,000
pages of documents on JFK's death, many of which had
not previously been seen.

These documents actually provide an abundance of important new information. There is no smoking pistol, but
no one had ever expected such a thing from the FBI,
whose JFK cover-up role has already been documented
by the Senate in the Schweiker-Hart report of 1976. The
real wonder is that the FBI files contain so much.

Yet all the networks and all the big dailies and weeklies
spoke in prompt choric unison to report that there was
nothing new in these papers, no suggestion of conspiracy, nothing to imply that Oswald fired fewer than all the
shots or that Ruby was more than a second lone nut.

This in the teeth of new discoveries showing conclu-
sively:

Clandestine America, vol. 2, no. 5, Jan.–Feb. 1978.

- That an aggressive cover-up scheme was imposed at the direction of LBJ's White House, which moved in the early hours of the case to secure control of the investigation and to define Oswald as the lone assassin.
- That Jack Ruby was linked to the FBI as a "PCI," i.e., a "potential criminal informant," with strong ties to organized crime as well as to the Dallas Police Department.
- That the FBI took deliberate secret steps to counter the early Warren Commission critics.
- That Hoover thought the FBI misled the Warren Commission.

To its eternal credit, ABC's "Good Morning America" news show gave representatives of the AIB interviews of about five minutes each on December 8 and January 19, the days following the two FBI releases. But except for these two little sniffs, the big media turned their news noses as far away as they could from any scent of a Dallas conspiracy—unless, which was much worse, it was to imply that Oswald was actually under the control of Castro.

This was indeed a favorite media ploy at the time of the December release of 40,000 pages. All three networks and several big papers and magazines hinted darkly that, even though the new documents showed "not the slightest indication of conspiracy" (NBC), there might after all be a slight shadow falling on Castro. This ploy was based on no new evidence but on resurrection of the curious but well-known "Pedro Charles" letters (two letters mailed from Cuba implying that Castro was paying and instructing Oswald to kill Kennedy).

When they came to the FBI's attention late in 1963, these letters were quickly recognized by Hoover as "some type of hoax" since they were postmarked after the assassination and typed on the same typewriter, though purporting to come from different people and places in Cuba. The media revivals of this non-story all mentioned the hoax angle, but only in passing, so that the main result of their bringing up the matter at all was to strengthen the public impression that Castro may have been materially involved in the assassination.

The real importance of these letters lies rather in their power to make immediately self-evident the fact that somebody was trying to frame Oswald and, through him, Castro for the death of JFK. *Who could have been doing this?* In view of subsequent discoveries about the Bay of Pigs connection, about the alliance of crime and the CIA and the Cuban exiles, the question is surely a burning one. Yet for all the FBI's vaunted investigative thoroughness, this is one lead Hoover turned his back on from the start without the least hesitation. The letters are hoaxes—he says—period, no more worrying about the hoaxer's identity and game.

Our curiosity about all this only grew greater when we found out from the most recent FBI releases that there were in fact *four* "Pedro Charles" letters. Until now only two were thought to exist. Behold the following from Hoover's letter of January 17, 1964, to Warren Commission chief counsel J. Lee Rankin:

"The FBI has been furnished four letters written from Cuba indicating or alleging that the assassination of President Kennedy was undertaken by Oswald under the direction of a Cuban agent, one Pedro Charles, who reportedly gave Oswald $7,000 for this mission."

Hoover then summarizes the contents of these four letters. The first, as noted, is from Pedro himself. "The other three letters," writes Hoover, "purport to be from individuals who have knowledge that Charles conspired with Oswald to kill the President. However, examinations by the FBI Laboratory have shown that all of these communications were actually prepared on the same typewriter and that several of the envelopes used came from the same source. It is, therefore, clear that this represents some type of hoax, possibly on the part of some anti-Castro group seeking to discredit the Cuban government.''

Now what we want to know from our friends in the mass media is why they cannot see this Pedro Charles thing at least as clearly as Hoover saw it. Why do the presumably independent-minded mass media reporters encourage the false and dangerous impression that the least fragment of hard evidence exists to attach Oswald to a Castroite assassination conspiracy?

And why are they so busy telling us there is nothing new in these files that they miss the quite significant fact of the additional letters? Two letters might have been the work of an idle mind. But four, all connected, make a lot more sense, just as Hoover said, as ''some anti-Castro group seeking to discredit the Cuban government.'' The media never even make it to that level of analysis, basic as it is.

The January FBI release gave us a fascinating variation on the above method of casting shadows. Once again a significant event was clouded over by a false analysis, this time in connection with one of the few moments of comedy in the assassination drama, the famous scene in which a frantic Marina is said to have held Oswald a prisoner in the bathroom to keep him from going out to kill Nixon.

The story of this fateful bathroom struggle is currently being coupled with the older story that Oswald once tried to assassinate General Walker, the famous Dallas right-winger. The purpose of these stories is to prove that Oswald was a homicidal person. In the Walker case, the police were unable to match the 30.06-caliber bullet dug from Walker's wall with Oswald's 6.5-mm rifle. In the bathroom case the same: they were unable to match Marina's testimony to the realities. First she said she locked Oswald in the bathroom, but investigation showed the door could be locked only from inside. So Marina changed her story and said she planted her feet on either side of the knob and pulled with all her might to keep the door shut, complaining to Oswald on the other side that she might be endangering her pregnancy. Then it turned out that Nixon was not in Dallas that day after all. So she changed her story again, now saying it was Vice President Johnson whom Oswald was raging to assassinate.

Warren Commission lawyers recognized Marina's constant prevarication as a problem, but found it necessary in any case to base certain key parts of their case against Oswald on Marina's word (e.g., the question of Oswald's possession of the alleged murder weapon). But how solid is argument based on such a witness's word alone? That is the real story here—not the homicidal character of the imagined lone assassin, but the incredibility of Marina as a witness and the uselessness of her uncorroborated testimony.

We ask ourselves what price the glory of this continuing media support for the cover-up. Why should the Carl Sterns and Daniel Schorrs, the George Lardners and the Jeremiah O'Learys, the Ford Rowans and the Jack Andersons, not be proud enough to lend their might to hammer out the truth of this case?

Few of us are willing—so far—to conclude that the American media are being actively manipulated. Surely they are still in substance independent and in essentials free! But always we are driven back to the question of why the media still try to infuse new credence into the Pedro Charles hoax, of why they still rehearse the bathroom scene as though Marina were a credible witness, and over all of why they still hide from such strong and numerous signs that something about the Dallas events remains to be uncovered.

8

Legend,
Counter-Legend:
Figuring Out Epstein's
Angleton*

Media giants customarily scorn conspiracy theories of
the JFK assassination as products of weakened minds.
Edward Jay Epstein's new book, *Legend: The Secret
World of Lee Harvey Oswald*, seems to have turned this
inside out. All at once the *New York Times, Time*, the
talk shows and the Book-of-the-Month Club are joined
in praise of a book whose argument is (a) that JFK
was killed by a Soviet agent, (b) that this was concealed
through the work of a Soviet mole in the CIA, and (c) that
J. Edgar Hoover was a witting party to the cover-up. Surely
the scales have never fallen so hard.

Legend says that Lee Harvey Oswald was recruited by
the KGB while serving in Japan with the U.S. Marines in
1959, brought to the Soviet Union for espionage training,
then sent back to the United States as a redefector on some
unguessed-at mission.

But Epstein is careful to say he does not think Oswald

*AIB briefing paper, 1978.

killed Kennedy on Soviet orders. Indeed, for all the effort Epstein threw into the half-million dollar research effort (funded by Reader's Digest) to link Oswald to the KGB, he is strangely reluctant to say what the KGB's purpose with Oswald might have been, even though he calls a main section of his book "The Mission." If not to kill Kennedy, what did the KGB mean for Oswald to do? Epstein does not answer, yet he does not in the least blame the Russians for the President's murder.

How does he manage to prove Oswald a Soviet spy and yet acquit the Soviets for what their spy allegedly did? This is done by imagining that the KGB lost control of Oswald sometime in 1963, Oswald being impelled then to still yet another rebellion by a combined surge of sexual anxiety and a sudden new passion for Fidel.

A "legend," we are told, is spy-speak parlance for a cover story contrived to protect a secret operation. The legend in question in Epstein's book is the KGB's tale about Oswald's two-and-a-half-year stay in Russia, a tale the KGB hand-carried to the CIA a few weeks after the assassination by means, Epstein says, of a phony KGB defector, Yuri Nosenko.

The legend which Nosenko was sent to tell the CIA was that the Soviets had nothing to do with Oswald. They had not debriefed him, had not recruited him for spy work, had not appended Marina Prusakova to him as a co-agent, and had not ordered him to kill Kennedy.

The inference Epstein offers is thus the simple reverse of Nosenko's claims (except the last). If the KGB sent Nosenko to spread a legend denying a KGB-Oswald relationship, then such a relationship must exist. Otherwise why deny it?

Were this just another buff's outside theorizing, the reader could lightly make the most of such standards of proof. But what we have in *Legend* is probably something more intense than that.

For *Legend* may be a "legend" in itself. The Nosenko undressing is a story put together in Epstein's ear by one of the craft's more expert legend-spinners, retired CIA counterintelligence chief James Jesus Angleton, sixty, a grower of orchids, a friend of Modernist poets, and lately emerging, albeit dimly so far, as a principal figure in a top-level CIA power struggle that involved Richard Helms and William Colby. Angleton was Epstein's chief source for the narrative unfolded in this book.

Angleton's case against Nosenko is comprised of several points. First, Nosenko is a product of Soviet counterintelligence, the point of origin of all KGB penetration agents. Second, the information he turned over to prove himself was worthless to the KGB. The Soviet agents Nosenko burned were American soldiers who no longer had access to secret material anyway. Third, Nosenko was caught in lies about his KGB career. Therefore, reasoned Angleton, he must be a penetration agent—a mole.

Angleton put his staff to work on Nosenko and his story. For three years Angleton kept his adversary under intense interrogation and solitary confinement. The product was a 900-page document claiming that Nosenko had come to give us disinformation and was ultimately loyal to the U.S.S.R.

Some may have problems with this version of Nosenko, even on the basis of details supplied in the book. For one thing, Nosenko's decision to defect and his first contact with the CIA occurred well before the assassination. For another, Nosenko never abandoned his story in spite of the ordeal Angleton put him through. Another Soviet intelligence informer whom Hoover especially trusted, "Fedora," verified Nosenko's identity and sincerity. And Nosenko was regarded as clean by everyone else in the CIA command but Jim Angleton.

Whatever the truth about Nosenko, the dispute about him sundered the U.S. intelligence community as few disputes in its disputatious history have done. Hoover was just as tenacious in his conviction of Nosenko's veracity as was Angleton of his duplicity. The FBI broke off relations with the CIA over this very argument. Then inside the CIA, too, Angleton was rebuffed and thwarted on the Nosenko question, until at last he was thrown out over it.

Who in the CIA defied and overpowered Angleton? Angleton concluded that Nosenko's durability in the teeth of Angleton's best shots admitted of only one inference, namely, that someone inside the CIA must be protecting him. *There must be a KGB mole in the CIA!*

Who was—who is—this mole? *Legend* is nervous on this point, seeking at once to provoke and to obscure this question. Angleton will go only so far (through Epstein) toward hinting at the source of his in-house troubles. He observes that the man who beat him out in the power struggle of 1974 was Colby, the new director. It was Colby who leaked to the *New York Times'* Sy Hersh the story of Angleton's role in illegal CIA serveillance programs, then called Angleton and his aides in to give them the ax. It was Colby who added injury by thereupon recalling Nosenko from North Carolina pastures to put him to work in Angleton's old inner sanctum. It was Colby who, while chief of the Vietnam War's infamous Operation Phoenix, was seen with a Frenchman suspected of KGB connections. Colby never reported the contact. That was a serious breech of discipline.

Colby discounts the charge with a certain amusement. I reached him by phone at his Washington law firm to ask what he thought of the Angleton-Epstein thesis that he was a Soviet spy. He said he had not read Epstein's book but was willing to comment.

"I knew nothing about Nosenko," he said, "until I discovered in 1973 that the CIA had confined him, which was one of the CIA's improper acts." As to the bruising fight between him and Angleton, he said, "We had a professional difference of opinion about counter-intelligence and Nosenko, but nothing more." As to the penetration of the CIA by the KGB, he said, "We are the only comparable organization that has *not* found a mole. Some of Angleton's counter-intelligence work probably helped us from being penetrated from time to time." As to the specific insinuation about him and the KGB, his flinty voice laughing now almost heartily, he said, "I am not a mole!" Yes sir, good night.

Epstein did not talk to Colby even so little as this. Still he leaves Angleton's accusation against Colby stressed in the last line of *Legend*'s main text: "With Nosenko accredited and the counterintelligence staff purged [by Colby], the CIA had truly been turned inside out." Pure Le Carré.

Why should anyone believe a word of it? Certainly not on Angleton's say-so. He is an interested party. Then can we rely on Epstein? Has he shown an ability to understand this counterspy business and not get ripped off by high-energy types like Angleton? The prevailing notion is that Epstein's research was thorough, his factual base solid, his powers of analysis adequate to the task. Which is too bad. Non-expert readers will not know what hit them.

Take the area of technical flaws in the lone-assassin theory. The question of whether or not Oswald killed Kennedy is obviously the most basic of them all. One's sense of Oswald's motive clearly depends on one's sense of what he did. It is instructive to see Epstein's way with factual details in this area, where the evidence is all in the record. Two quick examples out of a dozen or so:

- "The Commission made a serious error," Epstein writes, in thinking that a particular oak tree in front of the sniper's building blocked the sniper's line of sight until Kennedy was a certain distance down Elm Street. Epstein reminds us that the commission was studying the site in June "when the oak tree . . . was in full bloom. But the assassination occurred on November 22, when the deciduous tree had no foliage." All Epstein had to do was to look at any one of dozens of pictures taken at the precise moment of the shooting to see that the tree in question was *loaded* with foliage. Confronted with this fact by Dave Williams, my colleague of the Assassination Information Bureau, Epstein's response was: "Maybe I'm wrong. I was told it was a deciduous tree." Told?

- Another problem for the lone-gunman theory is that the famous Zapruder film showed unambiguously that JFK's head and body were driven violently backward by the impact of the fatal headshot. From Newton's laws, this reaction stipulates a shot from the right front. But Oswald was supposed to be behind. Epstein here offers to solve this famous mystery by attributing JFK's motion to the sudden forward lurch of the limo: "The car was accelerating" (p. 332). Yet on page 243 he declares that the car was actually braking to a stop at this moment: "The limousine came to an almost complete halt. A third shot exploded the President's head."

This is how Epstein handles public facts. One can only wonder what he has done with his great stock of private interviews. He invariably paraphrases his sources. He rarely gives a direct quote. He chose not to print a single transcript. Buyer, beware.

Legend's appearance just now, the House Assassinations Committee being in deep ponder over the very questions this book further muddles, is all the more distressing to those who know the JFK case well enough to spot Epstein's errors because of the handsprings the major media are turning. The book is a main selection of the Book-of-the-Month Club. *Time* called Epstein "a careful, academic researcher" and said his evidence that Oswald was a Soviet spy was "strong." The *New York Times Book Review* called it "fascinating, alarming and perhaps enormously significant" and praised its "explosive qualities." The normally chaste Wilfred Sheed swallowed the whole Angleton kaboodle and chimed in on his own that "Cuba itself seems the most likely conspirator" with Oswald. "This one," he concluded, "is a beauty."

Time prated on to upwards of a thousand words without once mentioning that there was this chap named Angleton with whom Epstein enjoyed a certain relationship. The *New York Times* mentioned Angleton only in passing and said not a word about who he is, what he used to do for a living, how he lost his job, and what all this implies for Epstein and *Legend*'s unwary readers. This is like reviewing Woodward and Bernstein without mentioning Deep Throat. To his credit, Epstein does better than his praisers in this respect. He shows us Angleton. He does not try to hide him behind a cute name. He points out candidly, "I realized that I could never be sure that crucial facts were not withheld."

Well? And if they were? AIB interviewer Williams

pressed Epstein on this point and got an amazing answer: "The guys in the CIA," said Epstein, "all tell partial stories. It's not a question of Angleton being honest or dishonest. I can't think of an instance of his being dishonest, but he'll tell you one thirtieth of what there is to know, which is a way of being dishonest. You don't have to lie, you just tell a person part of the story. I agree with your point. I think one day I'll write a long appendix on the sources."

In the meantime, our warning lights should be on for this book. Is the *Times* really so sure it wants to embrace Angleton's account against Colby's denial? Has *Time* really considered the implications of the Angleton-Epstein theory that Nosenko was and is a Soviet spy? Does Sheed actually want to say now with Angleton that there was and is a KGB mole in the CIA? That J. Edgar Hoover knew about this and helped conceal it? That maybe Colby also knows something about this and helped conceal it? That Castro ordered the assassination of Kennedy? That the CIA has been "turned inside out"? Are Epstein's enthusiasts truly prepared to accept and defend all this, and all on the say-so of a creature of shadow the likes of Angleton?

Here is conspiracy paranoia with a vengeance! And from the very voices, mainstream all, who have been so keen to reassure us, lo these many years, that there is nothing new or sinister to find out about the JFK murder.

Fascinating! So now we are all to be conspiracy buffs together, differing in feather only and all acknowledging that we are the children of the age of scientific disinformation.

And what are the media and journalists like Epstein supposed to do about that? How are the social organs of mass information to guard against manipulation by secret conspiratorial elites? In such a context, what is the real merit or demerit of the old privileged relationship between the anonymous source and the reporter who would face jail rather than reveal his source? In an information-burning political system such as ours, how can news reporting institutionalize a permanent resistance to colonization by the intelligence bureaucracies?

In a previous book, *Agency of Fear*, Epstein persuasively argued that we need to rethink the commitment to silence about sources. And especially, I would add, when sources from the disinformation shop are involved. For how are readers—and Epstein himself—to know they are not being deceived by Angleton? Or Woodward by Deep Throat, or Hersh by Colby?

Epstein's candor about Angleton is a big improvement over the *Washington Post* team's secretiveness about Deep Throat. Epstein is too much Angleton's advocate and not enough the skeptically "objective" journalist of our ideal, but he is straight up about it, and that gives us the chance to take the relationship into account when we assess his book. It is too bad that Epstein, having been so frank, should then leave careful readers feeling that his critical independence languished in the Angleton contact.

9

The Man Who Came in from the Cold. Maybe.*

One of the more intriguing figures in the JFK assassination case is Yuri Ivanovich Nosenko, a former KGB officer who defected to the United States fifteen years ago with a story to tell about Lee Harvey Oswald's sojourn in the Soviet Union. Nosenko was the highest-ranking Soviet intelligence officer ever to defect to the United States, and for a brief moment he enjoyed his status as a major prize of the spy wars. But soon the CIA began to doubt the truth of his information and to suspect he might be a Soviet penetration agent—a "mole." The agency clapped him into a five-year imprisonment, complete with torture. Years later, after a bitter internal dispute within the CIA, his tormentors changed their minds again, declared him a good-faith defector, and brought him onto the CIA payroll as a consultant. There he remained for ten years until a congressional investigating committee fingered him as a suspicious character and a liar after all, raising again the question of whether he might also be a Soviet mole, as had originally been suspected.

*Boston Magazine, October 1979.

These sharp changes in Nosenko's fortunes with the CIA define the main twists of a spy story that has become basic to our understanding of the JFK assassination, the conflict within the CIA, the apparent murder a year ago of a covert CIA officer named John Paisley, and the still-unfolding drama of alleged Soviet moles in the top levels of the CIA. Dormant for years, the Nosenko affair may now be growing into the most important spy story since that of Nathan Hale.

Oswald reached Moscow in October, 1959, announced his defection, and applied for citizenship in the Soviet Union. His quid pro quo was that he had important military secrets to divulge, an offer that (as we now know) put him in the secret sights of the Second Directorate of the KGB's Seventh Department, the unit responsible for counterintelligence surveillance of tourists and defectors. Yuri Nosenko was deputy chief of this unit. Thus, he was the administrator of the KGB's Oswald file.

In the Soviet Union, Oswald was an enthusiastic comrade at first, but then grew disenchanted and homesick. In February, 1961, he applied to the U.S. embassy in Moscow for repatriation to the States. In March, he met Marina Pruskova. In April, he married her. A year later, in June, 1962, he and Marina left the Soviet Union for Texas.

Nosenko, then serving as the KGB security escort to the Soviet delegation at the arms-control talks in Geneva, also made a big move that month. He found a private place and moment to ask an American diplomat to put him in touch with an appropriate U.S. intelligence officer. He had a proposal to make.

Soon Nosenko was talking secretly with the CIA's Geneva counterintelligence officer, Tennant "Pete" Bagley. Nosenko's story was that he had gone on a foolish drunken spree and spent nine hundred Swiss francs belonging to the KGB. He had to replace it quickly. Otherwise he would be discovered, fired, and heavily penalized. But if the United States could meet his small financial needs, he could survive. For such support, Nosenko would supply certain pieces of information in which he was sure the United States would be interested, such as the location of the KGB bugs in the American embassy in Moscow or the identities of Soviet agents working within the U.S. intelligence system. He did not want to defect overtly. He had a family in the Soviet Union. He would not give them up. Nor would he talk to the CIA inside the Soviet Union, only when he was in Geneva.

Bagley encouraged Nosenko. An agent-in-place was the most useful of all defectors, because he could maintain a constant flow of fresh intelligence and be directed toward specific targets.

But soon a doubt began to form in Bagley's mind about Nosenko. The problem was with the quality of intelligence Nosenko was delivering. A previous Soviet defector, Anatoli Golitsin (called Mr. X in the House Select Committee on Assassinations' final report), had given the U.S. much the same information in even sharper form. The Soviets knew, of course, that Golitsin had already divulged or compromised the information that Nosenko was now fobbing off as hot new stuff. As Bagley later told the Assassinations Committee in executive session, he had begun to think that Nosenko was in fact "a sent KGB agent dispatched to deflect and negate" the authentic information of Golitsin. Bagley came to think, moreover, that Nosenko was not the man he said he was, that he had never been the deputy chief of the Second Directorate, that he had never administered Oswald's KGB file, and that the whole story was a "legend," a cover story for a deep-penetration mission.

* * *

In September of 1963, Oswald was in Mexico City. He applied at the Soviet embassy for a visa to the Soviet Union. Nosenko later told his CIA and FBI questioners that he had personally reviewed and rejected this application, even though he was not now connected with the Second Directorate. He also said that in late November, after the killings in Dallas, he had reviewed the entire KGB Oswald file.

But now came a sudden change. On January 23, 1964, on Nosenko's first visit to Geneva after the assassination of JFK, Nosenko told Bagley that he had changed his mind about defecting. He was disillusioned with the Soviet system. His family would be taken care of. He wanted to come to the United States and begin a new life.

Bagley hesitated. His suspicions of Nosenko had not yet hardened but were hard to deny. He put Nosenko off.

Then, a week and a half later, Nosenko forced the issue. On February 4, he informed Bagley that he had just received a wire from KGB headquarters calling him home. He was sure he had been found out or was about to be. If he went back to Moscow, he would never come out again. It was now or never. Bagley swallowed his misgivings, and the CIA spirited Nosenko off to Washington. He was almost a free man.

Nosenko had already been questioned twice about Oswald by the CIA while he was still in Geneva, on January 23 and 30, 1964. Having arrived in the States in late February, he was questioned again on Oswald, this time by the FBI.

The FBI accepted Nosenko's story of Oswald's stay in the Soviet Union: that the KGB had been hardly interested in Oswald at all, that it had carried out only the most perfunctory and routine surveillance of his activities, and that in no way—this was the bottom line and the real point—was Oswald a KGB assassin in Dallas. Nosenko's message was: Oswald may have looked like a juicy intelligence morsel, but the KGB had declined the bait, had paid him no special attention, and if he had killed the President, the U.S.S.R. was not to blame.

A plausible message. What Soviet need to see JFK eliminated could have been so piercing as to motivate the immense risk of an assassination scheme? But senior officers of the CIA, like Bagley, did not accept his claim.

What made Nosenko's story impossible for the CIA to accept in those early days was what he said about Oswald and the KGB. For what Nosenko told his CIA questioners about the KGB's attitude toward Oswald didn't correspond at all with the CIA's best idea of the Soviet spy manual. The CIA could not believe that the Soviets would ignore a target like Oswald, who bragged of his information on U.S. radar and hinted (some said) at knowledge of the U-2 aircraft—at that point the CIA's most secret secret. As Bagley told the House Assassinations Committee much later, "the KGB . . . would face an American swimming into their sea . . . like a pool of piranhas."

So when Nosenko said the piranhas only yawned at Oswald, Bagley couldn't believe it. Nosenko had to be lying. If he was lying about this, what else was he lying about?

And this was important. Deputy director of the CIA Richard Helms told the House committee in September 1978: "It is difficult to overstate the significance that Yuri Nosenko's defection assumed in the investigation of President Kennedy's assassination. If Mr. Nosenko turned out to be a bona fide defector, if his information were to be believed, then we could conclude that the KGB and the Soviet Union had nothing to do with Lee Harvey Oswald in 1963 and therefore had nothing to do with President Kennedy's murder.

"If on the other hand," continued Helms, "Mr. Nosenko had been programmed in advance by the KGB to minimize KGB connections with Oswald, if Mr. Nosenko was giving us false information about Oswald's contacts with the KGB in 1959 to 1962, it was fair for us to surmise that there may have been an Oswald-KGB connection in November, 1963, more specifically that Oswald was acting as a Soviet agent when he shot President Kennedy.

"If it were shown that Oswald was in fact acting as a Soviet agent when he shot President Kennedy," Helms went on, "the consequences to the United States of America and indeed to the world, would have been staggering. Thus, it became a matter of the utmost importance to this government to determine the bona fides of Mr. Yuri Nosenko."

By March, 1964, Nosenko's credibility with the CIA had totally eroded. No one believed him about Oswald, and few believed him about anything else. Helms, Bagley (by this time promoted to deputy chief of the Soviet Bloc Division), and Bagley's superior, David Murphy, were united with the chief of CIA counterintelligence, James Angleton, in viewing Nosenko, as Bagley put it, as "a false defector on a disinformation mission."

Nosenko may have still thought at this time that he carried a little clout. Through the FBI, he offered to tell the Warren Commission all he knew about Oswald. The offer was rejected. Nosenko's name does not appear in the Warren *Report*.

On April 4, 1964, meeting what he thought was a doctor's appointment, Nosenko was arrested by the CIA and transported to a specially prepared safe house in North Arlington, Virginia, where he was confined in a cell that his current CIA defender, John Hart, told the committee was "most comparable to a bank vault." When Nosenko failed a lie-detector test, the CIA became convinced that he was an unregenerate Soviet agent. But Nosenko refused to budge from his story.

This led the CIA to the use of inquisitorial methods. Under the control of David Murphy's interrogation team—including John Paisley, an officer who will reenter the narrative much later as a corpse—Nosenko was isolated in solitary confinement in his CIA bank vault for more than three years. He was tortured during this time. Overall, the CIA kept him in custody for about five years.

The revelation last fall of this sorry episode was at once logged in as yet another CIA scandal. The CIA's John Hart, part of the pro-Nosenko group that took charge of Nosenko in 1968, flatly called it "an abomination."

To which Bagley replied before the committee, "Please bear in mind that I find this case . . . just as 'abominable' as Mr. Hart does. Its implications are ugly. It imposed immense and unpleasant tasks upon us and strains upon the agency, which are all too visible today in your committee's hearings."

The central problem facing the CIA, Bagley said, was "Nosenko's credibility and what lies behind his message to America concerning the KGB's relations with Lee Harvey Oswald." He went on, "The detention of Nosenko was designed initially to give us an opportunity to confront him with certain contradictions in his story . . . Our aim was, as Mr. Hart said, to get a confession: either of KGB sponsorship or of which lies could, finally, form some believable pattern."

The sticking point in Nosenko's story was his stubborn assertion that Oswald had not been of serious interest to the KGB. David Murphy told Assassinations Committee counsel Ken Klein, "The Soviet Union with foreigners don't do that,'' and went on to explain the importance to the Soviets of Oswald's technical knowledge of the U-2 spy plane. That Nosenko should maintain that the KGB did not question Oswald or closely watch his activities in the Soviet Union despite this knowledge, explained Murphy, ''is one of the things that created an atmosphere of disbelief, [a feeling] that there must be something to this case that is important, vitally important, to the Soviet Union, and we can't understand it.''

Nosenko had had other problems with the CIA as well. His leads had not been useful. Golitsin had already told it all. The CIA's background check was turning up indications that Nosenko was not the person he said he was. Two previous defectors whose usefulness to the U.S. had been established were skeptical of him. But his biggest problem remained his story about Oswald. That was the story he seemed to have come to tell, and that was the story no one could believe.

In 1966 Nosenko was given another polygraph examination. Again he failed. Helms knew, too, that Murphy and Bagley were preparing a gigantic document, called ''The Thousand-Page Report,'' fully stating their argument that Nosenko was a KGB plant.

But Helms faltered at this point. ''I made the decision,'' he told the committee, ''that the case simply could not go on in that fashion; it had to be resolved.'' In October, 1967, Helms assigned Bruce Solie of the CIA Office of Security to review the case. Solie at once objected to the isolation of Nosenko and had him moved to comfortable quarters.

In February, 1968, the CIA Soviet Bloc Division submitted a four-hundred-page condensation of the original report, concluding that Nosenko was a liar. But Nosenko now had a CIA defender in Bruce Solie. Solie responded to the four hundred pages with eighteen pages of his own, criticizing the Murphy-Bagley conclusion and saying that Nosenko was a good-faith defector who was telling what he thought to be the truth about Oswald and the KGB. Solie recommended further interviews by new people and another lie-detector test.

Nosenko's third polygraph exam was administered in August, 1968, under the supervision of Solie's Office of Security rather than Murphy's Soviet Bloc Division. There is no ready explanation for the fact that Nosenko was said to have passed this third test. But ten years later, the House Assassinations Committee brought in an independent polygraph expert to review the 1964, 1966, and 1968 tests. The expert concluded that only the second of these was valid—one of the two, of course, that Nosenko failed. But that was ten years later. In 1968, the new test appeared to put Nosenko back on the sunny side of the CIA.

Then in October, 1968, Nosenko-advocate Solie issued an in-house memo disputing all the findings of the Murphy-Bagley report. "Nosenko," wrote Solie, "is identical to the person he claims to be." As for the Oswald-KGB question, said Solie, that was "an FBI matter." He had no reason to disbelieve Nosenko or question his sincerity on this point. Solie told the committee that he "did not have all the facts" on Oswald because Oswald was not a main area of CIA interrogation of Nosenko. The statement directly conflicted with Helms' testimony that Oswald's stay in Russia constituted—"no question about it"—a major area of CIA questioning of Nosenko.

Later in 1968, over the anguished protests of Murphy and Bagley, and their interrogation team, the CIA formally conceded Nosenko's good faith and authenticity. On the first of March, 1969, Nosenko was compensated for his time under arrest and "employed as an independent contractor for the CIA" at a salary of $16,500 a year. "I was imprisoned for the whole five years," said Nosenko to the House Assassinations Committee, "and I started my life in the U.S.A. in April of 1969."

By 1973, Helms and James Angleton, strong Nosenko skeptics, had been pushed out of the agency. John Hart authored a CIA internal study of the Nosenko controversy and found that Nosenko, though not reliable on the Oswald-KGB question, was sincere.

Nosenko was thus vindicated. Soon he was lecturing CIA and FBI classes on Soviet intelligence. But his problems were not over.

In 1976 Congress created the House Select Committee on Assassinations to look into the controversies surrounding the murders of President Kennedy and Martin Luther King, Jr. By the middle of 1977, a deputy counsel for the committee, Ken Klein, was assigned full time to the Nosenko question. Said one of Klein's colleagues on the committee staff, "Kenny was in a bit over his head on Nosenko and the whole Kennedy case, but he worked on nothing but Nosenko for a year, and finally he broke him down."

The breaking of Nosenko, after all these years and efforts, took place early in the summer of 1978. Klein put Nosenko through some twenty hours of hostile interrogation, playing constantly upon the myriad contradictions and inconsistencies in Nosenko's story. "He just went to tatters when we got to him," said the staffer.

What did the breaking of Nosenko reveal? While the transcript of this particular encounter is not available, it is known that, in the end, "the committee was certain Nosenko had lied about Oswald."

Under the pressure of Klein's questioning, Nosenko changed his Oswald story in two particularly important respects. The first, key one involves the KGB file on Oswald. Nosenko formerly characterized this file as all but nonexistent. He insisted that the KGB had carried out no surveillance of Oswald and that he personally had "thoroughly reviewed Oswald's file." Now he told the Congress that this file comprised "seven or eight thick volumes," most of them containing "information relating to the surveillance" of Oswald by the KGB, and only one of which Nosenko said he had a chance to look at.

Second, Nosenko had always maintained that the KGB didn't know anything about Oswald's relationship with Marina until they were married. "There was no surveillance on Oswald to show that he knew her," he told the FBI in 1964. But in 1978, when counsel Klein asked him, "If [Oswald] met Marina on March 17, how long would you estimate it would take before the KGB would know about her?" Nosenko's answer was: "In the same March they would have quite a big batch of material on her."

So a completely different picture of the KGB's interest in Lee and Marina Oswald emerged, and with it a completely different picture of Nosenko's defection. The committee does not go so far as to say that Nosenko was—is—a Soviet plant. "In the end," reads its final report, "the committee [like the Warren Commission] was unable to resolve the Nosenko matter." But as a staff member confided shortly after the report was published last summer, "Yeah, basically I would really have to go with the theory that he's a plant."

Suppose this is correct. If Nosenko lied when he said that Oswald had not been closely watched and questioned by the KGB, was he also lying when he said that Oswald had not been recruited by the KGB and that he was not a Soviet agent or assassin when he returned to the States? One's first impulse, of course, is to assume that whatever a liar says is the opposite of the truth. If Nosenko is a liar and says Oswald was not a KGB agent, then Oswald must have been a KGB agent. If Nosenko, the liar, says that the Soviet Union did not send Oswald to kill Kennedy, then the Soviet Union must be the one to blame.

Is *that* what the CIA thought about the JFK assassination until the middle of 1968? *That the Russians did it?*

Bagley protested to the committee that, even though he thought Oswald a KGB agent, he did not think the Soviets had ordered him to kill Kennedy. Nosenko's "message," said Bagley, "hides the possibility that [Oswald] is or could have been a Soviet agent. [But] by 'Soviet agent' I don't mean a Soviet assassination agent. I mean something quite different . . . Perhaps he was a sleeper agent . . . They may have said, 'We will get in touch with you in time of war' . . . But then if he is on their rolls as a sleeper agent or for wartime sabotage or something of that sort, they would be absolutely shocked to hear their man had taken it upon himself to kill the American president." And as Bagley says elsewhere, "The Soviets have shown a proclivity to use tricky methods like this to give us messages through clandestine means." Thus, he thinks the KGB "might indeed change the mission of another man of another operation [Nosenko] in order to get this message over to us, that they really had nothing to do with [the assassination]."

But this fine distinction was lost as the CIA's interpretation of Oswald's alleged act percolated up to President Johnson. Earl Warren writes that he at first resisted Johnson's request that he head up the JFK inquiry, and that Johnson "then told me how serious were the rumors floating around the world. The gravity of the situation was such that it might lead us into war, he said, and if so, it might be a nuclear war. He went on to tell me that he had just talked to Defense Secretary Robert McNamara, who had advised him that the first nuclear strike against us might cause the loss of forty million people. I then said, 'Mr. President, if the situation is that serious, my personal views do not count. I will do it.' He thanked me, and I left the White House."

What can this mean if not that the CIA's theory of the JFK assassination led Johnson, and thus Warren, to fear that the price of the truth in this case could easily be World War III? Nosenko's apparent lies about Oswald in Russia became the basis of that fear.

But this view of Nosenko and Oswald did not, and does not, prevail. The Assassinations Committee finally declared that "there is no evidence that the Soviet government had any interest in removing President Kennedy, nor is there any evidence that it planned to take advantage of the president's death before it happened or attempted to capitalize on it after it occurred." The committee concluded, therefore, "on the basis of the evidence available to it, that the Soviet government was not involved in the assassination."

Well, if it is true that Oswald was not a Russian agent assigned to shoot the President, then Nosenko told the truth on that count. If Nosenko is nevertheless thought to have lied substantially about Oswald and the KGB, what could be the explanation for his strange mixture of truth and lies?

And to come to the practical heart of the whole Nosenko mystery, why, if the Russians had nothing to do with Kennedy's death, would they have contrived so intricate a method of conveying this critical information as that of a false defector? Said Bagley, "Why they might have selected this channel to send [this information], and what truth may lie behind the story given to us, can only be guessed at . . . I couldn't find any logical or any illogical explanation for why [Nosenko] said what he said about Oswald.''

A source on the Assassinations Committee staff expressed the same bewilderment to me: ''You'd have to assume that Khrushchev and even Brezhnev would have had to make the decision to send Nosenko in here like that. And it would have looked so risky. I just can't see why they would have made that decision. When [Nosenko] breaks down, he sobs, he gets real bitter, and he says he doesn't care what we believe, but if we ever try to torture him again, the word is going straight out to Daniel Schorr!''

I needed clarification on this. Was there any suggestion that Nosenko had a *continuing* espionage role?

''No,'' said the source, ''nobody says that. The theory is that he was sent to do the JFK stuff.''

How does this bear on CIA internal power struggles?

''Well, Angleton and those people [i.e., the anti-Nosenko group] really had to go. They were the most sinister of all people there.''

''Really?'' I asked. ''More sinister than William Colby?'' (Colby took over for Helms as CIA head in 1973.)

''Oh, sure!''

''The Colby who supervised the assassination of some 50,000 Vietnamese people in Operation Phoenix?''

The source laughed. ''Oh, well, that! But I mean, apart from mass murder, you know, Colby's pretty straight!''

I have a simpler explanation—a rather innocent explanation, in fact—for why the Soviet leadership might have chosen the Nosenko method of communicating to the United States leadership that Kennedy was not a Soviet victim.

Grant Bagley's point about the "piranhas" of the KGB and assume that Oswald, indeed, had been questioned at length and in detail by Soviet intelligence people. Assume, too, that the Soviets at the same time remained wary of Oswald and found him too unstable and mysterious for recruitment. The KGB took what it could get from him, was very possibly surprised at the usefulness of his information, rewarded him with a nice job and a comfortable apartment and the privilege of owning and shooting a rifle, and kept him at arm's length.

So Oswald goes home, and in a year and a half, Kennedy is killed. The Soviets are shocked to see their friend Oswald accused, then killed himself. Their urgent review of the KGB Oswald file discloses that a paranoid imagination could easily be led to see Oswald as a KGB recruit. That was not true, but it *looked* true, just as though Oswald had been groomed for that very purpose. Was someone trying to frame the KGB for the Kennedy assassination? How could the Soviets convincingly inform the wounded, suspicious Americans that appearances were, in this case, deceiving? A convincing reassurance could not be given by officials because, if the assassination of JFK were an official Soviet act, naturally, Soviet officials would be sworn to keep it secret.

So if the Soviets' message that Oswald was not a KGB assassin were to be delivered as a fact commanding belief, then they would have to deliver it through somebody in a position to *know* it for a fact. That meant the message had to come from the KGB, because only someone from the KGB, and indeed from the specific KGB section that handled Oswald, could even begin to know whether Oswald was or was not a target of serious KGB surveillance while he was in Russia, or whether he was or was not dispatched to the United States as a sleeper, assassin, or whatever by the KGB.

In fact, such a message could only be delivered by a KGB defector. *KGB* in order to know the truth, and a *defector* in order to want to tell it to the Americans. No other communication channel would even be logical. No matter how risky the Nosenko method must have looked, the very logic of the situation, as in a game of chess, may have demanded it.

On the afternoon of September 25, 1978, ten days after John Hart, CIA, defended Nosenko before the House Assassinations Committee and just three days after Richard Helms, CIA, restated the case against him, the skipper of a crab boat in lower Chesapeake Bay looked up from his work to see bearing down on him a graceful sailing sloop, *Brillig.*

The wind was brisk. The *Brillig* was light in the water and clipped along in the light chop rapidly on a collision course. The crabber finally realized the *Brillig* had not seen him, though the day was clear. He hit his engines. He barely managed to clear the *Brillig*'s charging bow. Angrily he radioed the Coast Guard to complain. It is not known if he noticed there was no one aboard the *Brillig.*

Coast Guardsmen discovered the empty sailboat grounded a few hours later, farther down the bay. Aboard they found an open jar of mustard and a half-made sandwich in the galley, a folding table torn off its hinges, secret CIA documents relating to Soviet military capability, and a highly classified burst transceiver, used only to transmit and receive sophisticated radio codes. The tiller was unlocked.

In just a few hours the *Brillig* was identified as John Paisley's craft and Paisley was identified as a ''former'' high-level official of the CIA now working for the agency on a consulting basis on a highly sensitive study of CIA assessments of Soviet capability. When last heard from in a routine radio call he had sent earlier that day, announcing that he was coming in, Paisley was aboard the *Brillig*. Now the *Brillig* was beached and Paisley was missing.

When Paisley's estranged wife, Maryann, heard of the beaching of the *Brillig*, she sent their son, Eddie, twenty-two, to check out his father's apartment. Eddie found the place ransacked and all of Paisley's papers gone. Several 9-mm bullets were scattered on the closet floor. Mrs. Paisley was all the more distressed to hear of this break-in because Paisley's apartment was in the same building, on the same floor, and off the same hallway as apartments of Soviet embassy employees whom Maryann Paisley knew to be under constant CIA surveillance.

On October 1, 1978, the Coast Guard pulled a body from the bay. It was bloated and badly decomposed. Positive identification was impossible. But a consensus emerged among examiners, insurance agents, and two Paisley acquaintances who saw the body that it was John Paisley's—despite such disturbing physical differences as the fact that Paisley stood 5′11″, weighed 170 pounds, wore a beard and a full head of hair, while the body fished out of the bay was four inches shorter, 30 pounds lighter, beardless, and bald.

There was a 9-mm gunshot wound behind the body's left ear. There were thirty-eight pounds of diving weights strapped around its waist.

The official verdict was suicide, but Maryann Paisley did not believe it. She retained longtime family friend Bernard Fensterwald, the Washington attorney who handled James McCord during Watergate days, to try to fight the cover-up.

Mrs. Paisley called attention to her own ''CIA background'' in a furious letter she wrote at the beginning of 1979 to CIA Director Stansfield Turner, protesting the CIA's "hands-off" attitude toward her husband's death.

"I was particularly anxious for Mr. Fensterwald to talk with Katherine Hart," she wrote, "because it is her husband, John, who is the agency's expert on Yuri Nosenko. You know that John Paisley [whose "activities," she wrote elsewhere, "were certainly not confined to the overt side"] was deeply involved in Nosenko's indescribable debriefing. It has crossed my mind, and that of others, that my husband's fate might be somehow connected with the Nosenko case."

So Paisley was part of Nosenko's "indescribable debriefing," was he? It is known from other sources that in 1972 and 1973 Paisley was also involved heavily in a CIA-wide search for a suspected Soviet mole. Paisley's job was then to determine if Soviet defectors were double agents, and he directly questioned Nosenko and another Soviet defector who came over at the same time, Soviet navy captain Nicholas Shadrin, who disappeared while walking through a public square in Vienna in 1975.

Thus, Paisley was a part of the group that regarded Nosenko as a false defector. So we can add his name to a group made up of Helms, Bagley, Murphy, and Angleton, none of whom are working for the CIA anymore, either.

Nosenko, however, is currently drawing a CIA salary of $35,325 a year and lecturing our counterintelligence trainees and future foreign-liaison officers on the Soviet practice of the intelligence arts, as well as playing some direct role in current CIA counterintelligence operations.

This is not, alas, a finished story. Questions abound. Was it really Paisley's body that was found so sea-changed in Chesapeake Bay? If not, who might have orchestrated the cover-up that identified the body as his?

And why? Is there substance to Maryann Paisley's belief that her husband was deeply involved in covert CIA operations and the Nosenko interrogation? Could Paisley's strange disappearance, as his wife suspects, have had anything to do with the Assassinations Committee's breaking of Nosenko's Oswald story shortly before? Was Nosenko a false defector sent to conceal a Soviet role in the assassination of Kennedy? Or to convey, through a calculated lie, the essential truth of Soviet innocence in the JFK murder?

On such mysteries, the Nosenko matter—perhaps from now on it should be called "the Nosenko-*Paisley* matter"—hangs in uncertainty and suspense, waiting for someone's next move.

10

Reflections on
the Assassination Media*

A reporter for one of the big outlets chanced one day to be the only one of the major media people at the Assassinations Committee's hearings to get the real point of what had happened that day. Chairman Stokes had presented a major blast at the FBI and raised the question of FBI co-responsibility in King's death. It was a dramatic moment. Stokes is a fine speaker, he cared a lot about what he was saying, and his statement was well conceived and written. The reporter who picked up on it had caught a strong story, clearly the lead of the day. And all the other majors missed it.

The reporter came in the hearing room smoldering the next day, slouched to his place muttering darkly about getting chewed out by his boss. Chewed out? For what? For that story about Stokes' speech on the FBI, he said. But that was a great story, nobody else got it. That's the point, he said. Why? Because my bosses say that if the rest of the press didn't get it, too, it must not have happened, and it looks bad when one of us says something so different from the rest.

What an educational exchange! One had heard things

*Clandestine America, Jan.–Feb. 1979.

about "scoops" and journalistic courage, and now it turned out that the real key to success in the big time was something else. You had to know how to run with the pack, because what the "news" actually was, boiled down, was the collective opinion of this same pack. If the pack thinks JFK was killed by a lone nut, then anybody who thinks something else must be another one.

How often on the lecture circuit in the old days the Warren critic would hear someone say that if any of these doubts were actually valid, and if there was anything at all to the monstrous idea that the President was killed by a conspiracy, then surely by now our bright, ambitious people of the media would already have found out all about it and won Pulitzers, like Woodward and Bernstein. Since there are no Woodward and Bernstein of the JFK assassination issue—and no Pulitzers—there must actually be no issue.

All ye who have ever thought that particular thought, take heed and ponder this tale of the bright, ambitious reporter who got rebuked for his scoop, while the ones with the blandest and emptiest impressions of what happened that day in the hearing room cruised on through their career-week without a ripple. Pack journalism is, to our mind, a very special problem in the conspiracy cases because pack journalists are so timid and vicious. As other interviews make clear, there are many faults to find with the HSCA's hearings. But their performance was a hundred times in front of the mainstream media in terms of curiosity, investigative vigor, and courage to face tough possibilities.

If the press had reported each day on the actual contributions the committee was making instead of constantly blunting everything that said conspiracy and overplaying everything that said relax, then the 80 percent of us who today sense conspiracy in the JFK death would be not only more numerous, but also more aroused and more insistent that the whole truth be found. The committee told us that Oswald was hanging out around Carlos Marcello at the very time Marcello was threatening JFK's life, and the press hardly blinked. The committee told us it did not think Ruby got in to shoot Oswald the way Warren said but may have had help from the police in getting in, and the press sat on its pencils as though the story meant nothing. The committee ran out a never-before-heard acoustic tape in evidence, an actual recording of the gunfire, and all the press said was that there was a 50-50 chance it didn't mean a thing.

A peroration on this theme: One has no doubt that a free press can help us all be free. But when it does not choose to *use* its freedom, how can its freedom make a difference? And if it doesn't make a difference, how can it be real?

11

Did the Mob Kill Kennedy?*

A lot of people wish it would go away permanently, but the murder of John F. Kennedy now begs, more than ever, for serious detective work in search of conspiracy.

Beyond the mechanics of what happened in Dealey Plaza, we are now confronted with larger questions and the elusive outline, at least, of a plausible conspiracy. This is certainly not the time to heave a collective sigh and let it drop, but rather to pose the next question: What kind of conspiracy? Was it big or small, left or right, foreign or domestic?

It is still not widely understood that the House Select Committee on Assassinations developed two conspiracy arguments, not one, and that its original finding was not based on the sensational acoustics evidence that struck home late in December when the committee's time was all but over. Before the acoustics experts testified that they were "more than 95 percent certain" of having detected proof of a second gunman, other evidence had persuaded most committee members that a conspiracy was "likely." The acoustics findings jumped "likely" to

*Washington Post, February 25, 1979. With Jeff Goldberg.

"probable," but the basic decision had already been made by a majority of the committee and its senior staff.

That decision was based on circumstantial evidence indicating that Lee Harvey Oswald, lone gunman as he may or may not have been, and Oswald's killer, Jack Ruby, were quite possibly under the control or influence of mob figures now known to have been threatening the lives of both John and Robert Kennedy.

The chief of these was Carlos Marcello of New Orleans, regarded by experts on the mob as one of the most powerful Mafia bosses in the country, just below Meyer Lansky and the New York Gambino family. Now aging, Marcello still bosses a crime system whose take in Louisiana alone has been estimated by the New Orleans Crime Commission at over $1 billion a year. His influence extends through the Southwest, including Dallas.

The committee staff's initial conspiracy theory had the peculiar property—and perhaps the virtue—of justifying both sides in this long and often acrimonious debate. To the Warren Commission and its children, it gave support for the views that Oswald was the only gunman of Dealey Plaza. To the critics, it gave support for the theory that Oswald was linked to a larger conspiracy that recruited or duped him.

If the committee is right about the acoustics evidence, then clearly any lone-gunman theories are forever obviated. But that only makes more important the evidence suggesting Oswald and Ruby's ties to the mob.

A Substitute Father

The Oswald link to Marcello bears on his relationship to three men during 1963—Charles (Dutz) Murret, David Ferrie and W. Guy Banister.

Murret is mentioned in the Warren *Report* but identified only as Oswald's uncle. According to committee sources, Dutz was Oswald's substitute father during his childhood. Oswald apparently was attached to him. When Oswald moved from Dallas to New Orleans, his birthplace, in April 1963, it was Uncle Murret who initially put him up while he looked for work and a place to bring his family.

What you will not find in the Warren *Report,* however, is information developed by the House committee that Dutz Murret was not your run-of-the-mill uncle. According to recently retired New Orleans Crime Commissioner Aaron Kohn, Murret, who died in 1964, was an important bookie tied into New Orleans organized crime. As such, according to Kohn, he "certainly knew who Marcello was."

A House committee source goes further, calling Murret "a top deputy of a top man in Carlos Marcello's gambling apparatus." Adds this source: "Oswald was aware of his uncle's [organized crime] ties and discussed them with him in 1963."

More intriguing is Oswald's relationship with David Ferrie, which was rediscovered and confirmed by the House committee (Jim Garrison's investigation was onto the Ferrie link in 1967 when Ferrie died). We still have much to learn about it, but the tie is important because Ferrie is known to have worn two quite different hats.

Under one hat, he worked inside the Marcello operation. He was Marcello's personal pilot, the man who flew the crime lord back into the United States after Marcello's summary deportation to Guatemala in 1961 by Attorney General Robert Kennedy. Within the organization, he also was an "investigator" for Marcello's top lawyer and adviser. Ferrie was, in fact, at Marcello's side in court at the moment of the assassination.

Under his other hat, Ferrie was a contract operative

for the CIA who had trained pilots for the Bay of Pigs invasion.

When Oswald and Ferrie first met is still cloudy. The committee's final report will note that Oswald was a teenager cadet in the same Civil Air Patrol unit in which Ferrie was once a captain and instructor. Also unclear is when and how often the two met in New Orleans in 1963. The committee has been impressed by the credibility of three witnesses who said they saw Oswald on several occasions in Ferrie's company in Clinton, Louisiana.

Oswald and Ferrie also both occupied offices at the small building then standing at 544 Camp Street, the address stamped on the pro-Castro leaflets Oswald passed out in August 1963 in downtown New Orleans. This building was then the headquarters of anti-Castro activity throughout the region.

The Camp Street operation was directed by an ex-FBI officer, W. Guy Banister, whose private detective agency was a cover for his role as go-between for the CIA and the Cuban exiles involved in anti-Castro operations.

Marcello's man Ferrie also worked for Banister as a private investigator at that time. We know that Banister, aided by Ferrie, acted in the areas of gunrunning and the training and staging of Cuban commandos. Banister's Camp Street office was surrounded by Cuban-exile organizations, including at one point the Cuban Revolutionary Council, a CIA front group set up by, among others, Antonio de Varona, the Cuban exile leader. It was Varona who received from mobster John Rosselli the poison pills which had come from the CIA and which were intended for the Castro brothers and Che Guevara.

Yet it was to this building, a hotbed of anti-Castro activity, that young Oswald, self-made Marxist, came to find an office for his pro-Castro one-man band, the New Orleans chapter of the Fair Play for Cuba Committee.

''There has to be a connection between Oswald and those who operated in the building,'' says one House committee source.

Adding substance to this view, committee sources also confirm that they have found reliable eyewitness evidence that Oswald and Banister may have been together during the summer of 1963. At least one of these witnesses, retired CIA operative William Gaudet, first said publicly in a 1977 Canadian television documentary that he saw Oswald and Banister together at a New Orleans garage close to the Camp Street headquarters. Gaudet had not spoken of this earlier. According to a committee source, ''he kept his mouth shut because that's what agency procedure was. Plus he's paranoid and thought he was going to be killed. And probably more importantly, nobody ever asked him.''

The ''nobody'' included the Warren Commission, which concluded that ''extensive investigation was not able to connect Oswald with that address,'' 544 Camp Street. This apparently was because the FBI withheld information on the point. The House committee knows, as the Warren Commission did not, that the FBI had a pre-assassination file on Oswald linking him to that well-known address. The committee also knows, as the Warren Commission did not, that the 531 Lafayette Street address provided by the FBI as Banister's office was simply a side entrance to the Camp Street building.

No Sudden Impulse

The committee also found evidence that Jack Ruby was acting under no sudden impulse when he murdered Oswald. The Warren Commission thought Ruby's act unpremeditated and accepted his story to the effect that sympathy for the President's widow was his only motive.

But the House investigation found indications that Ruby was stalking Oswald in the Dallas jail for at least a full day before he killed him, and that far from coming into the jailhouse basement via the driveway ramp, as the Warren *Report* had it, Ruby appears to have gone through an altogether different entrance and may well have had inside help in doing so.

The implication is that Ruby was out to keep Oswald from standing trial. Could Oswald, as he claimed, have implicated accomplices? Possibly acquitted himself in a trial? Identified those who might have framed him?

This raises the further question of what or whom Ruby was protecting. The Warren Commission concluded that "the evidence does not establish a significant link between Ruby and organized crime," even though in a secret meeting on Jan. 24, 1964, Warren Commission Chief Counsel J. Lee Rankin informed the commissioners that Ruby "has apparently all kinds of connections with the underworld." Indeed, House committee Chief Counsel G. Robert Blakey calls Ruby's presence in the story "the greatest single justification" for raising the question of mob involvement in the assassination.

Warren Commission members knew that Ruby's mob ties went back to the 1940s and that he went to Cuba in 1959. The House committee reported that he made at least three mob-related trips to Cuba that year. He met in prison with Florida crime boss Santos Trafficante, who had been jailed by Castro. He also met with his closest friend and Trafficante's manager at the Tropicana casino, Lewis McWillie. His aim included helping smuggle Trafficante's cash out of the closed casino and back to the United States.

The Warren Commission also knew that in the two months before the assassination, Ruby was in telephone contact with key figures of the New Orleans, Chicago and

Florida crime families. Initiated by Ruby, who somehow had access to their unlisted phone numbers, these calls went to mobsters Barney Baker, a feared enforcer for Teamster boss Jimmy Hoffa; Lenny Patrick, a hired killer working for Chicago boss Sam Giancana; Nofio Pecora, one of Marcello's most trusted aides; and Trafficante's man, McWillie.

Ruby also talked to Murray (Dusty) Miller, a national Teamsters official close to Hoffa, and Irwin S. Weiner, chief Teamsters bondsman and a top Hoffa adviser. On Nov. 20, 1963, two days before JFK was shot, Ruby was visited at his nightclub by another notorious mobster, Paul Roland Jones. And on the next night, Ruby had drinks with a friend who had been in recent phone contact with Marcello's aide and Oswald's friend, David Ferrie.

So what? So Ruby was a hood. So Oswald hung around with a few colorful types in New Orleans. What's the angle? What could it add up to? The answer may lie in the tangled, turbulent history set in motion by the Cuban revolution of 1959.

The Mob and the CIA

Most of us are aware that before the Cuban revolution the Mafia held a strong position in Havana, controlling vice and gambling rackets through an arrangement between Cuban strongman Fulgencio Batista and U.S. crime boss Meyer Lansky. When Castro overthrew Batista in early 1959, he expropriated and closed Havana's casinos and jailed or banished their owners or operators. That infuriated the mobsters—especially Marcello's ally, Santos Trafficante, whom Castro imprisoned.

Trafficante and Marcello were the pillars of a southern wing of the crime syndicate, and Cuba was vital to them.

No sooner had Castro driven them out than they started plotting how to get back in, wondering how to get rid of Castro.

Others were pondering the same problem, notably Vice President Richard Nixon, who was then the ranking political member of the National Security Council's so-called 5412, or Special Group, which would essentially decide (during Eisenhower's illness) what U.S. policy would be toward Castro. Nixon interviewed Castro privately when Castro came to New York to the United Nations in 1959 and concluded that he was a threat to U.S. security and would have to go. Plans for the invasion of Cuba were drawn up and set in motion before 1959 was out.

By August 1960, at latest, about the time JFK was being nominated as the Democratic presidential candidate, Allen Dulles' CIA had initiated its now infamous arrangement to have Castro killed by the Mafia. Thus, two powerful covert organizations, the CIA and the Mafia, were secretly joined for a joint strike against Castro.

Kennedy's election meant the invasion would occur under a President who hadn't been in on it from the start and who didn't share Nixon's anti-Communist zeal. Kennedy had tried to look even tougher than Nixon on Cuba during the campaign, but once in office he limited U.S. participation in the invasion. He rejected the CIA proposal to kill Castro (according to the Church Committee) and refused to unleash CIA B-26s waiting in Guatemala to support the strike.

Everyone came out of the Bay of Pigs Fiasco infuriated. Kennedy fired future Warren Commission member Allen Dulles from the CIA and promised to "splinter" the CIA "into a thousand pieces" for having deceived him on Cuban feelings toward Castro.

The invasion team and its partisans said Kennedy had

betrayed them at the beach. He betrayed them again, they said, in the October 1962 missile crisis when he secretly promised Soviet Premier Nikita Khrushchev that he would stop the exiles' commando raids against Cuban targets, raids staged from bases in Florida and Louisiana—home territories, respectively, of Trafficante and Marcello.

The Anti-Crime Drive

It was not Cuba alone, of course, that drove the mob to flash-point anger with the Kennedys. There was motive enough in the campaign to extirpate the mob from U.S. life.

RFK had had Marcello physically seized off a New Orleans street and deported to Guatemala in April 1961 (two weeks before the Bay of Pigs), without giving him a chance to see a lawyer or pack a bag. When Marcello reentered the country two months later in a private plane piloted by Oswald's soon-to-be-made acquaintance, David Ferrie, he was already in a state of permanent rage over the Kennedy brothers. Specifically angry with Robert Kennedy, the mobster, according to a House committee informant, also fulminated against the President in September 1962, citing a Sicilian adage that to kill a rooster "you don't cut off the tail, you cut off the head," and adding that JFK should be killed "by some nut." About the same time, Marcello ally Trafficante told Cuban exile leader Jose Aleman not to worry about JFK: "He's going to be hit."

Teamsters leader Hoffa, close to Marcello, was possibly even angrier at the Kennedys. Hoffa, who had become RFK's special target, was finally about to be imprisoned. According to a House committee source,

"The Hoffa threat [against RFK] is absolutely confirmed. We believe it and [our final report] will say so."

The committee has learned that in August 1962, in Hoffa's Washington office, he discussed two plans to kill RFK. The first was to firebomb RFK's Virginia estate with plastic explosives. The second was to shoot him with a high-powered rifle as he rode in his convertible in a southern city.

The committee will not pretend that it has found a smoking gun to support its Mafia theory. Nor will it say that the 1962 expressions of murderous hatred for the Kennedys by Marcello, Trafficante and Hoffa prove that they were embarked upon a JFK assassination plot as of that moment. Indeed, the committee's investigators find it unlikely that these threats would have been voiced before such low-level figures as Aleman or the Marcello informant if a plot actually had existed at the time.

The committee also will not pretend that it can clearly outline how a Marcello-Trafficante-Hoffa conspiracy would have selected and recruited Oswald, whether as assassin or patsy.

It will not explain (and Chief Counsel Blakey is known to be troubled about this) how some of the world's most hardened mobsters might let the weight of a supremely hazardous plot fall on an unknown quantity of the likes of Oswald. "What doesn't seem to add up," said JFK Subcommittee Chairman Richardson Preyer (D-N.C.) in early January, "is how other conspirators might have picked somebody as unstable as Oswald to carry out their plot."

What is important, though, is that the committee has established that Marcello, Trafficante and Hoffa all had motive, means and opportunity to assassinate the President, that the three were sufficiently close for individual motivation to have combined to produce an assassination conspiracy, and that they had access to Oswald and Ruby in the half year preceding the assassination.

The final committee report will tell what concrete opportunities exist for further investigation of the New Orleans angle. Chief Counsel Blakey has promised "to lay out in full detail the situation in New Orleans" in the final report: "What Oswald was up to and with whom he associated."

A Question of Trust

What about the larger meaning of it all?

Committee Chairman Louis Stokes (D-Ohio), who helped rescue the panel from the shouting matches that nearly destroyed it in its first year, says, "All of us know that organized crime permeates the society. Society is helpless. . . . It is not powerless, but government utilizes that power only where they want to, and organized crime is not where they really want to use it."

Chief Counsel Blakey has other thoughts. He is no firebrand. He is an Ivy League academic who does not express opinions impetuously. But, stepping out of his committee role for the first time publicly, this is what he told a meeting of lawyers on January 25 in New York City:

"I can tell you that not one institution of my society served me well in 1963 . . . The FBI did not adequately investigate the conspiracy . . . The CIA, what did they do for us? . . . The Warren Commission itself represented in many ways the best in our society . . . They studied the case as best they could, arrived at their judgments in good faith, and were fundamentally wrong on the conspiracy question.

"And they made what in my judgment was a serious mistake. They stated their judgment . . . as [though] they mistrusted the American people. They should have said, 'We've done the best we could, we know who shot the president, we're not sure whether others were involved,' and then trusted to the maturity of the American people to accept it as such.

"They didn't. And this let into our society a kind of poison that has run through the body politic since. We call it Watergate today—a lack of credibility in governmental institutions. There are a lot of young people who have thought this case through who will never trust the government again . . .

"If there is any message to take out of this case, it can be summed up in two words—*never again!* The next time this happens—and it will happen: one in four of our presidents has been shot at—I hope indeed that people will have the courage and the integrity to stand up and say, 'I will pursue this as far as I can, and if I can't go all the way, because I'm human, I will tell people of that.' "

12

Conspiracy Found*

The sound of a shot from the grassy knoll has been heard by the House Assassinations Committee since last we met, and the committee has thus been obliged to conclude in its final report that a conspiracy in the JFK assassination was "probable."

The immediate result was shocked, hurt, angry, incredulous outcries from the defenders of the lone-assassin faith, wails of disgust and disbelief from the FBI, a counterattack through the mass media, and the disintegration of the celebrated "non-partisanship" of the select committee, all the Democrats but one going along with the conspiracy finding, all the Republicans but one dissenting.

But this gets ahead of the story. Our purpose here is to look back on the committee's progress, review the main events that brought it to its last-minute reversal, then take a look beyond to guess what the new situation may be like.

The Shot

We heard the pre-echo of the knoll shot, the shock wave of it, as the acoustics people might say, on Septem-

Clandestine America, vol. 3, no. 1, June 1979.

ber 11, the fourth day of the committee's public hearings on JFK. It would be three and a half months more before we would hear the blast itself.

The chandeliered hearing room was expectant that bright September morning. The word was out that this was to be the big day for the outside critics, that we were perhaps even to be vindicated by the testimony that the acoustics expert was scheduled to give.

Certainly the first three days of the hearings had given the critics no comfort. The members gazed down in seeming contentment as their chief counsel, G. Robert Blakey, systematically went after the arguments advanced against the lone-assassin theory by the first-generation critics. Like a prosecutor in a trial, he set about to pull the magic-bullet theory back together, explain away the backwards head snap, and shrug off the relatively undeformed condition of bullet CE399.

To the satisfaction of the media, Blakey was clearly beating the critics back. Maybe now, they thought, the JFK question was at long last about to be shut down.

Then at the end of the third day a new word was out. A major upheaval was now expected.

New acoustics evidence was about to be presented that would turn the whole case around, weighty scientific proof of conspiracy. Where Warren said three shots were fired, the new evidence said four. Where Warren said all shots came from one gunman firing from behind, the new evidence said one of the shots, the third, was fired from the front, from the area of the grassy knoll.

The physical basis of these conclusions was a Dallas Police Department Dictabelt recording of the gunfire made automatically through an open mike on a DPD motorcycle riding escort in the motorcade about 120 feet behind the limousine.

This acoustical record of the assassination was known

to the Warren Commission, but the commission and the FBI were apparently satisfied that it had little evidentiary value. The critics, especially the Texas group led by Penn Jones and the magnificent Mary Ferrell of Dallas, knew there was important and indeed decisive information on this belt, but lacked the financial and technological means to retrieve it. And there the question lay.

Time passed. The debate alternately sputtered and raged, would not be quelled, and then finally in 1976 the House set up the Assassinations Committee. In 1977, Mary Ferrell informed this committee of the existence of the belt and turned over a copy of it from her archives. With help from a former Dallas Police Department assistant chief, Paul McCaghren, the committee was able to find and procure the original belt, formerly thought lost or destroyed.

The next step was to send the tape out for analysis to the outfit most experienced and competent in this kind of work, the Cambridge, Massachusetts acoustic laboratory, Bolt, Beranek and Newman. BBN had a long list of scientific and technological achievements to its credit, conspicuous among which was the fact federal courts had directed it to testify as an expert witness in two of the major political court cases of our time—the Kent State shootings and the Nixon 18½-minute gap.

The BBN technical analysis of the DPD belt was reduced finally to two propositions derived from two different kinds of scientific activity. First, BBN used a matched-filtering process to retrieve the possible sounds of shots from the Dictabelt's noise. Second came the analysis of the signals thus identified. This analysis was carried out by means of the detailed acoustical examination of the specific signals isolated in the first step—the ''impulses'' that might be sounds of gunshots. The method was to reproduce these impulses as waveforms and compare them to the waveforms of rifle and pistol shots recorded on August 20, 1978, by the BB&N project team in Dealey Plaza.

The waveforms are complex patterns that contain a great deal of specific information. The waveform produced by a rifle shot can be distinguished from that of a motorcycle backfire, for example, because the bullet, being a supersonic projectile, produces a distinctive shock wave preceding the blast wave. And a shot fired in Dealey Plaza can be distinguished from shots fired in all other places, because the buildings bounding the plaza and their overall configuration and physical relationship to each other give the plaza a unique acoustical "fingerprint." If the Dealey Plaza test patterns coincided with the Dictabelt patterns, then the Dictabelt impulses were of shots fired in Dealey Plaza or its exact acoustic replica.

So having found the shots and determined their points of origin, BBN's chief scientist and project leader, Dr. James A. Barger, was about to tell the committee and the world that the Warren Commission was wrong, that there were two gunmen after all, establishing a presumptive case for conspiracy.

Not so fast. As we would find out later, Barger had grown more and more sharply aware, as the time to testify publicly approached, of the enormous impact his testimony would have. The implications awed him. The more he considered the matter, the less did he want his testimony, his analysis, to bear the whole weight of a conspiracy verdict. He developed cold feet.

The night before he was to testify, Barger told senior staff people he was nervous, but the word didn't seem to reach the committee members, who convened their public session that morning still expecting to hear a possible scientific refutation of the Warren theory. Thus there was real surprise among them as it dawned that morning that they were not about to get that.

For Barger now seemed to be saying that there was only a 50-50 chance that there were four shots instead of three. It was 50-50 that one of the four shots was a "false alarm," and the shot among the four that would most likely not be a shot, after all, but a false alarm—that was shot number three, the positive shot from the grassy knoll.

One by one the reporters drifted out of the hearing room to phone in retractions of the morning's headline news. By three that afternoon the media were back on the lone-assassin team, looking smug, like people who had just survived a dangerous detour.

Actually Barger had merely allowed himself to be mis-understood. The point he was making to the committee was that the probability mechanics of his study allowed him to state with certainty that no more than two of these four shots were real shots. That all four were real was only 50-50.

The mass media people were in no mood to absorb fine distinctions. They thought they had been offered a direct proof of conspiracy and then had it snatched back. They were tired of the whole thing suddenly. They might have bought a little conspiracy evidence, but they would not tolerate the sort of technical ambiguities and com-plexities that could not be snugly fitted into a standard news story lead. There were either four shots or not, and if it can't be determined that there were four, then the assumption, please, will be that there were three and that the Warren Commission was right all along.

So the critics had no sooner stuck out their necks to get their medals than they found themselves in a noose instead. The reporters were again ready to write the whole thing off, more disgusted with conspiracy freaks than ever. "See?" one of them said to an AIB staffer at the lunch break that day, "there's nothing there at all."

And when the AIBer begged leave to differ, he sneered, "You guys are just as crazy as Mark Lane!"

But if 50-50 on the knoll shot was a de facto win for the Warren Commission in the eyes of the media, it was fortunately not so viewed by the committee. Frankly, the committee could have gotten away with dropping the whole acoustics kaboodle right there. But the committee decided it had to move the probability of conspiracy off the 50-50 mark, one way or another, and that new tests were therefore required.

This was the point at which the two new acoustics experts were put under contract. Their assignment was to review the BB&N tests and carry out additional analysis to determine whether or not the existence of a second Dealey Plaza gunman was indicated in the DPD belt.

The new experts were professors Mark Weiss and Ernest Aschkenasy of Queens College, New York. They are said to rank with Barger in level of expertise. They, too, have done fancy acoustics work for the military. They, too, were court-appointed to study the Nixon and Kent State tapes.

And employing nothing more complex than the classical laws of the physics of the propogation of sound, plus accurate architectural and acoustical data on Dealey Plaza, Weiss and Aschkenasy found themselves scientifically forced to state with "a better than 95% certainty" that there were four shots and that the third of these was fired from the knoll. There were two gunmen.

That was the Christmas present the acoustics people handed the committee on December 29, 1978: scientific proof of conspiracy.

Was this a verdict that the staff, the committee, and the Congress had wanted to accept? On the contrary. The new advocates of conspiracy theory were dragged kicking and screaming the whole way. They had not wanted this result.

But once they had found this evidence, there was little they could do but face its implications and speak the words, "conspiracy probable in JFK assassination." Chief Counsel Blakey was in a sense disarmed by his own weapons in this climax. It had been his strategy, as a lawyer confronting certain technical problems of proof, to define "best evidence" as "scientific evidence," and to give less weight to the things people said they saw or heard. He was saying in effect, "You can be fooled by what you think you hear or see. Let's see instead what kind of facts we can ascertain through the use of objective scientific examinations of material pieces of evidence. Whatever can be determined scientifically will be regarded as having been determined absolutely, and any contradictory direct testimony—'I saw this, I heard that'—will be discounted."

This is why, for example, Blakey was forced to insist that all shots that hit JFK were fired from behind. He had a body of "medical evidence" consisting basically of x-rays. The nature of these x-rays was such that expert study of them could determine the physical details of the shots. And one of the details shown by the x-rays, said Blakey's medical panel, was that the headshot bullet came from behind. Therefore, any evidence indicating that the headshot came from the front—the Zapruder head snap, certain eyewitness testimony—would simply have to be refuted or discounted or explained away. The scientific evidence was the best evidence, and the best evidence would predetermine the value of all the other evidence: good if it supported science and bad if it did not.

Now this self-same standard of evidence had reversed its bearing and was committing Blakey and the committee inexorably to a conspiracy conclusion. Science was best and science said two gunmen, period. A government body that was very probably created to silence the conspiracy buffs, freaks and paranoids now found itself cast among them.

Elite Reactions

As all know, the overwhelming majority of the American people have thought pretty well all along that the Warren *Report* was not the last word. But this is absolutely the other way around among the "issue elite," the politicians and media groups who produce the picture of the world we see in the evening news and the daily gazette. If eight out of ten ordinary people believe JFK was killed by a conspiracy, then eight out of ten reporters, eight out of ten academics, eight out of ten politicians, eight out of ten arbiters of fashionable opinion believe that Warren was essentially correct, that there was nothing to gain from further questioning, that there was nothing new or significant to be learned, that the whole thing didn't make any difference anyway. Remember this always, that such have been the views of the mainstream "makers of public opinion," in diametrical opposition to what that opinion actually is.

And these makers have been ruthless in their error. Bad enough to refuse the truth, how much worse to calumniate as well those who will not do so. We cannot forget an especially noxious *Washington Star* editorial (12/9/77) which dared suggest that the money spent by this committee would have been better spent on finding "a pill" with which "to neutralize the peculiar body chemistry of compulsive conspiracy theorists."

Well, time went by, the committee heard the arguments, weighed the evidence, and concluded that Warren and the *Star* and those of like mind were wrong. There was a conspiracy, after all. How now, *Star?* Do we hear an apology? A little self-criticism? Nothing of the sort enters the *Star*'s mind. Right straight on it marches with its hackneyed arrogance. "Modern witchcraft," it grumbles of the acoustics evidence, "esoteric," "highly inferential," "exiguous."

Then worse, on its news pages of March 16, the *Star* unleashed its Jeremiah O'Leary in an incredible-to-behold effort to muddy the acoustics issue by quoting radically out of context certain passages from the final report submitted by Weiss and Aschkenasy in order to make it appear that these two experts had reconsidered and retracted their former testimony on the front shot.

Nothing of the kind was the case. The *Star* story is child's play to see through for anyone the least educated in the issue. But to the lay public, the impression will have been supported that there is something serious to argue about in the acoustics evidence. Perhaps there will prove to be, but that will be revealed to us *only* by new scientific work on the Dictabelt, not by O'Leary's clumsy deceptions or the ignorant posturings of the *Star*'s editorial writers.

The thought returns that even more contemptible than the role of the agencies and institutions of the federal government in the JFK affair has been the role of the independent mass media. It is they most profoundly who deformed the facts and distorted the public context of the Kennedy debate, and who continue to do so even after the evidence against them is definitive.

The media elite will eventually come around on JFK, nevertheless, if only in their inner mental set. We noticed with bemusement the all but prurient investigative zeal with which the *New York Times* prowled and reported the Nelson Rockefeller deathbed scene. On this kind of gossip the big media will all be weekend-warrior conspiracists. But they will still fail to report the JFK case responsibly because they are so afraid of it, no doubt properly so, since they have so badly burned themselves on it in the past.

But probably it doesn't matter. If 80 percent of us can see through the Warren concoctions when 80 percent of the mainstream opinion elite are preaching to us how solid these concoctions are, then what the "opinion makers" think and say must not make that much difference.

What to Do Now?

The big question now pending as the final report's publication date keeps being slipped back is what kind of response will the report get from the Justice Department. Justice might say, "Ah ha! The culprits are still loose. To horse!" But it also might say, "Alas, too late, the whole thing is too boring."

The initiative has yet to shift formally from the committee to the Justice Department because the report has not yet been published, so even though the committee stated its essential findings last December, Justice has not yet been obliged to say what it means to do. No doubt persons of some inner sanctum have been using this winter hibernation to mull the question over, and the step we finally see taken by the government will be well considered. The committee is careful in its final report draft to caution Justice against seeing its options too simplistically. "The choice," reads the draft final report's last paragraph, in part, "is not between a full-scale reopening of both cases or making an effort to forget them. There are in both cases limited areas that may profitably be explored further. What the committee found out in both cases that previously had not been known must be used for rethinking what was done before."

The problem here is that these "limited areas" would all apparently involve the FBI, so that if one favors reopening the case, one finds oneself in the bizarre position of arguing for the FBI to take it up.

No way. The FBI, poor thing, stands *indicted* in this case. It stands exposed in moral and all but legal complicity in the murder of King. It stands accused of the grossest misfeasances in the JFK investigation, including the destruction of primary pieces of physical evidence and the deliberate deception of the Warren Commission on significant matters of circumstance. The FBI may not be exactly a suspect in these murders, but neither is it a blameless bystander.

The assassination-conspiracy question takes us into the heart of American darkness: What role did the Mob play? What role the police? What role the intelligence agencies and the covert operations elements? What role the military and other foreign powers? What role the political system?

A whole separate, independent investigative capability is required to probe such questions. It will have to be recruited from the existing agencies, but it will have to be run by an office as detached as possible from the regular government.

The *Philadelphia Inquirer* is the one and only major American daily newspaper the AIB has seen that squarely faced this requirement. "Because of its actions," said the *Inquirer* in an editorial of January 4, 1979, "any findings by Justice [i.e., the FBI] would be suspect, particularly if it should determine that there were no conspiracies in either case." Therefore, President Carter should "appoint a special prosecutor, independent of the Department of Justice."

The AIB supports this idea. Appointment of a special prosecutor represents the best possible further official development of the case. The problem is that it also requires

President Carter to act, and Carter may have reasons for not wanting to act.

Future Critique

As for our critical community, besides agitating however we can for a special prosecutor, we no doubt have very real and quite different kinds of tasks confronting us. My own sense of these (I will not try to be programmatic) will appear in the following observations.

a. There is no need to keep pounding on a long-locked door whose hinges have just sprung loose. The closed door to the JFK assassination will never come unbolted. Like every really important closed door, it comes open first by the wrong side.

Just so with this select committee. From the critics' standpoint, it did everything wrong. It coddled sensitive witnesses like Marina Oswald Porter, Richard Helms and Dr. James J. Humes. It sucker-punched critical witnesses like Robert Groden, Cyril Wecht and Jack White. It let itself be bullied by the CIA. It led off with a strong anti-critical, no-conspiracy snobbism.

But in spite of all that, it turned the JFK case around. To be sure, momentum can very easily be lost again, but as of spring 1979, there is a better chance of forward movement in the case than ever before. And that is because this anti-conspiracist committee, despite itself, found conspiracy.

b. My impression is that some critics have a hard time seeing this and taking it into strategic account. It means something that a congressional committee has essentially supported the critics, even if it was trying to destroy them. Some of our fellow critics find it tempting in this circumstance to vent their feelings against the committee. They have reason, but they should recall that the sage warned us of old to celebrate our victories as funerals and keep our eyes open.

c. The other side of the same coin, however, is that the struggle over the truth is about to rise to new levels of intensity. The article on the committee that Jeff Goldberg and I recently wrote for the *Washington Post* (see Chapter 11) provoked a small but measurable reaction from the underhaunts of New Orleans, wicked city, home of Mafia superthug, Carlos Marcello. The monsters one has long recognized through pure inference thus materialize within our tangible world. It gives one a thrill of dread to behold it.

This, I hope, is not to sound too deliriously paranoid or self-dramatizing. It is a basic fact about the new situation which all critics and critically-minded people should bear in mind.

d. The JFK question bears subtly and powerfully on the situation of presidential politics as we start toward the 1980 elections. We would not pretend to know all the ways and reasons why. We merely point out again that the previously buried partisanships of the Assassinations Committee members were rudely awakened by the conspiracy conclusion. There is a lesson in that. The sense here is that the innermost struggle going on in the country, to the extent that such a thing could be represented at all adequately in the careers of any two public figures, is going on between John Connally and Ted Kennedy. If there is or was an anti-Kennedy conspiracy in the same sense in which there was or is an anti-Castro conspiracy, then its exposure and containment are obviously basic to Kennedy's ability to survive and endure in this struggle. Sooner or later will come the moment of truth.

e. The question of Martin Luther King's murder is not to be slighted. But the link between the assassination of King and the national power struggle underlying it is actually best seen in connection with the Robert Kennedy assassination. That is because King and RFK were murdered within a few weeks of each other and their deaths were equally of a piece with the general context of 1968.

The Kennedy coalition that exploded at Dallas in 1963 was a northern liberal coalition with the conservative Democrats of the South and Southwest, straight out of the FDR handbook: liberal North plus conservative South equals certain victory at the polls, even if it also equals enormous internal problems.

But RFK's coalition of 1968, which implicitly included King and King's constituency, was totally different. By 1968 the remnants of the JFK coalition had been destroyed by the Vietnam War and the domestic protest movements. Thus, as "Old South" Johnson resigned, RFK forged a coalition with the "New South," with the forces represented by King. The formation of that "New Politics" coalition, the RFK-King coalition, defined the general situation in which King and RFK were assassinated. That is why it makes more sense to study King's and RFK's assassinations together. Only in the context of 1968 does it become clear how *political* was King's assassination, how heavy was the impact it had on the processes of the system of power. When we take the King case in the same breath as JFK, we tend to start seeing it as an event of 1963, thus distorting and sentimentalizing it. King's assassination as a study in raw national power politics will come more to the foreground and better in focus as the revision of the history of the U.S. 1960s continues to gain ground.

13

Media Reactions*

Nobody quite expected the mass media to roll over and play buff merely because a few acoustics experts had given the world scientific proof of conspiracy. Old ways dic hard.

Nonetheless, it has been quite an education to see the editorialists of the nation go to work on the problem of the JFK acoustics evidence. Following is a compendium of the choicer utterances.

The *New York Times* (Jan. 7, 1979) leaped directly into a metaphysics of language to hit at the use of the word "conspiracy." "To the lay public," the *Times* intoned, as though it were talking to somebody else, "the word is freighted with dark connotations of malevolence perpetrated by enemies, foreign or political. But 'two maniacs instead of one' might be more like it."

The *Washington Post* (Jan. 6, 1979) was very angry. The conspiracy finding, it noted, "appears to be based *solely* on scientific, acoustical evidence," and it found that not to its taste. "All that is left is a theory of conspiracy stripped of the international or domestic intrigue on which many of the Warren Commission critics have focused . . . There seems little reason for the Justice De-

Clandestine America, June 1979. With Jeff Goldberg.

partment to use its resources exploring the dead ends and pursuing the cold trails that the committee is presenting it in the Kennedy case. . . . Leave the matter where it now rests: as one of history's most agonizing unresolved mysteries." Quite an amazing position to take, when you look at it. On one hand, agony, mystery, unresolution. On the other, take two aspirin and try to sleep it off.

Or take the *Washington Post* columnist, Richard Cohen (Jan. 7, 1979): "This is . . . a conspiracy between Lee Harvey Oswald and someone like him—Oswald Harvey Lee. Make up a name. It's a clone of the same man. He allegedly fired the shot that never hit, if he fired it. If he was there. . . . The fact of the matter is that I no longer know why I believe what I believe." Well put.

Newsweek (Jan. 1, 1979): Conspiracy theory is "sorely lacking." "Many people may question the use of arcane mathematical and computer techniques to recreate complex physical events from a crackly tape." *Newsweek* further misinformed its readers by saying, falsely, that "the recording [of the gunfire] . . . was never made available to the Warren Commission."

The *Boston Globe* (Jan. 4, 1979) could not resist the usual dig at the motives of the independent critics who have led the chase so far. "For those who have long propounded conspiracy theories for both murders, the report was, in its bizarre way, reassuring." Then as though by deep reflex the *Globe* moved to defuse the implications of the new evidence: "The conspiracies the committee seems to perceive are of a much lower order, involving the private hatreds of private men." Whatever that means; i.e., is Carlos Marcello a private man?

The *Chicago Tribune* (Jan. 5, 1979) huffed, "This is scant value for the time and money spent. . . . We beg to be spared from any more of these 'official investigations' which squander money and produce little but more speculation.''

The amazing heights to which no-conspiracy editorialists can soar when pressed by hot evidence is not a spectacle confined to the bigger papers.

The *Cedar Rapids Gazette* (Jan. 4, 1979), for example, really unloaded on the conspiracy finding. The acoustics analysis, it sneered, gave us ''no hard goods to see and touch. . . . What Congress has come up with on the Kennedy assassination, as it stands, establishes a plot behind it no more solidly with *saying* one was there than someone else's *saying* there was no conspiracy refutes a plot. The scientific shot-tape data no more clinch the presence of conspiracy than radar blips and pictures of something on film establish UFOs as bringing visitors from outer space.''

The *Indianapolis Star* (Jan. 9, 1979) roared, ''It is old, rehashed stuff. . . . The pointlessness and lack of substance of this outlandishly expensive venture in amateur detective play and theatrics is [sic] measurable in terms of its failure to produce any solid new lead or body of evidence sufficient for so much as one criminal indictment.''

The *Norfolk Virginian-Pilot* (Jan. 4, 1979) also put a very confident face on to tell its readers, ''But after all the hullaballoo by conspiracy entrepreneurs, neither the House Select Committee nor anyone else has unearthed persuasive evidence of far-reaching plots to kill Mr. Kennedy or Dr. King. Those compelled to seek the sinister in high places and law will not be reassured, but, alas, they never are.''

Denver's *Rocky Mountain News* (Jan. 4, 1979) assured its readers that the conspiracy question was based ''solely on the belated analysis of a fuzzy tape recording that may well be questioned by other experts. . . . The verdict of the Warren Commission stands unshaken.''

The *Austin American-Statesman* (Jan. 4, 1979): ''Conspiracy buffs don't need supportive evidence to bolster their conclusions. But the majority of the American people is not so credulous as to believe everything it hears, especially on tape.''

Said the *Phoenix Republic* (Jan. 3, 1979): ''It was time and money wasted.''

But here and there, twinkling away in the vast night of the media's collective mind, there were points of brilliance, little stars of understanding and elementary intellectual honesty, and one of these was the Keene (N.H.) *Sentinel* of Jan. 25. The *Sentinel* editorialized when the acoustics results first came out ''that it would be interesting to observe the reaction of those in the media who had been assuring us for 15 years that Oswald had acted alone and that any suspicion to the contrary was the result of a psychological inability to believe that a lone madman could kill a president.'' The editorial then mentions many of the reactions of ''lone-assassin buffs''—a nice turn of phrase, that—which we have ourselves been reviewing here. We liked what the *Sentinel* had to say:

''If, as a nation, we are disinclined to examine possible conspiracies when our leaders are shot down in the street, perhaps we would be more honest to pass a constitutional amendment stipulating that, in the future, prominent Americans can be assassinated only by deranged individuals acting alone. That would clear the air.''

14

Is the Mafia Theory
a Valid Alternative?*

For close to two decades now, the vast majority of American people have believed, contrary to the Warren Commission, that President Kennedy was killed by a conspiracy.

Within the broad popular rejection of the lone-gunman theory of the crime, however, there is enormous difference of opinion as to what the nature of this conspiracy might be.

Jim Garrison has laid out in *On the Trail of the Assassins* the theory that I believe most serious students of this mystery will recognize and accept as the most complete, most natural, and most straightforward way to read the totality of the current evidence. Speaking for myself as a writer and activist on the JFK case for many years, I see compelling documentary support for Garrison's leading ideas, which I would paraphrase as follows:

(a) Rabidly anticommunist elements of the CIA's operations division, often moving through extra-governmental channels, were deeply involved at the top of the assassination planning and management

*"Afterword" to Jim Garrison's *On the Trail of the Assassins* (1988).

process and appear to have been the makers of the decision to kill the President.

(b) The conspiracy was politically motivated. Its purpose was to stop JFK's movement toward détente in the Cold War, and it succeeded in doing that. It must therefore be regarded as a palace coup d'etat.

(c) Oswald was an innocent man craftily set up to take the blame. As he put it, "I'm a patsy."

For all its structural logic and its virtually audible resonance with contemporary American experience, Garrison's theory of the crime is perhaps too challenging, too frightening, and too deeply contradictory of very basic American myths (e.g., that we are a law-abiding republic) to stand a chance of official recognition or even civil consideration by the intelligentsia and the media.

Garrison's line of reasoning raises basic questions about the legitimacy of the American state. Never mind that Garrison is a staunch patriot with Grant Wood roots and a long, happy career in the U.S. Army and J. Edgar Hoover's FBI before joining the district attorney's office in New Orleans; his vision of this crime is, I believe, nonetheless the most radical and cogent statement we can find of the predicament of American constitutionalism. One cannot follow Garrison's reasoning in serenity. Though Garrison is the furthest thing from a Marxist, an American cannot face his analysis without risking a crisis of political faith.

He threatens to make Hamlets of all who listen to him—children of a slain father-leader whose killers, for all we know, still in secret possess the throne. He confronts us with the secret murder at the heart of the contemporary American dilemma. His whole terrifying narrative forces down upon us appalling questions. Of what is our Constitution made? What is our vaunted citizenship worth? What is the future of democracy in a country where a President can be assassinated under conspicuously suspicious circumstances while the machinery of legal action scarcely trembles?

That is a brutal subtext. Garrison's reconstruction of the murder of the President tells us, in so many words, that what we call our Constitution has become, to some of us, secretly and shamefully, a laughingstock. Key components of government, critical to the integrity of policy intelligence systems, appear to have been occupied and manipulated by a secret force that we can barely identify and hardly conceive of opposing.

Maybe Garrison's political and historical realism will prove too intensely challenging for general consumption. We Americans like to regard ourselves as pragmatic about politics, but this seems to mean that we tend to believe what makes us happy and not to believe what confuses and depresses us. Garrison's analysis of the JFK murder challenges us to be unhappy about our political environment and to adopt a perspective that could easily put us at odds with it. This is not the way to be popular.

So Garrison's theory of the crime, despite being the most reasonable, the most realistic, and the most securely grounded in the totality of the evidence, is therefore not the official theory. The official theory used to be the Warren Commission's idea that Oswald was like a heart attack, something out of the blue, without significance beyond himself. But the Warren Commission's theory fell away bit by bit to the digging of patient volunteer researchers, and in 1976 the House of Representatives voted to create the Select Committee on Assassinations in order to reinvestigate the case. This was in effect a vote of no-confidence in the Warren Commission.

The House Assassinations Committee then proceeded to spend more than a year and $3 million in reinvestigating the JFK case and reconstructing the official theory.

This new official theory—semi-official, perhaps we should say, since the FBI will still have none of it—was framed and adopted by the House Select Committee on Assassinations in 1979 in its final report and then amplified and extended in 1981 in *The Plot to Kill the President,* by the committee's chief counsel, G. Robert Blakey, and its senior staff writer, Richard Billings (himself an important minor character in Garrison's narrative).

For comparison with Garrison's theory, the leading ideas of Blakey's theory can be summarized as follows:

(a) Oswald alone shot and killed JFK, as the Warren Commission deduced.

(b) An unknown confederate of Oswald's, however, also shot at the President, firing from the celebrated "grassy knoll." This shot missed.

(c) Apart from the question of the number of assailants in the attack, Oswald acted as the tool of a much larger conspiracy.

(d) The conspiracy behind Oswald was rooted in organized crime and was specifically provoked by JFK's anti-crime program. Singly or in some combination, prime suspects are Carlos Marcello and Santos Trafficante, godfathers respectively of the New Orleans and Tampa Mafias, and Teamster racketeer James Hoffa. Each one had the motive, means, and opportunity to kill JFK.

Blakey is an accomplished academic and a Washington lawyer of considerable experience and connection. He is close to the Kennedys. He was on Robert Kennedy's organized crime strike force. He wrote the RICO statute, which makes it possible for citizens to bring conspiracy charges against racketeers. He taught at Cornell Law

School before coming to the committee; he now teaches at Notre Dame Law School. He is not conventionally pompous and yet presents himself as an embodiment of scholarly values and tends to condescendingly judge those who do not share his views.

In his book, Blakey cannot simply ignore Garrison, since Garrison's investigation turned up key individuals (Ferrie and Banister) whom Blakey finds crucial to his own theory. Instead, Blakey viciously attacks the former New Orleans district attorney.

Garrison, Blakey writes, was motivated by "a thirst for publicity. National headlines were what he was after when he agreed to brief representatives of *Life* and CBS." Yet Blakey knows that "national headlines" were in the nature of the subject, that the strong involvement of the media and the public were required in order to move the stone of the federal cover-up, and that in any case it was *Life* and the rest that came to Garrison first, not the other way around. Blakey's co-author, Billings, was in fact the *Life* editor dispatched by upper management in 1967 to sound Garrison out on his willingness to collaborate against the conspiracy.

But Blakey cannot stand to credit Garrison's work even when he must admit its importance to his own. Garrison "stigmatized . . . by his conduct" whatever "bona fide evidence" existed in his "array of charges," Blakey writes, continuing:

> It would require the surprising disclosure of the findings of a Senate committee on intelligence in 1976 to prevent Garrison's probe from effectively ending any hope that the federal government would take a second look at the work of the Warren Commission. In short, Garrison's case was a fraud.

It is preposterous to blame Garrison, of all people, for the federal government's refusal to take this case by the horns. Blakey tries to pretend that there was something about Garrison's "conduct" that "stigmatized the evidence." It had nothing to do with Garrison's "conduct" as a district attorney, however, when federal officials in Washington, D.C. refused to serve his subpoenas. It was not because Garrison's charges were unfounded that the governor of Ohio refused to extradite an extremely critical witness (Gordon Novel) to Louisiana. It was because the government does not want the people to know the truth about the JFK assassination.

Moreover, it was not the Church committee as such or any of its "surprising disclosures" that persuaded the House to reopen the JFK case; it was the growing insistence of popular concern and, in the aftermath of Watergate, the murders of John Rosselli and Sam Giancana while they were sworn witnesses under federal protection.

Blakey's basic accusation against Garrison—insinuation is the better word, since Blakey is too much the lawyer to slander Garrison outright—is that Garrison approached the JFK case as the stooge of Carlos Marcello. Here is how Blakey and Billings phrase it in their book:

> As for the organized-crime aspect of Oswald's associations in New Orleans, where it had been overlooked by the F.B.I. and the Warren Commission, it had been studiously avoided by the District Attorney for reasons we believed had become apparent.

What were these reasons, "apparent" as Blakey believes they had become? Without ever actually saying it explicitly, Blakey conveys the impression that Garrison must have been secretly under Marcello's control. Blakey even unearths charges of which Garrison was acquitted long ago and writes as though the charges were borne out:

> Garrison was tried but acquitted in 1971 of federal charges of taking payoffs from underworld pinball operators, despite evidence that included incriminating tape recordings of Garrison and the seizure of $1,000 in marked money from Garrison's home.

Blakey sees fit not to explain why these "incriminating tapes" and this "marked money" failed to convince a jury that Garrison was guilty. Blakey chooses not to tell his readers that Garrison's chief accuser in the pinball trial, Pershing Gervais, publicly admitted that he had been pressured and rewarded to perjure himself against Garrison. Why does Blakey pass silently over the abundant indications that Garrison was framed in the pinball case by enemies at the federal level who wanted him out of the district attorney's office?

But what of Blakey's theory that Oswald was the agent and JFK the victim of Marcello?

On first look, there is much to recommend it. The attitude of certain mobsters toward the one administration in American history that actually did try to destroy them is a fascinating and perhaps pivotal aspect of this case (and one which Blakey was hardly the first to see); but Blakey knows very well that his Mafia hypothesis has never been rigorously probed and contested.*

Clearly, the Mafia is present in the drama of John Kennedy's 1,000 days. It appears in JFK's life before his presidency, is embroiled and entangled with his admin-

---

*David E. Scheim's *Contract on America* (New York: Shapolsky Publishers, 1988) essentially restates Blakey's theory without adding to the evidence.

istration, and survives his attempt to throttle it. The now-familiar instances of this presence are basic:

- The Mafia may have stolen the Illinois vote for JFK in 1960, thus delivering the White House.
- The Mafia supplied Kennedy with mistresses such as Judith Campbell Exner during the first year of his White House tenure.
- Mafia assassins answered the call of the CIA to try to kill Castro in 1961 and 1962 and became formal agents of the U.S. government.

And yet throughout Kennedy's tenure, paradoxically, the same Mafia was locked with the Justice Department in an unprecedented struggle that for a while seemed to threaten the Mafia's continued existence.

Furthermore, Jack Ruby was certainly a Mafia errand man. He may have been on a Mafia-directed errand when he shot Oswald. If it was really the Mafia that killed Oswald, then that might be because the Mafia wanted to keep the case out of court. What might have motivated such an interest? Why should the Mafia have cared enough about Oswald to liquidate him? Unless the Mafia had something to do with the assassination of Kennedy, why should it have cared about Oswald at all? It is only natural to suppose that the Mafia had something to hide; it is easy to jump to the conclusion that the Mafia must be the principal culprit.

However, a longer historical perspective makes it equally clear that the presence of the Mafia in illicit affairs of state does not necessarily mean that the Mafia stands there alone and unsupported. Besides the aforementioned CIA sponsorship of Mafia hit men against Fidel Castro, the best-established historical examples of positive association between the Mafia and elements of the U.S. government are ones in which the Mafia served as the junior partner:

- The Navy's Operation Underworld of the World War II years in which the U.S. government bought Mafia protection against Nazi sabotage on the East Coast docks in exchange for favors involving Lucky Luciano.
- The Army's alliance with the Mafia in General George Patton's Sicilian campaign in World War II.
- The CIA's use of Mafia force to destroy Communist-dominated unions in Marseilles during the early Cold War.

In none of these cases was the Mafia dominant over the government; in none did the Mafia provide the motivation for the relationship or the leadership within it. The Mafia, for example, did not invite itself into the CIA's secret war against the Cuban revolution. The Mafia was recruited into the campaign by Richard Bissell and Colonel Sheffield Edwards, top-level CIA operations officers. Similarly, if the Mafia was present in the Dealey Plaza assassination, it remains to be seen whether it was present as a principal or as an agent, whether as a prime mover or as a secondary technical service responsible to a larger combination secretly licensed by disaffected elements of the national intelligence services.

The Mafia theory of the JFK assassination is most helpful and interesting when viewed as a step in the evolution of the official perception of the case. It is an improvement over the lone-assassin theory, but its basis in fact still seems tenuous.

For example, if Marcello knew Oswald at all, never mind well enough to see what kind of an assassin he would make, and if Marcello or his lieutenants therefore reached out to Oswald, either to recruit him directly or to find means of controlling him indirectly—all of which is implied by Blakey and is necessary to his theory—then there must have been a bridge of some kind, a link, a connection, between Marcello and Oswald. How did Marcello know, or know about, Oswald?

The House investigation discovered a total of four people who were known both to Oswald and to individuals at the middle and lower levels of the Marcello organization. The first was Oswald's mother, Marguerite, who once had dated men connected with the Marcello organization. The second was Oswald's uncle and surrogate father, Charles Murret, an alleged bookie in the Marcello gambling apparatus. The third was not even an acquaintance of Oswald's, but a man named Emile Bruneau who filled in for the absent Murret in helping Oswald get released from jail in August 1963 following the leafleting incident.

The only Oswald-to-Marcello contact of any substance was the fourth, David Ferrie, who is indeed extremely interesting. Ferrie is said to have piloted Marcello back from Guatemala after he was deported there by Attorney General Robert F. Kennedy. He occasionally free-lanced as an investigator with an attorney, G. Wray Gill, who sometimes represented Marcello.

But investigation also determined that Ferrie had piloted for the CIA as well (on a contract basis at the time of the Bay of Pigs) and that he was close to intriguing individuals who were *not* Mafiosi, *not* distinguished by any special connection to Marcello. One of these was a leader of the anti-Castro Cuban Revolutionary Council (CRC), Sergio Arcacha Smith. Another was W. Guy Banister, an ex-FBI officer and professional anti-Communist engaged in the training and equipping of commando units for paramilitary actions inside Cuba.

Oswald himself knew Banister directly and associated with CRC exiles.

Thus, the one individual who might conceivably link Oswald to Marcello in any serious way, Ferrie, can much more readily be seen linking Oswald, through Arcacha Smith and Banister, to the CIA, with which both Banister and Arcacha Smith were associated.

Further, the Mafia theory fails to explain the evident complicity of the government in the cover-up. One of the major aspects of this case is the fact that members of the national intelligence community—the FBI, the CIA, possibly the Office of Naval Intelligence—have continually tried to suppress information bearing on some of its core issues, such as other CIA assassination projects, Oswald's military counterintelligence background and Ruby's ties to the mob. If it was just a few dons and thugs who condemned the President, why did the government's entire investigative apparatus stand paralyzed?

The most questionable step that Blakey took in the projection of his Mafia theory, however, was to classify as secret (or silently allow to be classified as secret) a 280-page report prepared for the Assassinations Committee by one of his own principal researchers, a young attorney named Edwin Juan Lopez, on the question of Oswald's mysterious trip to Mexico City in late September and early October 1963.

This trip is important in Blakey's case against Oswald because it was in Mexico City at that time that Oswald was said to have phoned and visited the Soviet embassy and the Cuban consulate, loudly announcing his name and, by one disputed account, his belief that JFK should be killed. It is suggested by some in fact that Oswald, during his stay in Mexico City, specifically met with the Soviet KGB's master of assassins.

The Assassinations Committee's investigation, however, turned up compelling suggestions that the Oswald seen in Mexico City was a completely different person from the Oswald known to all. (1) A CIA photo said to be of Oswald leaving the Soviet embassy is not Oswald's image. (2) A tape recording of Oswald talking on the phone with a Soviet diplomat is not Oswald's voice. (3) A Cuban diplomat who had three angry confrontations with Oswald said repeatedly and in detail that the Oswald of Mexico City was not the Oswald of Dallas. (4) The one eyewitness who said she saw Oswald in the Cuban consulate could not describe him correctly to House investigators.

The capstone of this is that Lopez himself, the author of the suppressed report, had risked violating his oath of secrecy to say publicly and under oath that he believes Oswald to have been impersonated in Mexico City by people who were trying to set him up. Surely if Oswald was being impersonated and belied by people who wanted him remembered as a dangerous person, then this fact in itself, apart from all the other evidence exculpatory of Oswald, would lend great credibility to his basic protest that he was framed.

And would this not be important news? That someone or some group had framed Oswald to take the blame for the assassination? Would this not oblige us to put back into suspense our official condemnation of Oswald? If he were in prison now and these facts were found, would he not deserve a new hearing and a new presumption of innocence? Not to Blakey.

Blakey pretended to be dispassionate and objective and to serve only the cause of truth when he came to the Assassinations Committee in 1977. He began his tenure with a promise "to let the sun shine in" on whatever he found. Blakey nonetheless suppressed the Lopez report, paid no attention to the doubts it apparently raises, declined even to mention the Lopez investigation or report in the more than 400 pages of his book, and plunged straight on with the inherited myth that Oswald was not only madman enough to shoot the President but madman enough to spread advance warning of his intentions directly and profusely in the beam of U.S. intelligence systems.

As a Washington co-director of the Assassination Information Bureau, which was created early in the 1970s to build a movement for a new JFK investigation, I watched Blakey from a short distance and sometimes close up over a period of about a year and a half as he prepared and presented his theory of the assassination for the committee's review and approval. At first I supported his Mafia theory for basically strategic reasons. It was at least a conspiracy theory that was not right-wing, it could command an official consensus, and it thus appeared strong enough to get the case properly reopened and activated by the Justice Department. Blakey believed the committee's then-fresh leads pointed to the Mafia. Many of us who were watching thought he was mistaken, and that the leads would punch right through the Mafia cover and track straight back to several departments of official U.S. intelligence. That was the gamble and the deal: let the government start pulling the Mafia string, we thought, and we will see what else it brings with it.

Then came the Reagan era and the total freeze-out from government sympathy of any project in the least memorializing of the Kennedys. Blakey did not take the offensive when the FBI rudely closed the Justice Department's door in his face, basically telling him and the committee, "We don't buy it, so you're out of luck."

Why did Blakey choose not to fight harder and more publicly about it? Why did he seem to retire from the fray?

But then, why did he try to crucify Garrison? Why did

he not credit Garrison for the contribution Garrison has made to the development of this case, though working with a fraction of Blakey's resources and under the intense pressure of an active covert opposition?

Why did Blakey ignore the evidence turned up by his own investigators that the Cuban exile community was equally well positioned to kill a President as was the Mafia? Why did he ignore the fact that this Cuban exile community was the creature of the CIA's operations directorate?

Perhaps there is, after all, a simple explanation for these curious lapses. At the very end of the Blakey-Billings book, sandwiched between the list of principal sources and the bibliography, there is the following paragraph, the book's final utterance:

> Pursuant to agreement with the Select Committee on Assassinations, the Central Intelligence Agency and the Federal Bureau of Investigation reviewed this book in manuscript form to determine that the classified information it contained had been properly released for publication and that no informant was identified. Neither the CIA nor the FBI warrants the factual material or endorses the views expressed.

This may be one of the most significant paragraphs in the book. It should be printed in the front instead of the back, where people would be sure to read it and have it in mind as they encounter the steps of Blakey's argument.

There is, in any case, no such addendum to be tied to the work of Jim Garrison. *On the Trail of the Assassins,* you can be sure, was not reviewed, censored, and approved for publication by the CIA and the FBI. Garrison's voice indeed emerges here as one of the great uncensored voices of our day.

15

Growing Doubts
about Dallas*

The media reacted with disbelief last year when the House
Select Committee on Assassinations published its conclusion that John Kennedy's assassination in Dallas, seventeen years ago this month, was "probably" the work
of a sophisticated conspiracy animated by organized
crime.

Of some two score major news dailies that commented
editorially on this finding, only one, the *Philadelphia Inquirer,* was sympathetic. The rest followed the *New York
Times* in complaining that the conspiracy conclusion had
not been reached scientifically.

The committee based its conclusion on the high-tech
analysis of a crucial piece of material evidence that had
slipped through the fingers of the Warren Commission.
This was a recording of the gunfire in Dealey Plaza made
at a receiver in Dallas police headquarters through a microphone accidentally left open on a motorcycle in the
motorcade. Analysis of this acoustics evidence by two
independent sets of experts (one of them Cambridge's
Bolt, Beranek and Newman, which also analyzed the
Nixon tapes) showed that four shots were fired, not three

Boston Magazine, November 1980.

(as the Warren Commission thought); that the first, second, and fourth were fired from the sixth floor of the Texas School Book Depository building behind the President; and that the third was fired from a point on the grassy knoll in front of him.

To the House committee's mind, two widely separated points of simultaneous gunfire implied two gunmen, and two gunmen implied a conspiracy. But the *New York Times* rejected this reasoning. And *Times* senior editor Tom Wicker had the cheek to write a negative introduction to the *Times'* own rush edition of the committee's final report without taking an opportunity to read it. In this introduction, Wicker acknowledged that his skepticism was "possibly a stubborn refusal to face facts," but insisted that he did not find the acoustics evidence "compelling."

About a year later, on a chilly, drizzly night in New York last June, Wicker was briefly confronted on these opinions by novelist Norman Mailer, long a friend of the case, and British author-investigator Anthony Summers, whose JFK-assassination study, *Conspiracy,* was just being brought out by McGraw-Hill. The occasion was a gathering of about forty New York media people at the swank Central Park West apartment of Jean Stein, a friend of Mailer's and his hostess for a series of evenings, of which this was the first, featuring authors of interesting new books and aiming (as Mailer put it) "to keep up the general level of culture." Mailer had asked me to come because he knew of my special interest in the JFK case.

Over in one corner was hard-edged novelist Elizabeth Hardwick. Over in another, Robert Silver, editor of the *New York Review of Books.* In another, Tom Wicker himself, with his wife, Pamela Hill, vice-president of ABC News Documentary. And in another corner, G. Robert Blakey, the balding, fortyish Notre Dame law professor who was chief counsel to the House committee and thus the main architect of its finding that the President was probably killed by organized crime.

We crowded into the library and Mailer got the thing going. He was brief in his introduction of Summers, sober and intense in the few words he said about the JFK issue. Speaking in his usual quiet staccato bursts, with short jabbing arm movements, Mailer said, "One recognizes that the Kennedy assassination may seem by this time to have the character of a national obsession. But the walling over of obsessions is a mark of old age and apathy in the individual personality, and it may be so in the life of the nation as well. In view of what Blakey's committee and Summers's book are teaching us about the assassination in Dallas, one must wonder if our media have served us courageously in this respect."

Given that it was a media house, the question had a good hang time. Could the real question of the Kennedy assassination be one of courage or cowardice within the media elite? Mailer turned things over to the night's guest author.

Summers is a short, thickset Londoner in his mid-thirties with woolly hair and a tough-guy face. He worked his way to his chair before an elegant little writing table and spread out two pages of notes, which he promptly forgot about. He at once took up Mailer's media theme.

"I came to the Kennedy case," Summers began, "as a BBC television journalist with many connections in the U.S. media. I expected to find that the case had been pored over by professional journalists. I found instead, to my astonishment, that there was a veritable reporting vacuum on the Kennedy case. My book went to press with a hundred pages of sources containing only a handful of references to the work of American reporters. It was not for lack of looking."

Summers mentioned no names but homed in on Wicker. When the House published its probable-conspiracy finding, Summers said, "the American press reacted true to bad form. One newspaper even ran an editorial suggesting blithely that perhaps two lone nuts were at work in the same moment within a hundred yards of each other.

"Particularly offensive," Summers said, his voice stronger, "was the foreword written by a *New York Times* editor to the Bantam edition of the final report. This foreword was generally negative and critical, even though it was written before the author could even have seen the final report, much less have read and digested it. This journalist simply announced, without giving his reasons, that the acoustics evidence did not convince him, as though that were the only or the most interesting evidence behind the committee's conclusion."

Summers went on to outline the key points of his book, then opened the floor for discussion. It was hard not to wonder what Wicker was thinking. He knew these barbs were for him, and so did many of the people in the room. But he seemed disinclined to pick up the gauntlet. So I heard myself saying, "The *New York Times* editor who has been referred to several times this evening, though not by name, happens to be present. Would he care to respond?"

The room stiffened. There was a brief pause. Then lanky Wicker stirred where he sat on the floor against the wall at the farther side of the room, dressed in jeans and a tweed jacket. He leaned forward and in his deep Southern gentleman's voice said a touch defensively that whether he was right or wrong—"and I could be wrong"—the fact remained that he did not like the acoustics evidence. He thought it was inadequate grounds for the committee's claim to have proved a conspiracy "scientifically."

Summers could not keep an edge off his voice. "I can't believe the *New York Times* editor really looked at the acoustics evidence. I think he was afraid of finding a conspiracy."

Would there be a little scuffle? Mailer was standing at the mantle behind Summers and now he stepped forward again. Addressing Wicker directly, but first assuring him that he had always respected him and admired his work, Mailer said shortly, "I wonder what you think now about the conspiracy. I get the feeling you think a lot of things would be lost if you crossed the line to conspiracy."

Wicker cleared his throat, considered his words, and spoke a bit sternly, seeming to sense the rebuke implicit in Mailer's gently worded question.

"There's a lot of disquieting information in Summers' book and the committee's report," Wicker said, "but I think it's wrong to claim that conspiracy has been scientifically proved."

Summers answered quickly, "I'd have felt better about your editorial if you'd said that, as well as knocking the acoustics evidence."

Wicker chose not to answer. Mailer did not prod him further. The little confrontation subsided. But the fact that Wicker had been even so briefly challenged on the JFK question by a peer before peers—put on the defensive about a question he is much more used to treating with disdain, if not contempt—this was something new. One could not fail to hear in the subtext of that brief encounter the creaking of deep foundations.

Another sign of this intellectual sea change came later that evening, when Elizabeth Hardwick told me that she had been turned around by Summers' book and for the first time she now believed that a conspiracy must have been afoot at Dallas. She said *New York Review* editor Robert Silvers had sent the book out to Queens College political scientist Andrew Hacker, a regular contributor to the *Review*'s pages. Hacker's piece, Hardwick said, would be appearing soon, and it was "highly favorable to Mr. Summers."

The New York Review of Books, mind, that highly influential organ of liberal opinion, had long ignored the whole conspiracy question, except to disparage those who raised it, as though there were something shabby about the mind that could so preoccupy itself with the lurid details of JFK's death, something malformed about the intelligence that could hypothesize the existence of sophisticated criminal conspiracies. This has been the attitude of the media at large, and until last summer, it was all but monolithically the attitude of the liberal press.

Then came Hacker's review of Summers's *Conspiracy.* Hacker began by noting the difficulty intellectuals have had with the conspiracy question, summarized the elements of Summers's argument, passed approving judgment on his reasoning, and laid down a conclusion as new for him as for the pages of the *New York Review:* "We may never know who fired the fatal bullets," he wrote, "but we are closing in on why the deed was done. It is not a case at rest."

Hacker's voice was not alone. Many of the same newspapers—like the *Atlanta Constitution* and the *Los Angeles Times*—that had gagged editorially on the closely reasoned, cautiously worded final report of the congressional committee a year before were now printing sympathetic reviews of a book that actually went much further in its conspiracy claims. Even the conservative *BusinessWeek* joined the great spinning. What had "seemed the province of cranks and self-seekers" was now changed by Summers's work into a legitimate issue.

"From now on," said *BusinessWeek*, "the question of conspiracy must be taken seriously."

This question turns out not to hinge so exclusively on the sensational acoustics evidence as may have first appeared. Summers' thesis in *Conspiracy*, in fact, is that regardless of the grassy-knoll shot, Oswald was probably not even in the same room when his rifle was fired at the President by somebody else. The conspiracy that framed Oswald for the crime, suggests Summers, was probably formed of three institutional components, each with its own motive.

First, a "renegade element" within the CIA, connected with the "fiasco" of the invasion of Cuba at the Bay of Pigs in 1961 and furious with Kennedy for what they considered his treachery.

Second, Cuban exiles, Bay of Pigs vets and others, convinced that Kennedy had betrayed them.

Third, mobsters linked with the CIA and Cuban exile anti-Castro operations through their immense stake in pre-revolutionary Cuba (Castro had closed their casinos and kicked them out), and particularly angry with the Kennedy administration because of its all-out campaign to destroy organized crime in America—the first and last time there has ever been such a thing.

These forces, thinks Summers, joined hands to kill the President, specifically isolating Oswald as the patsy and going to great lengths to plant false clues that would seem to prove his guilt.

But another important book on the Kennedy assassination, due out November 1980 from Times Books, presents a substantially different and perhaps more convincing theory of the Dallas conspiracy. Called *The Plot to Kill the President*, this is Chief Counsel G. Robert Blakey's own account (co-authored with his chief editor on the Assassinations Committee, Richard Billings) of the committee's two-year investigation and what it proved.

Unlike Summers, Blakey is convinced that Oswald fired all the shots that hit the President, and that he did so much in the manner determined by the Warren Commission: a first shot that went wild, a second that hit both the President and Governor John Connally, and a third that struck the President's head and was clearly fatal. However, Blakey believes the acoustics evidence proves that another shot was fired, just before Oswald's last shot, this one by a second gunman situated on the grassy knoll. Blakey says this shot missed.

Who this second gunman might have been, Blakey thinks, is forever lost. "That guy's been at the bottom of Lake Pontchartrain for seventeen years," he told me recently. But as for Oswald, Blakey thinks we can establish much: first, that he was a genuine defector to the Soviet Union, not a U.S. spy on a mission; second, that he had real left-wing sympathies; third, that he was possibly recruited by Soviet intelligence and was in any case of great interest to the KGB.

Blakey goes much further than any previous writer in making a case that Oswald was the KGB's man when he shot the President. As Blakey told me, "Here's Tony Summers getting all uptight about a *possible* sighting of Oswald with a *possible* CIA agent, but we've got a *perfect* sighting of Oswald with a KGB assassin supervisor within a month of the assassination! Okay? You take Oswald with his demonstrable left-wing politics, you put him in the presence of a KGB assassin, and the next month he kills the President. That's a hell of a case!"

But even though he knows that "the KGB has been assassinating people around the world since the 1940s when they were the *Cheka*" and believes the Soviet regime morally capable of assassinating the President,

Blakey comes out thinking the Soviets were not the guilty party. Oswald's Soviet ties were relevant to the conspiracy scenario, he thinks, only in that they helped make him the perfect fall guy.

Similarly, Blakey takes up the possibility that Cuba ordered Kennedy's death. Here again he makes what he calls "a powerful case for the view that Castro did it," but finally rejects that theory, proceeding to the notion that the anti-Castro Cuban exiles may have been responsible. "This gets very complicated," Blakey says. "It is not entirely distinguishable from the question of whether organized crime did it, so it's a natural bridge to the chapters on organized crime."

Blakey chuckles that "one of the problems with this case is that it sometimes seems like the novel *Murder on the Orient Express,* where *all* the suspects come by and stab the victim." Nevertheless, he reaches and defends a strong conclusion in this book. As his subtitle says, "Organized Crime Assassinated J.F.K. The Definitive Story." The CIA, he thinks, played no role. "The problem I have with Tony's book," he said, "is that his perspective is slightly left of center. As a European intellectual, his preferences were to find a CIA involvement. And even if a few CIA people were corrupted, that only raises the question of who corrupted them."

The most likely candidate for mastermind and driving force of the Kennedy assassination, Blakey believes, is New Orleans crime lord Carlos Marcello, now close to eighty and still fighting deportation proceedings instituted against him by Robert Kennedy in 1961. Possibly acting in league with his Miami Mafia counterpart, Santos Trafficante, also an old man now and Jimmy Hoffa, Marcello "had the motive, the means, and the opportunity," according to Blakey, to kill the President.

The evidence that necessitates a mob-conspiracy theory of the crime, says Blakey, concerns Oswald's killer, Jack Ruby. Ruby's ties to organized crime, which the Warren Commission denied, turn out to be extensive, including specific ties to the Marcello and Trafficante families and killers associated with Hoffa. ("Did you know," says Blakey in a wonder-filled voice, "that Ruby was with the number-two guy in the Dallas mob the night before the assassination?") And Blakey believes he has proved that Ruby was stalking Oswald for two days before he got close enough to kill him. "Jack Ruby silenced Oswald on behalf of the mob," he says flatly, "and that is the heart of the matter. Even if the acoustics evidence had turned out to be a dud, the evidence on Jack Ruby still proves an organized-crime conspiracy."

Blakey concedes that *The Plot to Kill the President* demonstrates this proposition only at what he calls "the level of historical truth." As a careful lawyer, he knows that his case is not yet ready for court. "But give me twenty FBI agents and a dozen good Justice Department attorneys," he says excitedly, "and I could get indictments in six months."

Though Blakey is discontented with foot dragging in the Justice Department since the Assassination Committee turned its final report over to the attorney general a year and a half ago, he is confident that the case will sooner or later get the judicial attention it demands. "Our society has a difficult time dealing with sophisticated conspiracies," he says, "but notice that the motto of our book is the line from Chaucer, 'Murder will out.' "

Further delays not intervening, the Justice Department will soon announce steps to verify the acoustics evidence, which still looms large in the conspiracy argument because it is so simple to grasp and, as far as it goes, so conclusive, not necessarily because it is the strongest or most revealing evidence. To distance the government from the process as well as to secure credible finality in the results, the Justice Department has arranged to fund, through the National Science Foundation, a panel of Nobel-laureate scientists selected by the National Academy of Sciences. This panel will do only one thing: evaluate the scientific procedures employed in the committee's analysis of the acoustics evidence. If the finding is inconclusive, the panel will draw up new tests and carry them out. If the panel blows the committee's analysis out of the water, the matter will probably be put back to rest, *pace* the Summerses and the Blakeys and the Ruby evidence. If, on the other hand, as Blakey anticipates, the panel confirms the two-gunman finding, then a real investigation may begin.*

Of course, Blakey is annoyed that all the effort is being concentrated on the acoustics evidence. "We did it twice," he insists, "with two independent scientific groups applying different technological approaches, and it came out both times. How long do we keep pretending not to know there's a crime to be solved?" Meanwhile, Marcello, Trafficante, and the live leads Summers and Blakey say are there to be followed up are going untouched, the principals growing older.

The delay also creates subtler problems. One of the great achievements of the House select committee's work was to rescue the case from the "cranks and self-seekers" *BusinessWeek* complained about. But as time goes by and the government continues to procrastinate, the bad money comes back into circulation. A perfect case in point is British author Michael Eddowes's efforts to exhume Oswald's body from its Fort Worth grave. His argument for doing this is that discrepancies between

---

*For how the acoustics story came out—maybe that should be *failed* to come out—see the following chapter.

Marine and autopsy records indicate that someone other than Oswald may be buried in Oswald's grave. Snapped a former senior member of the House committee's investigative staff, ''The issue is not Oswald and never has been. The issue is who is controlling the people who fired the shots, whoever they were, whatever their names. And that is not going to be settled by measuring a seventeen-year-old skeleton. They'll dig him up and announce that it's Oswald's body, after all, and we should all go back to sleep again.''

But if its seventeenth anniversary finds the JFK case moving along at a lot less than top speed, still it is moving along discernibly. The world has new information, richer theories of the crime, new books with new levels of seriousness and detail, and in the immediate offing, new official steps.

Just as important, the media may be preparing to enter the lists for the first time in a positive way: to understand at long last that the question of a JFK conspiracy is forced upon our attention by the facts and the importance of the case, not by cranks or ghouls. If and when that understanding takes root and the media get nearly as cranked up about JFK as they were about Watergate, there's nothing to keep us from establishing the final truth in this matter, bringing a few conspirators to justice, and coming to more realistic terms with our recent political history.

16

A Farewell to Dealey Plaza*

In a technical report published in May 1982, an expert panel selected by the National Academy of Sciences attacked and overturned the so-called "acoustics argument" which four years earlier had convinced the House Select Committee on Assassinations that President Kennedy was shot at by two gunmen instead of one, and hence was "probably" the victim of a conspiracy. A scientifically sophisticated refutation of a scientifically sophisticated original claim thus delivered the Justice Department from any need to reopen the case.

Many counted this a blessing, weary of nitpicking disputes about bullet angles and the physiology of fatal trauma, but hardier followers of the case knew that the House committee had advanced more serious if more subtle conspiracy arguments wholly independent of the acoustics evidence and logically separate from the question of the number of gunmen involved. For the committee was suggesting that Oswald had been manipulated by a powerful anti-Kennedy group, and if this was the case, then a conspiracy would exist whether there was a second gunman or not. Yet the NAS rejection of the

*Memo to file, 1982.

acoustics evidence was taken by the Justice Department and the news media as a rejection in effect of all conspiracy evidence of any kind. Disbanded for more than three years, the Assassinations Committee was in no position to answer. Its refuted scientific experts were engaged by other work and not eager to be drawn into public controversy. The loose coalition of Warren Commission critics that had helped make the new investigation happen to begin with had spent itself in the effort to do so and fallen back, dispirited to have brought the case so close to resolution only to let it drop at the end back into the grave, there being apparently no other place to put it.

The John Kennedy murder case would never have been reopened at all if the President had been the only liberal hero for a while to die by violence. But the 1960s were streaked with the blood of social activists, and that fact alone helped maintain a high level of public anxiety about JFK. In the half year before Dealey Plaza, as though to blood the stage, civil-rights activists William Moore and Medgar Evers were shot and four black girls were dynamited to death. The year after came the lynching of the Mississippi three, in 1965 the gunning down of Malcolm X, then in 1968 the firearm assassinations of Martin Luther King, Jr. and Robert Kennedy. Nothing the public would learn about these and later, similar killings (the Kent State four, the Jackson State two, Orlando Letelier, Ronnie Moffit, Karen Silkwood) would teach it to believe, as myth had it, that only lone nuts kill for politics in America.

But America's literate culture—especially on its liberal side, where there has been such a long fight against right-wing conspiracy-mongering—is strongly biased against "conspiracy theories" (a somehow demeaning term) of any kind, the more so in the case of JFK because the debate about JFK has long since soured into mutual recrimination. It took more than a turbid, murderous social context and gaping contradictions in the Warren Commission's lone-nut theory to persuade the federal government to have another go at understanding what happened to America at Dealy Plaza.

The big blast against right-mindedness about conspiracies was Watergate, the heaviest blow to the no-conspiracy mindset since Cassius drew Brutus aside. Watergate opened up a broad (if impermanent) pathway to mass media credibility for a body of suspicions about JFK's death normally treated with contempt. After Watergate, arguments pointing to conspiracy could no longer be dismissed just because they pointed to conspiracy.

No sooner had the magnitude of Watergate begun to register on popular consciousness than the CIA's most embarrassing secrets, the so-called "Family Jewels," were exposed, so that now the world knew, and the patriot could no longer deny, that the American government was capable of the same abberrations that other governments were capable of. The government had conducted massive illegal spying operations against citizens exercising their constitutional rights of dissent. Searching for a "truth drug," it had run LSD experiments on unsuspecting citizens. It had tested biological-weapon delivery systems against unwitting American cities. It had plotted the overthrow of foreign governments, perceptibly casual about what it was doing.

At about the same time—just in case anyone still doubted the awful truth—came our first awareness that the FBI did this sort of thing, too. The FBI's major program was called "COINTELPRO," FBI-speak for "counterintelligence program." COINTELPRO consisted of a large (still incompletely disclosed) number of separate FBI missions against specifically targeted individuals in the civil rights and anti-war movements, an attack that grew more feverish and less legal—it was never at all legal—as those two movements began to merge in the mid-1960s. Discovery of COINTELPRO forced our first national recognition that J. Edgar Hoover's FBI was a politically motivated organization capable of stooping, without a solitary outcry, to dismember the Constitution.

Then in November 1975 came the highly detailed *Interim Report* of the Church committee (the Senate Select Committee to Study Governmental Operations with Respect to Intelligence Activities, chaired by Frank Church). The Church report disclosed that, in August 1960, the CIA set out to murder Fidel Castro and that it hired the Mafia to do the job. Church's investigators even raised the possibility that JFK's assassination was the work of a Castro infuriated at the CIA's attempts against his own life, attempts which he could only blame on Kennedy. This theory broadened the base of the movement to reopen the JFK case, because it created the possibility that there might be something in this for the right wing. If Dealey Plaza could be blamed on Castro, that might break the back of American resistance to a definitive military solution of the Castro problem. And at the least, it would put a muzzle on Castro's apologists everywhere.

Then in 1976 a former FBI agent, Representative Don Edwards of California, chairman of the House Constitutional Rights Subcommittee, announced his belief that there was a cover-up in the JFK case and that the FBI and the CIA were ''somewhere behind'' it. In this same period, Senators Richard Schweiker of Pennsylvania and Gary Hart of Colorado, both of the Senate Intelligence Committee, looked specifically into FBI and CIA performance in the JFK assassination investigation and came away wondering if Oswald's stance as a left-winger was not merely a cover for secret ties to the anti-Castro Cubans.

Meanwhile, we who were then active critics of the Warren theory siezed the moment. We believed that we could win the public debate. We believed we could oblige the Congress to respond to us. We believed that the critics acting together could keep any new investigation from becoming a cover-up. And we believed that any honest investigation would either be moved by the same reasoning that had moved us or else would be able to show us where we were wrong. If we could win the debate before Congress, we thought, then official recognition of a JFK conspiracy would galvanize an irresistible change in the government's attitude toward the case. The Justice Department would get cracking. Mainstream journalism would throw off its disbelief, organize investigative teams, assign star reporters, come alive with visions of Pulitzer prizes, and thus help crack the case. And even if it was too late to move on to grand juries and subpoenas, to indictments and trials, to convictions and punishments, still we might have somewhat beaten back the night of our ignorance of real politics. We might have glimpsed the devil's face and come away educated, chastened, matured.

And a surprising lot of this did happen. After Watergate, the critics intensified their efforts and handily won the debate on the campuses, forcing the issue into prime time in 1974 and 1975, with CBS producing lengthy specials that always supported the Warren theory yet always created new problems for it. It was a CBS-TV special, for example, that first showed the world how compelling was the evidence of a contact between our loner Oswald and a group of anti-Castro Cuban militants tied to the CIA's Bay of Pigs operation, men who nourished the most venomous hatred of JFK for his supposed "betrayal" of their cause.

Such new evidence called into question, if it did not

overturn outright, the Warren *Report*'s representation of Oswald as a recluse whose politics were unambiguously left-wing. And as a simple cognitive byproduct of live on-camera interviews with living figures in the story, the CBS attempts to rebut the critics only showed the world how fresh and fascinating the leads were, how politically significant and alive the case was. The TV rebuttals in fact created a previously lacking sense that we were dealing here with a current, still-unfolding event, not with ancient history.

Also essential in motivating the reopening of the case was Robert Groden's optical enhancements of the Zapruder film. Groden's work arrived at the best possible political moment, early in 1975, just as public interest in the question was once again on an upswing. The Zapruder film—the famous 8-mm home movie of the assassination filmed on Dealey Plaza by Abraham Zapruder—had never been shown on TV, mainly because *Life* owned the rights to it but perhaps also because, before Groden applied to it the arts of the modern film lab, it was not easy to see exactly what was in it. But working with a first-generation print (and Time-Life, Inc., by the way, never troubled him about showing it), Groden centered and steadied the image in the frame and added blow-ups, freeze-frames and slow-motion sequences of the crucial portion. Running less than a minute, his enhanced Zapruder film was perfect for TV. Millions saw it, whether on a network special, an early morning or late night program, or a local talk show. And what most who saw it thought it revealed was that the President—obviously—had been killed by a shot fired from the front. Therefore, he was not killed by Oswald.

Even if it said nothing whatsoever about who or why, such evidence seemed still a serious proof that conspiracy of some kind was to blame. This impression was strong. Multiplied by the powers of the international media, it was vastly felt. Coming in 1975, the Zapruder-Groden film took the debate beyond words and static images.

Similarly crucial to the reopening process, though much differently, was the obstreperous Mark Lane, radical attorney and controversialist, who did much to discover and to publicize the deficiencies of the Warren theory and to create a national constituency for reopening the case. Such other Warren critics as Sylvia Meagher (her *Accessories After the Fact*, 1967, remains one of the great books on the case) and the tireless Harold Weisberg were better scholars, more careful with factual detail. But Lane always saw the JFK case in political terms and was the first to see that the only way to create a congressional will to reopen it was to link it to the King case, thus mobilizing the powerful congressional Black Caucus. Lane not only saw this—he went to Washington and did it. He put JFK and MLK together.

He also alienated the world with his arrogance. After a point, Washington, city in love with the correct gesture, would have nothing to do with his snarling, agitating ways. I say with no joy that Lane was the one who gave the JFK case the shape it had to have in order to be reopened by the Congress, the only forum where the results could make the least difference.

Another contribution to the mix of forces that reopened the case came from a group that several other Warren critics and I organized in Cambridge, Massachusetts in 1972, the Assassination Information Bureau. The AIB tried to link up the more credible critics and to project a political conception of the case. In 1975 we organized a national conference at Boston University called "The Politics of Conspiracy," at which Groden first showed his enhanced Zapruder film. Later that year we helped introduce to the Massachusetts legislature a unanimously passed resolution formally calling on the U.S. House of Representatives to reinvestigate the Kennedy case. The next year, 1976, by a vote of 280 to 65, the House set up the Select Committee on Assassinations.

The mass media greeted the select committee, however, with editorial contempt, maybe because the media had all but uniformly stood on the other side of this argument and thus felt wounded by the Congress' decision in favor of the critics. The *New York Times* supported the new investigation only on the assumption that it would uphold Warren and forevermore end the disputes.

There was a period early in the committee's life when its leadership faltered badly. Its first chairman, Thomas Downing, Democrat of Virginia, did not run for reelection. Its second chairman, Henry Gonzalez, Democrat of Texas, broke into such an acrimonious public quarrel with its first chief counsel, Richard A. Sprague, that the House might well have closed the whole operation down out of sheer mortification. But whenever the committee seemed defenseless and doomed, House leadership behind Representative Tip O'Neill would move to keep it alive. Given O'Neill's ancient friendship with the Kennedy family, this implied that the Kennedys were not against this project. If true, this gave the committee's investigation a real chance of succeeding.

The committee acquired its third and final chairman, Democrat Louis Stokes of Cleveland and an influential member of the Congressional Black Caucus, on March 9, 1977. Shortly thereafter it also acquired its second and last chief counsel, G. Robert Blakey, then of Cornell Law School (now of Notre Dame Law), a well-respected academic lawyer then in his mid-40s with extensive Washington experience behind him, including a previous association with the Kennedys, having been a member of

Attorney General Robert Kennedy's organized-crime strike force in the days of Camelot on the New Frontier. Stokes and Blakey between them were shortly able to restore the committee's dignity, drive off and hold at bay the media jackals who had sensed an easy kill, and in quick order plan its two separate investigative programs, staff up and get going.

The Assassinations Committee staged its main series of JFK hearings in seventeen days of testimony between September 6 and 28, 1978 (the King hearings were in August). It became apparent on the very first day that, although Blakey had listened to the critics, he had not been persuaded by their arguments. For example, Blakey had hired Robert Groden as a technical consultant to the committee. And much of the first day's time was given over to Groden's presentation of the Zapruder film, other photographic evidence and his defense in complete detail of his belief that this evidence compelled a two-gunmen theory of Dealey Plaza.

But then in an aside to a conservative member who dared ask testily where all this was leading, Chairman Stokes let slip the truth. To outline the main points which the critics have made, he said, is "the sole purpose of hearing his [Groden's] testimony." As I noted in my journal of the hearings (I was there as an AIB observer), "In one way, yesterday looks like a clear solid good first inning for our side. Yet there's a sense of being behind the game. Obviously Blakey is setting out the conspiracy case in order to take it apart."

By the second day there was no doubt. The expert panels brought in their results, and it became clear that Blakey had rejected all the classical arguments of the critics. The "single-bullet theory," the timing of the shots, the anomalies in the medical evidence, the "forged" Oswald photos, the two-gunmen implications of John

Connally's testimony—one by one, Blakey struck back at these quintessential claims against Warren. And bit by bit, over the first four days of hearings, he put Warren's Humpty-Dumpty back together. There was only one gunman. This gunman was Oswald. There was no shot from the front. Any contrary impression conveyed by eyewitness testimony or the Zapruder film was false, an illusion. People thought they heard shots from different directions because of echo effects, and the President's body flew backward at the headshot not because the shot came from in front but because of a neuromuscular reaction to the trauma.

But now came an unexpected turn. For several weeks, the select committee's more garrulous staffers had been fretting within earshot of the critics about something they called "Blakey's Problem." Now, on day four, September 11, "Blakey's Problem" made its formal debut.

This "problem" had been in the making for almost exactly one year. On September 17, 1977, Blakey held a meeting in Washington to give the critics, once and for all, a chance to lay out all their complaints, all their evidence, all their leads, so that never could they say that this committee had refused to hear what the critics had to say.

Blakey recounts that at the end of the first day of this two-day conference, Mary Ferrell of Dallas, the principal archivist of the case, handed him a tape recording of channel one of Dallas Police Department Dictabelt KKB-364, covering the time period 10 AM to 2:15 PM, November 22, 1963. Ferrell explained to Blakey that in 1963 the Dallas police department routinely recorded all radio transmissions on a two-channel Dictabelt recording device at police headquarters, using two Dictaphone machines rigged in tandem. If any police microphone was open, its transmission would be recorded on that Dictabelt. Further, she explained, it appeared that a police microphone somewhere in Dealey Plaza had been open, perhaps by accident, at the moment of the assassination. Thus, she said, we possibly had on this Dictabelt a recording of the actual gunfire. We could perhaps use it to settle the old perplexing question of how many shots there were and at what intervals they were fired. If there were only three shots, Warren would be vindicated. Any more than three would support the critics. But the tape was of very poor quality, Ferrell said. The unaided ear could not tell if a burst of noise was random static or gunfire. Could the committee find some technical way to retrieve the signals from the noise?

Blakey asked the Acoustical Society of America to recommend a list of firms and individual scientists most competent to analyze this tape. By October 5, the select committee had reached an agreement with the Cambridge laboratory of Bolt, Beranek and Newman, which the Justice Department had retained to analyze the various tape recordings of the Kent State shootings of 1970, and whose president had chaired the expert panel assembled by the Watergate committee to study the 18½-minute gap in the Nixon tapes. The Ferrell copy of the DPD tape was too poor in quality to be useful to BBN, but in February 1978 the select committee located what it believed to be the original Dictabelt, as well as a first-generation tape of the critical section of channel one, in the files of a retired chief of the DPD intelligence division.

By March, 1978, BBN had set to work, its first objective being to show, if possible, that there were no shots at all on the tape. Showing this would obviate further work. Otherwise, BBN would have to go to Dealey Plaza to record actual gunfire and compare the pattern of echoes with those it could identify in the police tape. It could tell bursts of static from gunfire because gunfire would display an echo signature characteristic of Dealey Plaza. Once you knew what gunfire in Dealey Plaza looked like on a cathode ray tube, you could always distinguish it from static.

At first, there was nothing problematic to Blakey about Ferrell's tape. Blakey believed in a three-shot, one-gunman theory of the crime. He had no reason to doubt that this tape, if it did actually contain the gunfire, would support the Warren theory.

The first sprout of coming difficulties appeared on July 13, 1978, two months before the JFK hearings were scheduled to open. BBN's chief scientist, James Barger, called from Cambridge to report that there were definitely gunshots on the tape, and that there might be as many as six. BBN would have to go to Dallas to do test firing.

Early in August, the select committee briefed Senator Edward Kennedy and brought on another scientific team to doublecheck the BBN work, this consisting of a Queens College professor of computer science specializing in acoustics, Mark Weiss, and his assistant, Ernest Aschkenasy, who were on the ASA recommended list. Weiss and Aschkenasy looked at the preliminary data and agreed with BBN that the next step was to go to Dallas and duplicate the shots. Spectrograms could then be compared to the police tape to determine precisely which if any impulses were shots (instead of backfire or static) and, by analysis of echo patterns, where any shots were fired from.

The BBN's Dallas tests were held on August 20. BBN roped off Dealey Plaza and fired 57 rounds into sandbags at the spots where JFK had been hit. They recorded these shots through microphones placed at intervals along the motorcade route to approximate the changing positions of the motorcycle with the open mike as it traveled between the first shot and the last.

Ten days later, after these tests, BBN's Barger called Blakey to tell him the bad news. There seemed to be four shots. One of them seemed to come from the grassy knoll. Hence, "Blakey's Problem."

A week later, the JFK hearings began. Five days after that, on September 11, 1978, Barger came in to testify.

Barger proved to be the committee's most frustrating witness. As Blakey later wrote, he was almost "too precise," so that "the impact of his testimony was lost." Anxious not to blur the scientific niceties of his laboratory work, wanting the committee members to be clear that his product was probabilities rather than certitudes, and intimidated by the implications of his testimony, Barger would answer one member's exasperatedly straight-ahead question, "Is it your conclusion that you proved four shots?" by saying, "No, we demonstrated that if there were four shots, then the intervals between them are 1.6, 5.9 and 0.5 seconds." Or again, when Chairman Stokes asked him, "What do you conclude from what you hear?" Barger would only answer, "My opinion about the shots is of no particular value." Stokes: "Can I come to a conclusion from this tape?" Barger: "I think not. . . . This was not a stereo recording. . . . I can't reach a meaningful conclusion about how these sounds should be interpreted." Or again, another member asked, "I understand you've given the pros and cons, but as a professional, do you have an opinion as to three shots or four?" And Barger: "I do not believe the results of the test allow me to answer with greater certainty than I have."

So the hearing that might have produced the conspiracy-in-JFK headlines produced only the lamer news that one particularly prolix, guarded and unforthcoming Cambridge scientist thought there was a 50–50 chance of a shot from the grassy knoll. The press table was nervous and giggly at the beginning of the day's session, when it still feared that Barger was about to dump an unambiguous JFK conspiracy in the country's lap, but it visibly relaxed as Barger's testimony grew steadily less comprehensible. There would be no major story to file that afternoon.

The story of a major break in the JFK case thus had to be staged anew in a special hearing on December 29, when the second team of acoustics experts came to testify about the new tests they had performed to clear up Barger's uncertainty.

What Weiss and Aschkenasy told the packed committee room in a glare of TV lights was that an analysis based on simple principles of physics had been able to show that this police tape did indeed contain the acoustical record of gunfire, that there were in fact four shots fired in all, that the timing of these shots exactly correlated with the Zapruder film, and most dramatically, that one of these shots, the third, just as the BBN analysis had indicated, was fired from behind the picket fence on the grassy knoll. As though to dazzle any doubters with the power and sensitivity of their method, Weiss pointed out that their analysis of the echo patterns associated with each shot enabled them to pinpoint within one and a half feet the position of the open microphone, and examination of the photographic record had discovered a motorcycle at the very place. And also, just as they had predicted, the motorcycle had a windshield on it: they had detected its acoustical baffling effect in the tape data.

A few days later the outline of the Assassinations Committee's findings was formally published, a document of a few legal-size pages which would half a year later be buttressed by a 686-page final report and 25 volumes of supporting documentation. The select committee had spent about $6 million and had taken two and a half years to bring in its final report. What it had found for its trouble was that a conspiracy was "likely" in the case of King and "highly probable" in the case of Kennedy. "Blakey's Problem" had become America's problem.

Now for a while the headlines were as from a conspiracy buff's wildest dreams. Bannered the *New York Post:* "JFK Panel: There *Were* Two Gunmen. Warren Commission 'blown apart.' " Streamed the *New York Times:* "Assassination Panel's Final Report Backs Theory of Plot on Kennedy."

But the mass media opinion-makers did not roll over and play conspiracy. The nation's news pages became momentarily more open to the conspiracy idea, but its editorial pages were slammed shut. Of the country's major dailies, only the *Philadelphia Inquirer* would even concede that the Assassinations Committee had carried out a serious investigation and discovered worrisome evidence. More typical was the *Washington Star*'s sniff that the committee's report would be "a treasure trove for conspiracy buffs but otherwise of little value." Or the same thought from the *Chicago Tribune:* "While the report will provide new life to the industry in the conspiratorial theory of history, it does nothing to advance the cause for which it was established—to put a definitive end to the unhealthy speculation about these two horrible episodes." The *Los Angeles Times* picked up the leftover phrases: ". . . no credible evidence . . . full of speculation . . . lacking in relevant facts. . . ."

The FBI didn't like the Stokes-Blakey report either, though of course the FBI had more reason to complain, being named in it as a prime miscreant in the original JFK investigation. For this was a main new finding: that the FBI had failed in both the King and the JFK cases to carry out a proper investigation and to report its results without distortion. How could the FBI investigate the King assassination, since it had itself been long and deeply committed to a campaign to destroy King? How could it be trusted in the JFK case, since it had concealed its link to Jack Ruby?

Anticipating that the FBI would be a formidable adversary, the Assassinations Committee chose to saturate its report with counter-argument, stressing continually how tenuous were its findings, losing no chance to remind that it could bring no one to trial, that it was not after all a judicial body, that its only purpose was to sort out the basic controversies of fact and to suggest a next step. It would be nothing if not *objective*.

And in that frame of mind, the committee advised the Justice Department to resolve the acoustics question by having it reviewed by the National Academy of Sciences. The Justice Department readily agreed, since this was a way off the hook, but saw no need to hurry the NAS, which took more than a year finally to assemble a blue-ribbon panel (chaired by Harvard physicist Norman Ramsey).

And all the while there simmered a small duel of words between Blakey and the Justice Department. Blakey would accuse Justice of stalling, and Justice would answer that Blakey had failed to deliver certain documents. The FBI would issue a report criticizing and rejecting the conclusions of the committee's acoustics experts, and Blakey would take to a press conference to denounce the FBI's work as "cheap" and "sophomoric."

On May 14, 1982, about a year and a half after its formation, the NAS panel published its final report (formal title: "Report of the Committee on Ballistic Acoustics" of the National Research Council). This is a 123-page document that set out to destroy the acoustics argument for conspiracy.

The report acknowledges that "there are some valid arguments in support of the [select committee's] conjecture that the impulses may be due to a gunshot from the grassy knoll. The selected impulses [from the DPD tape] fit better than randomly the echo patterns of the test shots, the trajectory of the microphone inferred from the [committee] analysis is reasonable for a microphone attached to a motorcycle, and some interpretations of photographic evidence are consistent with a motorcycle being in approximately the correct location. However," the panel continued, "these points are not strong since there are many ways in which static-like impulses can be non-random, unreasonable microphone trajectories were rejected, there were many motorcycles in the area, and the impulse and echo selection procedures used by [the select committee's experts] could affect the results."

Ironically, the killing blow to the committee's experts was dealt not by the NAS experts but by a conspiracy buff named Steven Barber, a musician from Mansfield, Ohio. Barber acquired a copy of the Dallas Police tape printed on a plastic audio disc as a promotion device by a magazine, *Gallery,* with a long interest in the case. Listening on ordinary equipment to this mass-produced copy of the tape, Barber noticed that an almost unintelligible voice transmission that overlapped the putative gunshot sounds was Sheriff Bill Decker saying, "Hold everything secure until the homicide and other investigators can get there," a transmission that was perfectly clear on channel two of the two-channel recording system. A faint electronic image of this had somehow crossed over to the other channel, the one with the "shots" on it. Barber's point was that the "shots" had to be simultaneous with the voice transmission, since they were recorded together, and that it was known for a fact that Decker's transmission well after the assassination.

So the "shots" which the committee's scientific experts had so brilliantly discovered could not have been shots at all. The experts had charmed themselves into finding shots in random bursts of static. "Therefore," concluded the NAS panel, "reliable acoustic data do not support a conclusion that there was a second gunman."

The NAS report will not end the acoustics debate, although BBN and Weiss and Aschkenasy, a half year after the report's publication, still have not responded to it, except to say off the record that they do not agree with it.* Partly their delay expresses some pique at the leisurely pace of the NAS panel's review compared to the pressure under which they had to produce their results. Partly it expresses the technical subtlety of the issues: an appropriate response from the committee's side requires new study, which takes time and money, and there is no one now to pay for it.

But the amateur critics, if not the professional experts, will find lines of argument. They will sieze upon an apparent pro-FBI bias in the NAS report and ask why the panel handled itself so unscientifically. The critics will want to know why a highly visible participant in the Dealey Plaza debate, Berkeley physicist Luis Alvarez, for many years a vehement critic of the Warren critics, was invited to serve on the NAS panel in the first place, much less allowed (on report) to become its dominant and most active member. Alvarez had said of the acoustical evidence, when it was first presented, that he was "simply amazed that anyone would take such 'evidence' seri-

---

*BBN's Barger told Summers in 1989 that he stood by the four-shot finding.

ously." And yet the NAS offered him the chair of this committee!

The critics will insist that the acoustics correlations are too strong to be tossed out just because of a ghost signal from the other channel at a different point in time. First, attempts to erase something from one channel could have resulted in a false superimposition; second, there are indications that other police Dictabelts were tampered with (in connection with Patrolman J.D. Tippitt) and the NAS panel did not look into these; and third, the chain of custody of this particular piece of evidence, this particular Dictabelt, leaves its authenticity open to challenge. One of the committee's scientific experts said outright, though not for attribution, that discovery of the apparently simultaneous voice transmission from one minute after the assassination means that this Dictabelt could not be the original.

Moreover, the four disputed impulses are the only ones BBN selected as gunshots from the hundreds of noise bursts audible on the police tape. BBN selected these impulses as shots before knowing where they fell in the sequence of events and without knowing that their timing would line up exactly with the Zapruder film. Against the weight of these correlations, the NAS panel will be called on to produce a better explanation than to say dismissively, without citing a single example, that "there are many ways in which static-like impulses can be nonrandom," just as though that were the point at issue.

The acoustics debate, therefore, will not quickly be abandoned by those who care enough to follow its many technical intricacies. But there will only be a few who do. The intricacies have by this time built a forbidding wall on both sides, from the original scientific explanation that this acoustics method was as infallible as fingerprinting to the equally scientific, equally self-confident conclusion four years later that the first people were making shots out of static.

At each stage of rebuttal and response, the technical covercharge gets higher and the return in confidence diminishes. So people stop paying attention. They write the question off as undecidable and therefore irrelevant. Even if the committee's experts, whose scientific reputations are in some sense on the line in this matter, find the intellectual means of vindicating themselves and restoring their interpretation of the tape, the fact will remain that from a political standpoint the issue has been permanently denatured. In 1978 the acoustics evidence had the world wondering who killed JFK. In 1982 it only stirs a fog of technical questions. Great causes do not turn on evidence that becomes more ambiguous the more closely it is examined.

G. Robert Blakey, the chief counsel of the select committee, never wanted proof of a second gunman to begin with, so it's too bad his ideas about the assassination had to sink with the acoustical evidence. Although the question of one versus two assassins is conventionally at the center of the JFK controversy, Blakey's revised version of the Dealey Plaza conspiracy made it little more than a trivial distraction. A month before the dawn of "Blakey's Problem," for example, one of Blakey's staff assistants was confiding to my group, the Assassination Information Bureau, the outline of the coming public hearings in such language as the following: "No, no, no! There was only one shooter! That shooter was Oswald! But this does *not* mean that Oswald was necessarily alone in the crime!" Thus, for the Blakey probe, the core question was not "Who shot JFK?" but rather, "Who told Oswald to do it?"

The Assassinations Committee looked at several basic

possibilities—that Castro did it, angry at Kennedy for sending the CIA to assassinate him; that the anti-Castro Cubans did it, enraged at Kennedy for having, as they saw it, abandoned them at the Bay of Pigs in a fight they thought he had encouraged them to fight; that it was the Soviets, revenging national honor for the humiliation suffered in the Cuban Missile Crisis; that is was a cabal of disaffected military and intelligence operatives morally persuaded that Kennedy's policies were leading the United States into defeat at the hands of international communism. Each had something to recommend it.

But the theory the select committee deemed most probably correct was that the Mafia did it, suspicion narrowing in particular down to two top-class Mafia godfathers, Santos Trafficante of Tampa and Carlos Marcello of New Orleans, and their friend James Hoffa of the Teamsters. FBI wiretap and informant files opened by the committee showed that all three men hated the Kennedy brothers with an obsessive passion and that they explicitly threated violence against them.

The main cause of this hatred was the Kennedys' unparalleled campaign to destroy the American Mafia. There had been nothing like it before and there has been nothing like it since. The new attorney general, Robert Kennedy, not yet four months in office, even had had the audacity to pluck Marcello off a New Orleans street and deport him straightaway to his passport country, Guatemala, without stopping for legal ceremony. Marcello soon was back in the United States, piloted in by the same David Ferrie who would befriend Oswald in New Orleans a year and a half later, but notice had been served on the Mafia leadership elite that the new administration meant to destroy their organization.

The Kennedy-Mafia confrontation was sharpened to a complex irony by two exceptional circumstances. The first was that the Mafia, during this same period, was all but under formal long-term contract with the CIA to assassinate Castro. The second was that John Kennedy was himself in the Mafia's debt, first and more trivially through the easy women who reached him through the Hollywood Rat Pack, courtesy of Chicago godfather Momo Giancana, but much more substantially for the ten thousand nonexistent pro-Kennedy votes counted into the returns from Chicago's Giancana-dominated Ward Four in 1960, without which Kennedy would have lost Illinois to Nixon and thus the election. Kennedy's New Frontier Camelot owed its existence in this sense to the Mafia, yet it was trying to destroy the Mafia.

From such contradictions are state tragedies made. What was a man like Carlos Marcello to make of a man like John Kennedy, who with one hand would take secret criminal favors and share the most intimate sins, but with the other would bring down the full power of the state against his friends? Kennedy became the target of an impassioned Mafia conspiracy, in this view, because he wanted it both ways. His streak of hypocrisy made him a towering moral fraud in the eyes of men who had the most tangible need to destroy him.

The Assassinations Committee supported its Mafia-conspiracy theory with an analysis of Oswald's killer, Jack Ruby, showing that Ruby was deeply involved with organized crime, contrary to the impression formed by the Warren Commission. Ruby actually matriculated through Al Capone's organization in Chicago in the 1930s and was moved to Dallas in 1947 as part of the Chicago mob's drive to take over the Texas vice market. Ruby's ties to organized crime were in fact so strong, reasoned Blakey, that suspicion of a Mafia hand would arise from his mere presence in the drama. If Ruby wanted Oswald dead bad enough to kill him, it must be because the Mafia wanted him dead.

What was it, then, about Oswald that could have bothered the Mafia so? What could Oswald have known that the Mafia would want so badly to protect that it would risk sending in one of its own people to kill him on live TV?

The committee made a special effort to pin down Oswald's associations during the last few months of his life, and it found out some fascinating facts:

(a) Oswald spent time with anti-Castro Cuban militants, veterans of the Bay of Pigs Fiasco;

(b) Oswald spent time with Guy Banister, a former Chicago FBI officer whose New Orleans office was a center of illegal Cuban exile military activities; and

(c) Oswald spent time with David Ferrie, an odd-job man close to the CIA and Carlos Marcello. The Assassinations Committee also established that Oswald's uncle and surrogate father, Charles "Dutz" Murret, was a life-long functionary, a bookie, in Marcello's New Orleans Mafia organization.

From the above, Blakey deduced the following theory of the crime: A Mafia group probably centered around Marcello, Trafficante and Hoffa decided to kill JFK, motivated to do so by fear of federal prosecution and anger at having been betrayed by a politician they thought they had paid for. This group discovered Oswald, secretly recruited him, and manipulated him into carrying out the killing. Against Mafia plans, Oswald got out of Dealey Plaza alive and into police custody. Therefore, the Mafia plotters had to improvise a quick hit on Oswald, and Ruby was their best possible man because he was in the best position to get inside police security.

Not the most elegant theory. How can Blakey explain,

for example, the ability of his Mafia hit team to make total fools all at once of the Warren Commission, the FBI, the CIA, the Secret Service, the military intelligence arms, the Dallas Police Department and the mass media?

But finally it did not matter, because Blakey's theory was not going to be taken seriously in any case, elegant or not. The acoustics evidence had collapsed, and with it had gone everything else remotely attached to it.

Some Warren critics had thought at the beginning of their long sojourn with the JFK issue—I confess *I* had thought—that this country cared enough about JFK's office, if not about the entire man, to extirpate in sheer moral outrage any group that would dare take a President's life. If a Mafia hand in Dealey Plaza could be demonstrated at the congressional level, then surely the days of the Mafia would be numbered.

When no such swell of outrage emerged in 1978, after the committee first displayed its major findings; when the editorial pages of the nation greeted the conspiracy finding with a hostility to the issue even icier than before; when indeed the very appearance of what seemed at the time a serious scientific argument for conspiracy, incongruously, acted to shut the debate down rather than to open it up; then one had to admit that one had been wrong about this case. One had missed something in the American temperament, or in the situation. The JFK murder case was, in any event, no longer an issue of current political significance. With the silence that swallowed up the committee's claims even more deeply than the subsequent technical refutation, the JFK question had become, perhaps forever, a purely historical, speculative conundrum.

V

The Stone JFK

I am not sure what purely aesthetic standards are to be invoked in assessing Oliver Stone's remarkable *JFK*. This powerful, supremely self-confident movie hit popular as well as political culture with great force. It revived the topic from a long hiatus. It put the entire no-conspiracy faction on the defensive. It brought a new level of expression and legitimacy to popular fears about the JFK murder and launched a popular demand for release of the secret JFK files.

It also inspired what must be film history's most impassioned and widespread assault upon not merely a certain movie but upon the very *idea* of such a movie. Iran's attack on Salmon Rushdie's *Satanic Verses* was more powerful and effective, but one felt the Imam's presence in the tone of voice adopted by the likes of Tom Wicker in the *New York Times,* George Lardner, Jr. in the *Washington Post,* Jon Margolis in the *Chicago Tribune.*

What could motivate the virulence of so many of Stone's critics, or his critics' unseemly willingness to trash and condemn his project simply for what it had to say about an important public controversy? I have a thought on this.

The polls are currently saying—as of early 1992—that well over seven out of ten Americans reject the Warren theory and suspect a conspiracy in the JFK assassination. A large minority suspect that the CIA might have been involved. Imagine: almost half the American people find it thinkable that JFK was killed by CIA operatives.

Yet in sharp contrast, among news people the number of those who accept the Warren theory seems quite high. I have seen no data on this, but I would gamble that news people accept the lone-Oswald theory in roughly the same proportion—seven out of ten—in which most other people reject it.

Thus, the subtext of the debate about the JFK assassination is a parallel and mostly tacit debate about the credibility of news corporations. Nor is it simply a remote and abstract corporation that feels the rejection; it is real people with very prominent media images. It is a Ted Koppel, a Dan Rather, a George Will. Not only do they feel that an unwashed audience has wrongly judged them losers in the great JFK assassination debate, perhaps even more painfully, they are forced to see that their industry—in a sense the *reality industry*—has failed to establish its way of seeing the world as the only or even the best way to see it. At least not in respect to Dealey Plaza. Here they are, all these decades, *not* reporting the JFK conspiracy story except occasionally in the most derisive terms, and yet the public turns out to have been somehow hearing a radically different version of that story from other and, it seems, more convincing voices. Is that a big surprise to the newsroom? Is that a disappointment to those who lip-sync the daily news script? Does it sadden the pundits to see their reality simulation break up like a bad TV signal?

"Media Whitewash" reflects on—and responds to—the unprecedented attack launched against *JFK* by several mass-media outlets when it was still a half year from distribution. "The Conspiracy That Won't Go Away" used the Stone movie, then in production (1991), as a friendly pretext for talking at length with Jim Garrison again. Finally, "On *JFK* and Its Critics" records my impressions of the film and compares them with those of others who were, mostly, displeased with it.

17

The Media Whitewash*

Oliver Stone's current film-in-progress, *JFK*, dealing with the assassination of President John F. Kennedy, is still months from theaters, but already the project has been sharply attacked by journalists who ordinarily could not care less what Hollywood has to say about such great events as the Dealey Plaza shooting of November 22, 1963.

The attack on Stone has enlisted (at least) the *Boston Globe* (editorial), the *Boston Herald*, the *Washington Post*, the *Chicago Tribune*, and *Time* magazine, and several other outlets were known to have been prowling the *JFK* set for angles. The intensity of this interest contrasts sharply with 1979, when the House Assassinations Committee published its finding of probable conspiracy in the JFK assassination, and the mass media reacted with one day of headlines and then a long, bored yawn.

How are we to understand this strange inconsistency? It is, of course, dangerous to attack the official report of a congressional committee; better to let it die a silent death. But a Hollywood film cannot be ignored; a major production by a leading director must be discredited, and

Lies of Our Times, September 1991.

if it can be done before the film is even made, so much the better.

Garrison's Case

JFK is based chiefly on Louisiana Judge Jim Garrison's 1988 memoir, *On the Trail of the Assassins* (New York: Sheridan Square Press), in which Garrison tells of his frustrated attempts to expose the conspiracy that he (and the vast majority of the American people) believes responsible for the murder at Dealey Plaza.

Garrison has argued since 1967 that Oswald was telling the truth when he called himself a ''patsy.'' He believes that JFK was killed and Oswald framed by a right-wing ''parallel government'' seemingly much like ''the Enterprise'' discovered in the Iran-contra scandal in the 1980s and currently being rediscovered in the emerging BCCI scandal.

The conspirators of 1963, Garrison has theorized, grew alarmed at JFK's moves toward de-escalation in Vietnam, normalization of U.S. relations with Cuba, and détente with the Soviet Union. They hit upon a violent but otherwise easy remedy for the problem of JFK's emerging pacifism, Garrison believes, in the promotion by crossfire of Vice President Lyndon Johnson.

Stone hardly expected a movie with such a challenging message to escape notice, but he was startled to find himself under sharp attack while *JFK* was still being filmed. ''Since when are movies judged,'' he said angrily, ''sight-unseen, before completion and on the basis of a pirated first-draft screenplay?''

The Ignorant Critics

The first out of his corner was Jon Margolis, a syndicated *Chicago Tribune* columnist who assured his readers in May, when Stone had barely begun filming in Dallas, that *JFK* would prove "an insult to the intelligence" and "decency" ("JFK Movie and Book Attempt to Rewrite History," May 14, p. 19). Margolis had not seen one page of the first-draft screenplay (now in its sixth draft), but even so he felt qualified to warn his readers that Stone was making not just a bad movie but an evil one. "There is a point," Margolis fumed, "at which intellectual myopia becomes morally repugnant. Mr. Stone's new movie proves that he has passed that point. But then so has [producer] Time-Warner and so will anyone who pays American money to see the film."

What bothered Margolis so much about *JFK* is that it is based on Garrison, whom Margolis described as "bizarre" for having "in 1969 [1967 actually] claimed that the assassination of President Kennedy was a conspiracy by some officials of the Central Intelligence Agency."

Since Margolis and other critics of the *JFK* project are getting their backs up about facts, it is important to note here that this is not at all what Garrison said. In two books and countless interviews, Garrison has argued that the most likely incubator of an anti-JFK conspiracy was the cesspool of Mafia hit men assembled by the CIA in its now-infamous Operation Mongoose, its JFK-era program to murder Fidel Castro.

But Garrison also rejects the theory that the Mafia did it by itself, a theory promoted mainly by G. Robert Blakey, chief counsel of the House Assassinations Committee (HAC) of 1978 and co-author (with HAC writer Richard Billings) of *The Plot to Kill the President* (New York: Times Books, 1981). "If the Mafia did it," Gar-

rison told me "why did the government so hastily aban-
don the investigation? Why did it become so eagerly the
chief artist of the cover-up?"

More important, Garrison's investigation of Oswald
established that this presumed left-wing loner was associated in the period just before the assassination with
three individuals who had clear ties to the CIA and its
anti-Castro operations, namely, Clay Shaw, David Ferrie
and Guy Banister.

Garrison did not draw a conclusion from Oswald's ties
to these men. Rather he maintains that their presence in
Oswald's story at such a time cannot be presumed innoc-
uous and dismissed out of hand. The Assassinations
Committee itself confirmed and puzzled over these ties
in 1978, and even Blakey, a fierce rival of Garrison, ac-
cepts their central importance in the explanation of Oswald's role.

Lardner Grinds His Axe

The most serious attacks against the *JFK* project are
those of the *Washington Post*'s George Lardner, perhaps
the dean of the Washington intelligence press corps.
Lardner covered the Warren Commission during the
1960s, at one point ran a special *Post* investigation of the
case, and covered the House Select Committee on Assassinations in the late 1970s.

Lardner's May 19, 1991 article on the front page of the
Sunday *Post* "Outlook" section, "On the Set: Dallas in
Wonderland," ran to almost seven column feet, and by
far the greater part of that was dedicated to the contemp-
tuous dismissal of any thought that Garrison has made a
positive contribution to this case. Stone must be crazy
too, Lardner seemed to be saying, to be taking a nut like
Garrison so seriously.

And yet Lardner's particulars are oddly strained.

Lardner wrote, for example, that the Assassinations Committee "may have" heard testimony linking Oswald with Ferrie and Ferrie with the CIA. Lardner knows very well that the committee *did* hear such testimony, no maybes about it, and that it found this testimony convincing. Then Lardner implicitly denied that the committee heard such testimony at all by adding grotesquely that it "may also have" heard no such thing. Why does Lardner want unwary readers to think that the well-established connections between Oswald, Ferrie and the CIA exist only in Garrison's imagination?

Lardner next poked fun at the pirated first-draft version of Stone's screenplay for suggesting that as many as five or six shots might have been fired in Dealey Plaza. "Is this the Kennedy assassination," Lardner chortled, "or the Charge of the Light Brigade?" As though only the ignorant could consider a fifth or even, smirk, a sixth shot realistic.

But here is what the House Assassinations Committee's final report said on page 68 about the number of shots detected on the famous acoustics tape: "Six sequences of impulses that could have been caused by a noise such as gunfire were initially identified as having been transmitted over channel 1 [of police radio]. Thus, they warranted further analysis." The committee analyzed only four of these impulses because (a) it was short of funds and time when the acoustics tape was discovered, (b) the impulses selected for analysis conformed to timing sequences of the Zapruder film, and (c) any fourth shot established a second gun and thus a conspiracy. All four of these impulses turned out to be shots. Numbers one and six remain to be analyzed. That is, the acoustics evidence shows that there were at least four shots and perhaps as many as six.

Lardner's most interesting error is his charge that *JFK* misstates the impact of the assassination on the growth of the Vietnam War. No doubt Stone's first-draft screenplay telescoped events in suggesting that LBJ began escalating the Vietnam War the second day after Dallas. Quietly and promptly, however, LBJ did indeed stop the military build-down that JFK had begun; and as soon as LBJ won the 1964 election as the peace candidate, he started taking the lid off. Motivated by a carefully staged pretext, the Gulf of Tonkin "incident," the bombing of North Vietnam began in February 1965. It is puzzling to see such a sophisticated journalist as Lardner trying to finesse the fact that Kennedy was moving toward deescalation when he was killed and that the massive explosion of the U.S. war effort occurred under Johnson. In this sense, it is not only reasonable but necessary to see the JFK assassination as a major turning point in the war.

Strangest of all is that Lardner himself has come to believe in a Dealey Plaza conspiracy, admitting that the Assassinations Committee's findings in this respect "still seem more plausible than any of the criticisms" and subsequently restating the point in a tossed-off "acknowledgment that a probable conspiracy took place."

The reader will search Lardner's writing in vain, however, for the slightest elaboration of this point even though it is obviously the crux of the entire debate. My own JFK file, for example, contains nineteen clippings with Lardner's byline and several *Washington Post* clippings by other writers from the period in which the Assassinations Committee announced its conspiracy findings. The only piece I can find among these that so much as whispers of support for the committee's work was written by myself and Jeff Goldberg (Chapter 11. "Did the Mob Kill Kennedy?").

If the Warren critics were a mere handful of quacks jabbering about UFOs, as Lardner insinuates, one might understand the venom he and other mainstreamers bring to this debate.

But this is simply not the case. The *Post*'s own poll shows that 56 percent of us—75 percent of those with an opinion—believe a conspiracy was afoot at Dallas. And it was the U.S. Congress, after a year-long, $4 million, expert investigation, that concluded, "President John F. Kennedy was probably assassinated as a result of a conspiracy."

The Reluctant Media

So what is it with the American news media and the JFK murder? Why do normally skeptical journalists reserve their most hostile skepticism for those who have tried to keep this case on the national agenda? What is it about Dealey Plaza that not even the massive disbelief of the American people and the imprimatur of the Congress can legitimate this issue to the news media?

As one who has followed this case closely and actively for nearly twenty years—and who has often heard the charge of "paranoia" as a response to the bill of particulars—I find it increasingly hard to resist concluding that the media's strange rage for silence in this matter presents us with a textbook case of denial, disassociation and double-think. I hear frustration and fear in the reasoning of Lardner and Margolis and their comrades who constantly erect straw men to destroy, and whose basic response to those who would argue the facts is yet another dose of *ad hominem* character assassination, as we are beholding in the media's response to Stone and Garrison: frustration because the media cannot stop Stone's movie from carrying the thesis of a JFK conspiracy to a global audience already strongly inclined to believe it; fear because the media cannot altogether suppress a doubt in their collective mind that the essential message of *JFK* may be correct after all, and that, if it is, their current relationship to the government may have to change profoundly.

About Clay Shaw

It is true that Garrison could not convince the New Orleans jury that Shaw had a motive to conspire against JFK. This is because he could not prove that Shaw was a CIA agent. Had Garrison been able to establish a Shaw link to the CIA, then JFK's adversarial relationship with the CIA's Task Force W assassination plots against Castro would have become material, and a plausible Shaw motive might have come into focus.

But in 1975, six years after Shaw's acquittal and a year after his death, a CIA headquarters staff officer, Victor Marchetti, disclosed that Garrison was right, that Shaw, and Ferrie as well, were indeed connected to the CIA. Marchetti further revealed that CIA Director Richard Helms—a supporter of the CIA-Mafia plots against Castro—had committed the CIA to helping Shaw in his trouble with Garrison. What the CIA might have done in this regard is not known, but Marchetti's revelation gives us every reason to presuppose a CIA hand in the wrecking of Garrison's case against Shaw.

George Lardner is not impressed by the proof of a CIA connection to Shaw. He responds dismissively that Shaw's CIA position was only that of informant: Shaw, he writes, "was a widely traveled businessman who had occasional contacts with the CIA's Domestic Contact Service. Does that make him an assassin?"

Of course not, and Garrison never claimed it did. But

it certainly does—or ought to—stimulate an interest in Shaw's relationship to Oswald and Ferrie. Is it not strikingly at variance with the Warren Commission's lone-nut theory of Oswald to find him circulating within a CIA orbit in the months just ahead of the assassination? Why is Lardner so hot to turn away from this evidence?

How fascinating, moreover, that Lardner should claim with such an air of finality to know all about Shaw's ties to the CIA, since a thing like this could only be known for a certainty to a highly placed CIA officer. And if Lardner is not himself an officer of the CIA, then all he can plausibly claim to know about Shaw is what the CIA chooses to tell him. Has George Lardner not heard that the CIA lies?

18

The Conspiracy That Won't Go Away*

We are in a screening room atop the Westin Hotel in New Orleans. It is July 1991 and Oliver Stone is in town filming *JFK*, his latest assault on establishment sensibilities, a movie with the premise that we do not yet know the truth about the assassination of President John F. Kennedy in Dallas on November 22, 1963.

Stone has already filmed the Dallas scenes. He has brought his company to New Orleans because *JFK* is based on the work of Jim Garrison, a young and aggressive district attorney at the time of the JFK murder. The lights dim and an image flickers to life on the screen. The clapper board reads JFK, SCENE 30. We are in a cell in the Dallas County Jail. It is June 1964, seven months after Dealey Plaza.

The prisoner is Jack Ruby, a stocky, nervous middle-aged man whom the whole world watched murder accused JFK assassin Lee Harvey Oswald on live TV two days after Oswald's arrest. Facing Ruby across a table, erect and somber in a black suit, sits Earl Warren, Chief Justice of the Supreme Court and the reluctant chairman

Playboy, February 1992.

of the President's Commission on the Assassination of President John F. Kennedy.

It is a tense moment. Ruby has insisted on testifying even though no one wants him to, least of all Warren himself. "Do you understand that I cannot tell the truth here in Dallas?" Ruby says. "That there are people here who do not want me to tell the truth?"

But Warren says only, "Mr. Ruby, I really can't see why you can't tell us now."

Ruby's desperation is palpable. "If I am eliminated," he says, "there won't be any way of knowing." He waits for a reaction, but Warren seems a genius at not getting on Ruby's wave length. He does not ask, "Knowing what?"

Finally, exasperated, Ruby blurts it out: "A whole new form of government is going to take over our country," he says, "and I know I won't live to see you another time. My life is in danger here. Do I sound screwy?"

And Warren's voice resonates in its most mournful basso, the words lingered over, tasted, given all their weight: "Well, I don't know what can be done, Mr. Ruby. Because I don't know what you anticipate we will encounter." Now the camera turns more closely on the heavy, solemn figure of Warren and, for a moment, it almost is Warren, the right age, the right look of stolid pride.

But the figure isn't Warren at all, of course. It's Jim Garrison. Not Kevin Costner, who plays the part of Garrison in the film, but Garrison himself, the real Garrison, all six and a half feet of him. No soul in all creation stands more opposed to Warren on the question of what happened in Dallas than does Garrison, the embattled nay-sayer of New Orleans, who was one of the first to hold that JFK was felled by conspiracy, that the same conspiracy acted through Ruby to kill Oswald and thus prevent a trial, and that the commission to which Warren gave his name was the front line of the most serious cover-up in American history.

"Warren must have spun madly in his grave," mused Garrison the next afternoon as we talked about this scene. "I can only hope the afterlife has sharpened his taste for irony."

Yet Stone was not just indulging his own taste for irony in casting Garrison in this role. "Between adversaries," Stone told me, "there can sometimes be great respect." Had Stone not seen in Garrison that respect for the adversary, his casting move could easily have backfired. Let Garrison's portrayal of Warren seem the least bit vindictive and the entire movie could come out looking like a cheap shot.

Garrison leaned forward with delight. "I'll swear I never said it," he remarked in his soft New Orleans drawl, "but I think it was a minor stroke of genius for Oliver to offer me this role. The great thing about it is that the screenplay uses Warren's words. And the more I studied them, the more I could see that Warren had developed such empathy with Ruby that he couldn't control himself completely. Although I've never forgiven Warren for what he did, he was a basically warm human being. You could tell he felt sorry for Ruby even as he evaded him. And in that final line, he told him more than he intended to. He confessed his own weakness."

His smile brightened. "And I think I was just the actor to bring this out. If Warren could see it, I think he'd smile."

Garrison's enactment of Warren seems a perfect summation of a career that has been to an uncommon degree shaped by irony, by a relationship with the mass media predicated on equal parts of mutual need and rejection.

JFK is based on Garrison's 1988 memoir, *On the Trail of the Assassins*. This in itself is satisfying to Garrison, now a retired Louisiana appeals-court judge. He finds it satisfying to see himself portrayed by an actor as convincing and warm as Kevin Costner in a movie directed with the artistry and drive of Oliver Stone.

But the mere news that Stone was making this movie was enough to reawaken the media furies that have bedeviled Garrison since he first joined the great hunt for the JFK conspiracy in 1966.*

A man less confident of his vision may have been shaken, but Garrison long since has become inured. "Being attacked with such vehemence from so many sides and for such a variety of reasons, I admit, is not conclusive proof that one is right," he says with a smile and a shrug. "But surely it goes a long way."

The controversy that rages around Garrison is set against the fact that he started out so all-American. He was born in 1921 in Denison, Iowa, to a family of tall lawyers that soon moved to New Orleans. At the age of nineteen, in 1940, he joined the U.S. Army and, in 1942, was commissioned as a lieutenant in the field artillery. He volunteered for flight training and spent the war on the European front flying light airplanes on low-level and often dangerous spotter missions. He saw combat in France and Germany and was present at the liberation of Dachau.

He came back to New Orleans, earned his law degree at Tulane and joined the FBI, which sent him to Seattle to check out the loyalty of defense employees, a job he soon found "greatly boring." He left the FBI and returned to New Orleans to go into private practice as a

*See Chapter 17.

trial lawyer. Then he went to work in the district attorney's office. He ran for a judgeship in 1960 and lost, but then, in 1961, quarreled publicly with Mayor Victor Schiro—whom he accused of "laxity in law enforcement"—and District Attorney Richard Dowling, whom he called "the great emancipator" because he "lets everyone go free."

This was the first burst of controversy in his career and it immediately propelled him to a higher orbit. He campaigned for D.A. in 1961, without the backing of the Democratic Party and without a big war chest. But he had the strong support of both blacks and blue-collar whites, a unique coalition in the South of the early 1960s. "To my surprise and to the astonishment of many others," he says, "I was elected."

He moved immediately to make good on his election promises. "If this entailed raising the level of confrontation," he recalls, "my attitude was, well, let the good times roll." He clamped down on organized gambling and prostitution, made Bourbon Street safe for tourists, challenged police corruption and criticized eight criminal-court judges for refusing to approve funds for his fight against racketeering. The judges sued him for defamation of character and won a judgment of $1000; but he appealed, arguing that elected judges were not exempt from public criticism. He won a reversal.

Jim Garrison was on the map.

So was Fidel Castro.

Castro overthrew Cuban dictator General Fulgencio Batista and took power in 1959. He announced a communist program. Cubans opposed to his government began flocking to Miami and New Orleans. Many of them formed counterrevolutionary organizations with such names as Alpha-66, the Cuban Revolutionary Council,

Free Cuba, the Cuban Expeditionary Force and the Cuban Brigade. All were sponsored by the CIA.

Their aim was to reverse Castro's revolution. This was the objective of their major military assault, Operation Zapata, organized by the CIA and the U.S. military. The world came to know Operation Zapata better as the Bay of Pigs Fiasco of April 1961. This attempted invasion failed to inspire the mass uprising that was its major strategic premise. The Zapata guerrillas were pinned down on their beachheads without a chance to declare a provisional government. Instead of sending in U.S. military support, JFK opted to cut his losses, standing by as the invasion force was captured and paying a humiliating ransom to rescue the prisoners. An angry self-pity soon gripped the anti-Castro militants and their U.S. supporters. They blamed Operation Zapata's failure on Kennedy. He had put them on the beach, then fled.

Then JFK betrayed them again, as they saw it, in October 1962, when a spy plane revealed Soviet missile bases under construction in Cuba. In the year and a half since the Bay of Pigs, the CIA had helped the exiles stage a series of commando raids against a variety of Cuban targets. But in the secret deal that ended the Cuban Missile Crisis with the dismantling of the Soviet bases, JFK promised that this activity would end.

This arrangement deeply affected an ultra-right-wing acquaintance of Garrison's named W. Guy Banister, a key player in the anti-Castro games of New Orleans. Banister served in the office of Naval Intelligence during World War II and after the war joined the FBI, rising to head its Chicago bureau. He left the FBI to become deputy chief of police in New Orleans, then resigned in 1957 to set up a private detective agency.

In 1962, at the time of the Cuban Missile Crisis, Banister was involved in running a CIA training camp for anti-Castro Cuban guerrillas on Lake Pontchartrain, north of New Orleans. Garrison had no idea at the time that Banister was involved in this activity. But he did know that Banister was not just another gumshoe for hire.

Guy Banister Associates, Inc., hung out its shingle, according to Garrison, "across the street from the building that housed the local offices of the CIA and the FBI. And across from that building was the New Orleans headquarters of Operation Mongoose." Operation Mongoose was an array of anti-Castro projects being run by the CIA, the Defense Department and the State Department under the coordination of Air Force Major General Edward G. Lansdale. Its CIA component, called Task Force W, was dedicated to the assassination of Castro. Its deepest secret was the fact that the CIA had contracted out his murder to the Mafia. Its headquarters was the meeting place for Cuban exiles coming in from Florida. "They were sleeping in the hallways," says Garrison.

Banister's key associate in these anti-Castro operations was a peculiar man named David Ferrie. Ferrie was an ace pilot, a kitchen-sink scientist, an omnivorous reader in the occult, a well-known denizen of the New Orleans gay scene, a militant activist against Castro and a great hater of JFK. His on-the-job homosexual activities had cost him his pilot's job at Eastern Airlines, but he had flown several clandestine flights to Castro's Cuba and was part of the training staff at the Lake Pontchartrain guerrilla camp. A rare chronic disease *(alopecia praecox)* having taken all his hair, he wore a wig made out of mohair and drew on his eyebrows with a grease pencil. He worked out of Banister's office, but he also served as a free-lance investigator for G. Wray Gill, a lawyer who represented Carlos Marcello, the Mafia godfather of New Orleans. Ferrie reputedly flew Marcello back into the

United States after his deportation by Robert Kennedy in 1961. On the day of JFK's murder, Ferrie was with Marcello in a New Orleans court as Marcello won a verdict against RFK's effort to deport him again.

But far stranger still among Banister's associates in the summer of 1963 was a young ex-Marine named Lee Harvey Oswald.

At first look, Oswald seems to be a creature of contradictions. On closer examination, the contradictions become complexities.

There was, on the one hand, the patriotic Oswald, a true-blue if emotionally mixed-up American kid raised in and around New Orleans, New York City and Fort Worth by his widowed (and twice-divorced) mother with the help of Aunt Lillian and Uncle "Dutz" Murret, a bookie in the Marcello gambling net. As a teenager in New Orleans, Oswald joined the local Civil Air Patrol and there met David Ferrie, its commander, in 1955. He tried to join the Marines but was rejected for being underage. He went home and memorized the Marine Corps manual and came back to try again as soon as he reached seventeen in October 1956, this time succeeding.

Oswald served his three years ably, rated "very competent" and "brighter than most" by his officers. The Marines cleared him for access to the performance characteristics of the top-secret U-2. They put him in a program of Russian-language training and instruction in the basics of Marxism-Leninism, as though he were being prepared for intelligence work. Indeed, a Navy intelligence operative named Gerry Hemming had thought as far back as 1959 that Oswald was "some type of agent." The House Select Committee on Assassinations noted that "the question of Oswald's possible affiliation with military intelligence could not be fully resolved."

On the other hand, there was Oswald the traitor. With only three months to go in the Marines, rather than await the normal discharge process, he applied for a hardship discharge for no good reason (citing a minor and already-healed injury to his mother's foot), then hurried to the Soviet Union. After two and a half years of Soviet communism, Oswald recanted. Now with a Russian wife and a daughter in tow, he returned to the United States, explaining in a written statement that "the Soviets have committed crimes unsurpassed even by their early-day capitalist counterparts."

So was he a good patriot again? No, now he announced himself to be a member of the Communist Party and became the founding and sole member of the New Orleans chapter of the Fair Play for Cuba Committee, three times seen passing out pro-Castro leaflets in New Orleans.

Yet, paradoxically, Oswald's frequent companion that summer in New Orleans was the militant anticommunist David Ferrie, with whom he had joined in loud public condemnations of Castro and JFK. During this same period, Oswald also spent time with Banister. He stamped Banister's office address on his pro-Castro leaflets and stored his extra copies there. He and Banister twice visited the campus of Louisiana State University and made themselves conspicuous in discussions with students in which their main theme was that JFK was a traitor. Not once during this time did Oswald associate with anyone actually sympathetic to Castro.

Oswald left New Orleans on September 25, 1963, and on the next day in Mexico City, according to the Warren reconstruction, registered as O. H. Lee at the Hotel del Comercio, a meeting place for anti-Castro Cuban exiles. He spent the next several days trying to get visas for travel to Cuba and the Soviet Union. In the process, he got into a prolonged row with a Cuban consular official.

The CIA had the Soviet and Cuban embassies staked out. It was later able to produce several photos of Oswald taken at these sites—as well as to supply tapes of several phone conversations between a Soviet embassy official and a man calling himself Oswald. There was a problem with the photos: they showed a large, powerfully built man in his mid-30s not in the least resembling Oswald. And there was a problem with the tapes: the CIA destroyed them, and the transcriptions contained garbled Russian, whereas Oswald was considered to be fluent in Russian. Even the row with the Cuban official presented a problem: interviewed by the Select Committee on Assassinations in 1978, the official said his Oswald was not the same one as the man arrested in Dallas. Moreover, two CIA spies working inside the Cuban consulate in 1963 agreed that "the real Oswald never came inside." They told the House Committee that they sensed "something weird was going on" in the Oswald incident.

There is also abundant evidence that Oswald was often impersonated quite apart from the alleged Mexico City trip.

Item: An FBI memo dated January 3, 1960, noted that "there is a possibility that an impostor is using Oswald's birth certificate." The real Oswald was in the Soviet Union at this time.

Item: Two salesmen at the Bolton Ford dealership in New Orleans were visited on January 20, 1961, by a Lee Oswald in the company of a powerfully built Latino. Oswald was looking for a deal on ten pickup trucks needed by the Friends of Democratic Cuba. On this date, Oswald was in the Soviet Union.

Item: On September 25, 1963, a man calling himself Harvey Oswald showed up at the Selective Service office in Austin to request help in getting his discharge upgraded from undesirable. On this date, Oswald was supposedly in transit to Mexico City.

Item: A highly credible Cuban émigrée, Sylvia Odio, told the Warren Commission that she was visited in Dallas by Oswald and two other men recruiting support for the anti-Castro cause. On the date of this encounter, the Warren Commission placed Oswald either in New Orleans or en route to Mexico.

Item: On November 1, 1963, a man later identified by three witnesses as Oswald entered a gun shop in Fort Worth and made a nuisance of himself while buying ammunition. The Warren Commission had evidence that Oswald was at work in Dallas that day.

Item: On November 9, 1963, when Warren Commission evidence placed Oswald at home in Irving, Texas, a man calling himself Lee Oswald walked into a Lincoln-Mercury showroom in Dallas and asked to take a car for a test drive. The salesman found the ride unforgettable in that Oswald reached speeds of 70 miles an hour while delivering a harangue about capitalist credit and the superiority of the Soviet system. Oswald, in fact, did not know how to drive a car.

Curiouser and curiouser, this Oswald who was all over the map and all over the political spectrum, in New Orleans and Fort Worth and Austin and Mexico City all at once, here a radical and there a reactionary. What to make of this man?

"This question became a very practical one for me," says Garrison, "on the day the President was killed and Oswald's picture was flashed around the world. As his résumé filled in over the next day and we found that he'd spent that summer in New Orleans, it became my duty as D.A. to see what we could find out about him."

Garrison soon discovered Oswald's ties to Ferrie. He brought Ferrie in for questioning on Monday the 25th, the day after Ruby murdered Oswald, then turned Ferrie over to the FBI for further questioning. "In those days," Garrison recalls, "I still believed in the FBI. They questioned Ferrie, found him clean and released him with a strange statement to the effect that they wouldn't have arrested him in the first place, that it was all my idea. Then they put a SECRET stamp on their forty-page interrogation report. But what did I know? I had burglaries and armed robberies to worry about. I went back to the real world. I was happy to do so."

Garrison's happy life in the real world came to an end for good about three years later. He at first saw no problem when the Warren *Report* was published in September 1964, holding that Oswald was a lone nut and Ruby another one. "Warren was a great judge and, one thought, wholly honest." Here and there a few spoilsports—Mark Lane, Edward J. Epstein, Harold Weisberg, Penn Jones, Sylvia Meagher, Josiah Thompson—were discovering problems with Warren's double lone-nut thesis, but Garrison was inclined as most Americans were to go along with it. "It seemed the easiest position to take," he says, "especially since the war in Vietnam was getting nasty and Americans of critical spirit were now caught up more in the mysteries of Saigon than in those of Dealey Plaza."

Then in 1966 came a fateful chance meeting with Louisiana's Senator Russell Long. The conversation turned to the Kennedy case. Long astounded Garrison by saying, "Those fellows on the Warren Commission were dead wrong. There's no way in the world that one man could have shot up Jack Kennedy that way."

Garrison immediately ordered the Warren *Report* plus

the 26 volumes of its hearings and exhibits. He plunged in, dedicating his evenings and weekends to the case.

He expected to find "a professional investigation," he says, but "found nothing of the sort. . . . There were promising leads everywhere that were never followed up, contradictions in the lone-assassin theory that were never resolved."

In particular, he was troubled by evidence that:

- Shots were fired from the so-called grassy knoll to the front and right of JFK as well as from behind.
- The maximum number of shots the alleged murder weapon could have fired was inadequate to account for the total number of bullet holes found in Kennedy and Texas Governor John Connally (who barely survived) unless one of the bullets had magically changed its direction in mid-flight.
- Nitrate tests performed on Oswald when he was arrested supported his claim that he had not fired a rifle in the previous 24 hours.
- Oswald appeared to have been trained as an intelligence agent in the Marines, which implied that his awkward display of sympathy for communism was phony.

Any one of these possibilities, Garrison realized, was enough to reduce the Oswald-acting-alone theory to ruins. "I was stunned," he says. "There were nights I couldn't sleep."

Finally, in November 1966, as he puts it, "I bit the magic bullet." Basing his jurisdiction on Oswald's 1963 summer in New Orleans, he secretly opened an investigation into the President's murder.

* * *

Of the four New Orleanians of primary interest to Garrison, the most interesting of all was Oswald himself, since Oswald had in a sense become Garrison's client. But he was dead. Next most interesting was Guy Banister, clearly at the center of New Orleans' anti-Castro scene. But Banister had died, too, of a heart attack in 1964.

Third came David Ferrie, quite alive in 1966. Garrison's investigators started compiling a portrait of Ferrie as a talented and impassioned anticommunist, a far-right soldier of fortune whose relationship with the reputedly procommunist Oswald during the summer of 1963 posed a question crucial to the clarification of Oswald's purposes—namely, as Garrison puts it, "What the hell were these guys doing together?"

By reconstructing the 1963 relationships of Oswald with Ferrie and Banister, Garrison hoped finally to make sense of the bundle of contradictions that was Oswald. But he never got a chance to do a proper job of it.

A bright young reporter for the *New Orleans States-Item,* Rosemary James, was routinely nosing through the D.A.'s budget in February 1967 when she noticed some unusual expenses. Garrison's men had spent some $8000 during the previous three months on such things as trips to Texas and Florida. What could they be up to? A few questions later and she had the story.

D.A. HERE LAUNCHES FULL J.F.K. DEATH-PLOT PROBE read the headline on the February 17 *States-Item.* MYSTERIOUS TRIPS COST LARGE SUMS. James's lead ran, "The Orleans parish district attorney's office has launched an intensive investigation into the circumstances surrounding the assassination of President John F. Kennedy."

In the ensuing pandemonium, Garrison found himself under enormous pressure from city hall and the media. He felt he had begun to build a strong conspiracy case against Ferrie in that Ferrie clearly hated JFK and clearly had a tie to Oswald, but that it was still not time to arrest him. His staff was meeting to debate the timing of Ferrie's arrest when word came that Ferrie had been found dead in his apartment, killed by a brain aneurysm. The coroner ruled the cause of death as natural, but Garrison saw indications of suicide: an empty bottle of Proloid—a medicine that could have pushed the hypertense Ferrie's metabolism over the red line—plus two typewritten and unsigned suicide notes.

Within hours came a report that Ferrie's militant anticommunist comrade, Eladio del Valle, had been found in a car in Miami, shot point-blank through the heart and with his head hatcheted open.

Now what? The stage was filled with enough dead bodies for an Elizabethan tragedy, and two of Garrison's key suspects were among them. Just one other was left.

Clay Shaw, born in 1913, was one of New Orleans' best known and most impressive citizens, a charming, richly cultivated and cosmopolitan businessman, a much-decorated Army officer during World War II detailed to the Office of Special Services and a founder and director of the International Trade Mart, a company specializing in commercial expositions. Shaw retired in 1965 to pursue interests in the arts, playwrighting and the restoration of the French Quarter, where he lived. He was a silver-haired, handsome *bon vivant* with high cheekbones, a ruddy complexion and an imposing six-foot-four frame.

Garrison had come to believe that Shaw was part of the JFK conspiracy. Research had turned up indications that Shaw was the mysterious Clay Bertrand who had phoned New Orleans attorney Dean Andrews on the day after the JFK hit to see if Andrews could arrange legal representation for Oswald. Garrison had found that Shaw led a double life in the New Orleans gay community and that Shaw was a friend of Ferrie's, who had been his pilot on at least one round trip to Montreal. Garrison had a witness, Perry Russo, who claimed to have been present when Ferrie, Shaw and a man Russo thought was Oswald discussed assassinating JFK.

More important, one of the D.A.'s assistants, Andrew Sciambra, had discovered an Oswald-Shaw link in Clinton, a rural Louisiana town. Dozens of people had seen Oswald in Clinton on two occasions in early September 1963, once as a passenger in a battered old car driven by a young woman and later in a shiny black Cadillac with two other men who waited for hours while Oswald, the only white in a long line of blacks, tried unsuccessfully to register to vote. Five Clinton witnesses testified that the men with Oswald were David Ferrie and Clay Shaw. The local marshal, curious about strange Cadillacs in town, traced the license plate to the International Trade Mart. He talked to the driver and later, at the trial, identified him as Shaw.

Garrison knew that such fragments didn't add up to an airtight conspiracy case. When I asked him if he was surprised to lose, he said, "Not really. I'm too good a trial lawyer. So why did I go to trial against Clay Shaw? Because I knew that somehow I had stumbled across the big toe of someone who was involved in one of the biggest crimes in history. And I was not about to become the person who did that and then let go and said, 'Oh, I might be violating a regulation.'"

Looking back, does he think this was an error?

"If it was an error, then it was an error that I was obliged to make."

But Garrison did not leap blindly into the prosecution of one of New Orleans' leading citizens. He first presented his evidence to a panel of three judges. They told him he had a case. Then he presented the evidence to a

12-member grand jury. The grand jury also ruled that there was sufficient evidence to try Shaw. And at that point, the decision was out of Garrison's hands: the law required him to proceed. Shaw's lawyers went all the way to the Supreme Court with an argument that the case should be thrown out, and they lost. After Shaw was acquitted, he filed a $5 million damages suit against Garrison for wrongful prosecution; the Supreme Court dismissed it.

But Garrison's case ran into many strange problems. One of his assistants provided the list of state's witnesses to Shaw's attorneys. An FBI agent with detailed knowledge of anti-Castro projects in New Orleans refused to testify for the prosecution, pleading executive privilege. The U.S. Attorney in Washington, D.C., "declined" to serve Garrison's subpoena on Allen Dulles, CIA chief at the time of the Bay of Pigs, who was in a position to clarify the relationship between Ferrie, Banister, Shaw and the CIA. The governors of Ohio, Nebraska, Texas and California refused on technical grounds to honor Garrison's requests for the extradition of witnesses. A federal agent told Garrison privately—but refused to testify—that Ferrie, Shaw and Banister were involved in handling Oswald. A witness critical to establishing that Shaw used the alias Clay Bertrand, a key issue, was not allowed to present his evidence.

Some of these difficulties may have arisen because, as later became known, both Shaw and Ferrie were contract agents of the CIA. This was revealed in 1974 when a former aide to CIA director Richard Helms, Victor Marchetti, noted he had heard Helms wonder aloud if the CIA were giving Shaw and Ferrie "all the help they need."

Without this knowledge, the jury got the case on March 1, 1969, two years to the day after Shaw's arrest. It took a little less than an hour to conclude unanimously that Shaw was not guilty of conspiring to kill Kennedy. In post-trial interviews, some jurors said Garrison convinced them that a conspiracy existed but not that Shaw had been a part of it. The Garrison who two years previously had promised, ''We are going to win this case, and everyone who bets against us is going to lose his money,'' could now sit down for a long, slow chew.

The loss didn't hurt him at the polls. He recorded his most lopsided victory ever in the elections of 1969.

But the story wasn't over.

Garrison had just risen from his breakfast and was still in his pajamas and robe when the doorbell rang. It was a posse of IRS men, there to arrest him on a charge of allowing pinball gambling in exchange for a bribe.

This was June 30, 1971. About two years later, in August 1973, the trial was held, Garrison arguing his own case (with the donated help of F. Lee Bailey). His defense revolved around one powerful basic point, namely, that the government's star witness against him, his former wartime buddy and colleague, Pershing Gervais, had been bribed by the government to make the accusation.

Garrison was acquitted of the bribery charge as well as of a follow-up charge of tax evasion the government pressed against him in 1974. ''A thing like that,'' he says, ''can be enjoyable if you have a cause and you're wrapped up in it. I'd say it was one of the high spots of my life. It was nothing to feel sorry about. I never went to bed with tears on my pillow.''

But another kind of attack on Garrison began about this time, most often in the work of other conspiracy theorists who began to wonder why Garrison said nothing about Mafia involvement in the JFK hit. There were mobsters all around Jack Ruby. The New Orleans godfather, Carlos Marcello, was right in Garrison's back yard. A Marcello lawyer worked with Ferrie. Ferrie was with Marcello the day JFK was shot. Yet Garrison seemed to ignore all this.

The charge is raised by writers (notably G. Robert Blakey and John H. Davis) who champion a Mafia-did-it theory of the crime and who themselves spend little ink on the evidence pointing to renegade federal agents. But Garrison's position on Mafia involvement was reflected in the 1979 report of the Select Committee on Assassinations (Blakey was its chief counsel), which stated that "the national syndicate of organized crime, as a group, was not involved in the assassination." As for the presence of individual mobsters, Garrison was among the first to see it. An FBI memo of March 28, 1967, reported that "Garrison plans to indict Carlos Marcello in the Kennedy assassination conspiracy because Garrison believes Marcello is tied up in some way with Jack Ruby." According to another FBI memo, June 10, 1967, "District Attorney Garrison believes that organized crime was responsible for the assassination." The memo goes on to explain Garrison's fear that the Mafia wanted to blame the crime on Castro and thus spark a U.S. retaliation that would lead to restoration of the Mafia's control of Cuban casinos.

More recently, Garrison has written that "Mob-related individuals do figure in the scenario." After all, the CIA and the Mafia shared an interest in Castro's overthrow, as is evident in their murderous alliance of Task Force W.

But Garrison does not believe that the Mafia could have set up Oswald, controlled the investigation of the crime and influenced the conclusions reached by the Warren Commission. "The CIA hired the Mafia," he points out, "not the other way around. If Carlos Marcello had killed

JFK on his own, he would never have gotten away with it.''

The merits of the CIA vs. Mafia debate aside, however, this was not a great time for Garrison. He lost a close race in the next election, and in 1974 left the D.A.'s office after twelve years of service. He spent the next few years in what he calls his interregnum, a period of relative quiet in which he wrote his one novel, *The Star-Spangled Contract,* a fictional treatment of his view of the JFK hit. That period ended in his successful campaign for a seat on the Louisiana court of appeals in 1977. He was inaugurated to a ten-year term in 1978 and re-elected in 1987. He reached mandatory retirement age of 70 in November 1991.

During the 1970s, the JFK case suddenly shot forward. Watergate and the resignation of President Nixon had already put the country in a mood to listen to conspiracy theories when Mafia boss Sam Giancana was shot down in his home on June 19, 1975, five days before he was to testify to a Senate committee. On July 28, 1976, Mafioso John Roselli was asphyxiated, dismembered and dumped into Miami's Dumfoundling Bay. Giancana and Roselli had both been deeply involved in the CIA-Mafia plots.* The atmosphere created by these events persuaded the House of Representatives by a vote of 280–65 to establish the Assassinations Committee.

That was September 17, 1976. Two and a half years and $6.5 million later, this committee reported its findings: conspiracy was ''probable'' in the death of JFK and a ''likelihood'' in the 1968 death of Martin Luther King, Jr. In neither case could the House committee offer a solution.

*Eight months later, three more major Dealey Plaza witnesses died violently inside a week. See Chapter 6.

But then came the Reagan years. The new Justice Department found the conspiracy evidence unconvincing and decided not to bother about it. And there the case has stood for the past decade—"stuck," as Garrison says, "not for want of something to do but for want of a government with the will to do it."

But Garrison is not resigned.

"Who killed President Kennedy?" he demands, just as though he still expected an answer. "That question is not going to disappear, no matter what the government does or does not do. It may fade into the background sometimes, but something will always evoke it again, as Oliver's movie is about to do now. It's basic to who we are as a people. We can no more escape it than Hamlet can escape his father's ghost."

But what can Hamlet do three decades later?

"There's a lot to do," says Garrison, "and since well over half the American people still gag on the lone-nut theory, there would appear to be a supportive constituency."

Garrison's program:

"First, open the files that the Warren Commission and the House committee classified as secret until the year 2039.

"Second, declassify the House committee's so-called Lopez Report, a 265-page document on Oswald's supposed trip to Mexico. Lopez himself has said he believes Oswald was set up. Why is this report still secret?

"Third, declassify all the files on Operation Mongoose and the CIA-Mafia murder plots. The Mongoose group seems to be at the center of the JFK conspiracy. We need to know every detail about it.

"And, no, these steps will not crack the case, but they will help us understand it better, and we can move on from there."

Someone else who had put so much into such a cause and who had so often been abused for his pains might feel defeated to have to settle for such small demands as these, and to realize that, small as they are, they are almost certainly not going to be met.

But Garrison doesn't see it that way. "The fight itself has been a most worthy one," he says quietly. "Most people go through their lives without the opportunity to serve an important cause. It's true that I've made some mistakes and had some setbacks. But who knows? To manhandle a line from *The Rubáiyát:* The moving finger has not stopped moving on yet. The full story's not in."

His smile becomes a beam. A light dances in his eyes.

"Clarence Darrow lost the Scopes trial," he says. "But who remembers that today?"

On *JFK* and Its Critics*

Whoever would reflect on the relationship of Hollywood to real politics must from now on begin with Oliver Stone's *JFK*. No film ever made—not *Grapes of Wrath*, not *Mr. Smith Goes to Washington*, not *Metropolis*, not *Dr. Strangelove*, not *Guess Who's Coming to Dinner*—has produced so impassioned a reaction in the sphere of the news media nor so prompt and concrete a result in the sphere of practical events.

The media battle about the film had in fact been launched months before, and within a month of the film's debut on December 20, 1991, was raging at full intensity with little sign of abating. No presses had yet been bombed on *JFK*'s account, but there was not a magazine that had not run its big think piece, not a newspaper that had not found ways to write the movie up again and again as a news event. Indeed, a few days before it opened, the *New York Times* fired a warning blast of contempt and outrage by senior editor Tom Wicker, then greeted the premier with no fewer than four pieces in the same issue: an editorial going to bat for Clay Shaw, a self-defense by Stone, a feature story on Jim Garrison's life as a judge, and a review by Vincent Canby who called the movie

*Memo to file, February 1992.

"simultaneously arrogant and timorous" and said it would leave the "uninformed . . . exhausted and bored" but allowed that there may be something to the conspiracy claim nonetheless.

It is much more significant that the stir over the movie has already provoked movement in the case itself. Senator Ted Kennedy, Richard Nixon and Representative Louis Stokes (who chaired the 1977–79 House Assassinations Committee) have now called for declassification of the secret files.

The House JFK file sits today in the National Archives in 838 (by one count) cardboard boxes, currently classified as secret and sealed until the year 2029. A box might have 3000 pages in it, so the whole file might consist of more than two million pages.

Several other JFK assassination files exist apart from the House file. Late in 1991, the archivist discovered twenty boxes of previously unknown Warren Commission files. Along with over twenty specific CIA and FBI documents in the closed Warren files, these documents are sealed to the year 2039. The CIA, the FBI and the military branches apparently have (or have destroyed) secret JFK files.

As I wrote of *JFK* weeks before the movie's release, it was to wonder at the extraordinary haste with which such print heavies as the *Washington Post*'s George Lardner, Jr. and syndicated columnist Jon Margolis had leapt to attack a project which in the first place was far from finished and in the second place was known to them only in the form of a pirated first-draft screenplay.

Now I wonder if Stone's critics hurt their own cause by baring their fangs so early. One could get the idea they were defending something more important to them than mere moral, historical and aesthetic standards, such as their reputations.

But they make a few salient points. As several *JFK* reviewers have observed, even people who sympathize with Stone's point of view can come out of this film with questions on their minds.

For one thing, as a card-carrying assassination revisionist, I am used to making an effort to keep separate the various lines of evidence pointing to the variety of suspects. My assumption is that, although JFK suffered an embarrassment of enemies, probably the hit was arranged by only one of them, or maybe by a small partnership. So it startled me to see Stone hurling the suspects one after the other into the boiling cauldron of conspiracy—the Mafia, the CIA, the Pentagon, Texas fat cats, Cubans—as though they might all be guilty together.

As a born advocate for this movie, moreover, I was troubled by the fact that Stone so freely interlaces fact about the case with fiction about Garrison. An audience of students might be able to supply running footnotes from scene to scene, but I was not convinced that this is such a good way to treat so fact-heavy a subject. Especially I thought Stone was too willing to paint out Garrison's flaws and gloss over his mistakes.

Such a result was no doubt implicit in the use of Garrison's 1988 memoir, *On the Trail of the Assassins,* as the basis of the screenplay. I admire Garrison and his book,* but might Stone not have achieved a more compelling statement with a screenplay more complex in its treatment of the principal figure?

Yet in overview, there is so much more to be happy than unhappy about in this film that it is almost carping to name the flaws. The flaws are there. We all can see

---

*And indeed contributed an "Afterword" to it. See Chapter 14, "Is the Mafia Theory a Valid Alternative?"

them. As Norman Mailer remarked in his review for *Vanity Fair,* "it is one of the worst great movies ever made," but still "the first thing to be said about *JFK* is that it is a great movie."

Surely the operative term here is *movie*. The row about factual accuracy has been very intense, so it is probably time to be reminded that the movie is *not* a history, *not* a documentary, *not* a brief for the defense of Oswald, but in every respect a work of fiction. Yes, it uses the real names of historical figures and attempts truthful reconstruction of historical events, but that did not keep *War and Peace* from being fiction. Stone's willingness to speculate about the secret life of public facts is a part of this movie's power. But the movie's impact and importance do not lie in its ability to tell us things we did not know. It is not an educational film. On the contrary, *JFK* is most effective when it mirrors what most of us indeed believe we know already. That is its purpose and its point—to give body to our fears about JFK's death. The movie exists to crystalize the paradigm of conspiracy within popular culture.

Soon after the first generation of critics had gone over the Warren Commission's 1964 report, a groundswell of expert and then public rejection of the lone-assassin finding began to develop. By the end of the decade, and despite more than because of the distractions of the Vietnam War and the protest against it, more than half of the American people had come to reject the Warren *Report*. A majority of us had become conspiracy theorists.

That majority has remained constant ever since. No revisionist thesis in the history of the republic has commanded such solid support for so long. A poll taken by Time-CNN as the Stone film opened last December showed 73 percent of us rejecting the Warren lone-assassin theory. (Nor did this mean that 27 percent accepted it. Only about 13 percent accepted it; the rest had no opinion.)

Thus, the one *historical fact* that lies at the heart of this film—the one fact in this dispute to which Stone is required to be utterly faithful—is the fact that America rejects the Warren *Report*. Period.

This is why the movie's factual shortcuts and improbable conspiracy scenarios are trivial flaws. It is not up to Stone to tell the historical truth about the JFK assassination. Only a professional investigative staff could do something like that. It is up to Stone only to reflect back into public consciousness the long-standing public conviction that the facts of the case, as they are now generally known, imply a conspiracy. I believe Arthur Schlesinger, Jr. was on target when he wrote in the *Wall Street Journal* (January 10, 1992) that "the more enduring residue of *JFK* will be the questions the film raises about the adequacy of the Warren Commission inquiry. These questions are legitimate." I would add only that, of course, it is not just the Warren Commission that *JFK* raises questions about but the whole panoply of issues of the Kennedy period: the Bay of Pigs, the Missile Crisis, the Vietnam War.

Stone's movie does not exist to prove our fears about this period, but to embody them, and the fact that it does so with such passion and confidence is what makes it so welcome.

The Hamlet Factor

In an attack on *JFK* in December 1991 in *The Nation*, columnist Alex Cockburn was especially aggrieved about a passage from the Garrison character's long speech to the jury toward the end. This is the part where the character observes that the JFK assassination puts us all in the position of Prince Hamlet. Cockburn quoted the following speech from the movie:

> We have all become Hamlets in our country, children of a slain father-leader whose killers still possess the throne. The ghost of John F. Kennedy confronts us with the secret murder at the heart of the American dream. He forces on us the appalling questions: Of what is our Constitution made? What is our citizenship—and more, our lives—worth? What is the future of democracy where a President can be assassinated under conspicuously suspicious circumstances while the machinery of legal action scarcely trembles?

"Stone wrote those words himself," howled Cockburn, pouncing on them for their "truly fascist yearning for the 'father-leader' taken from the children-people by conspiracy" and for "the crippling nuttiness" of believing "that virtue in government died in Dallas."

Actually, Stone did not write these words himself, nor did Garrison, nor did the screen writer, Zachary Sklar. Stone (not Sklar) incorporated them from the "Afterword" I wrote for Jim Garrison's 1988 book, *On the Trail of the Assassins* (reprinted here as Chapter 14). My passage reads as follows:

> [Garrison] threatens to make Hamlets of all who listen to him—children of a slain father-leader whose killers, for all we know, still in secret possess the throne. He confronts us with the secret murder at the heart of the contemporary American dilemma. His whole terrifying narrative forces down upon us the appalling questions: Of what is our Constitution made? What is our vaunted citizenship worth? What is the future of democracy in a country where a President can be assassinated under

conspicuously suspicious circumstances while the machinery of legal action scarcely trembles?

I suppose Cockburn will not like the Hamlet analogy or this piece of prose any better for knowing they come from me, but he might as well know whom to blame. Besides, I think his attack on this passage tickets me to defend it.

Perversely, Cockburn reaches to find a "fascist yearning" in the concern with the JFK assassination. What fascist yearning? A man was killed. *Three* men were killed. The stage was strewn with corpses. And just as was the case with the young prince of Shakespeare's play, the American people feel a sense not of "yearning" but of loss, victimization and dread. They are uncertain what knowing the truth about JFK's death might demand of them and would happily evade the whole thing if only they could: "O, that this too, too solid flesh would melt."

And maybe some of us do grieve for JFK as for a lost father, brother, TV companion, who knows. But so what? That sort of thing is normal in leadership relationships. Grief for JFK is all right. What makes it "fascist" to grieve?

And why should drawing an analogy between Hamlet's father's ghost and the dead JFK suggest to Cockburn that one is idolizing JFK, as though the ghost exemplified "virtue in government"? "I was cut off even in the blossoms of my sin," as the ghost tells Hamlet clearly, and "with all my imperfections on my head." The analogy to JFK seems complete.

Prince Hamlet and America have no satisfaction in seeing this conspiracy. Both are frightened and angry, aroused and confused, bold and hesitant. The bumper sticker of the Dealey Plaza revisionism movement reads:

''The time is out of joint. O cursed spite, that ever I was born to set it right.''

The most baffling of Cockburn's objections to *JFK* is that the manner of Kennedy's death is inconsequential, that his death would have had the same result ''if he had tripped over one of Caroline's dolls and broken his neck in the White House nursery.''

Where has Cockburn been? It is *exactly* the manner of JFK's death, not the mere fact that he suddenly died, that has vexed American politics for nearly three decades now. The mystery of Dealey Plaza is the heart of it. Without that mystery, the ghost goes away.

Cockburn writes as though it were the Warren revisionists rather than the orthodox who have something to prove, a conceit common among the orthodox of both left and right. One sees this self-flattering assumption most vividly in the *New York Times* writers, egregiously in Tom Wicker, who despite all the evidence to the contrary continue to approach this story as though their audience shared their bias. With all the aplomb they can muster, they stand explaining to an empty room why no one believes the other side.

To fight JFK's deification, Cockburn tries to demonize him. How much more natural to say that JFK was, simply, a normal person with good and bad points, a man who sometimes learned from his mistakes but who never knew everything he needed to know. Then at least, instead of sanctifying or demonizing Kennedy, we could try to weigh him on the balances.

In that case, how do we weigh him on Vietnam?

Stone's movie says that JFK turned against the Vietnam War during his last half year of life, that he would have withdrawn us from the war once he was in his second term, and that he had perhaps already begun a withdrawal when he was killed. Cockburn says that JFK would have done just what Johnson did.

JFK came to office an unformed, unfinished and highly seductive person, driven probably by the simple will to power. Once he achieved power—the presidency—by hook, crook and seduction, he was confused for perhaps two years as to what to do with it. He allowed the CIA to make a contract with organized crime to assassinate Castro, then declared war on organized crime. He gave us both the Peace Corps and the Special Forces on impulses that were both divided and linked, equally highminded and cynical. He invaded Cuba, then stranded the expedition on the beach. He created the Alliance for Progress, then let the Special Forces and the CIA make violence an instrument of U.S. policy in the Third World. He gave the military and the defense industry a missile gap, then took it back. He gave American blacks a civilrights program that he probably knew he could not enact. He purchased a stylish rhetoric ready-made, then called it his own. He invoked the chivalry of Camelot, then womanized in the White House as though it were a bordello.

So would JFK have ended the war in his second term or escalated it as Johnson did? This has become the major point of controversy in the discussion of Stone's film, which is not the least of the film's achievements. The debate has too long been confined to a few academics and journalists. It is too important for that. As Stone is hardly the first but perhaps the most influential person to say, the Vietnam War is "the watershed experience of our times." It is important for us to know why and how we decided to fight it.

As with the debate about the assassination, the debate about JFK's Vietnam policy will not be resolved quickly. Certain secondary-source historians (e.g., Stanley Karnow, *Vietnam: A History,* 1983) and journalists (such as George Lardner, Jr. of the *Washington Post)* convince Cockburn that JFK "never entertained the idea of a settlement."

On the other side of the question, convinced that JFK planned and was even beginning a disengagement, are Senators Wayne Morse, Ernest Gruening and Mike Mansfield, Representative Tip O'Neill and Generals James Gavin and Bruce Palmer.

Many who were utter but fascinated bystanders to the politics of the Vietnam "counterinsurgency operation" in 1963, as was I (working for a defense company with Vietnam contracts), got the strong impression that Kennedy had become skeptical of the chances of an affordable military victory in Vietnam. The important new historical work by Army Major John Newman, *JFK and Vietnam* (Time Warner, 1992) picks up where Air Force Colonel L. Fletcher Prouty *(The Secret Team,* Prentice Hall, 1973) leaves off in articulating this argument. Newman's basic point is that during the summer of 1963 JFK made a decision to curtail further escalation in Vietnam and to start looking for a way out. He had decided, says Newman, that the game was not worth the candle. As Chapter 4, above, makes clear, I argued the same position in 1976.

But the issue is rich and complex precisely because it is to a certain degree enmeshed in the ambiguities and contradictions of JFK's quite unfinished personality. President Kennedy was a work in progress when he was killed. It is a great loss that we never got to see the finished product, but it was also a kind of national disaster that he chose to treat the White House as a finishing school.

VI

Theories and Action

This final brief section consists of a tabulation of the usual suspects in the case. The reader may have noticed a tilt toward the Mongoose theory in the previous pages, but I mean to decline a choice of scenarios at this point. Suspicions are one thing, convictions another. We have too much evidence not to be suspicious, not enough to be convinced.

As to what should be done to move our understanding ahead, the final piece in the book, drafted to begin with as a statement that others might sign as well, enumerates a set of basically straightforward and inexpensive steps the Congress and the President could take right now. They would not solve the mystery, but they might help settle certain outstanding technical questions about the shooting.

20

Round Up the Usual Suspects

If the single-bullet theory falls, then the lone-assassin theory falls with it. If the lone-assassin theory falls, then we must postulate a secret plot, an active conspiracy, and we must speculate about its people, purposes and organization.

There is no doubt also a psychological need to seek answers to the riddle of Dallas. The assassination of a head of state is not something to walk away from in casual frustration. If there were a satisfactory official account of the facts in the case, people would no doubt accept it (as they do, for example, in the shootings of Ronald Reagan and John Lennon). It is because there is no satisfactory official account and, further, because the official account seems cobbled together irrationally that so many have tried their hand at solving the riddle.

Warren defenders are doubtless correct in observing that conspiracy theorists often reflect their larger political beliefs in their attempts to explain the mystery, but that is equally true of the Warrenites. Why indeed would a George Will snarl that JFK conspiracy theorists are ''worse than those who deny the Holocaust'' unless he were trying to drive people away from the riddle and restore the security of the official theory? Surely it is not because he believes there is nothing to argue about in the case. Quite apart from the single-bullet theory and the direction of the headshot, there are immense uncertainties about the acoustics evidence, Oswald's intelligence ties, and Ruby's ties to the Cuban Mafia, to name just three other examples. People do not make these uncertainties up. They arise from the official record.

A tabulation of the basic alternative theories follows, giving the theory, its proponents, its scenario, its take on the assassination motive, its strong points and its drawbacks.

Who killed JFK?
There are as many theories
as theorists.
These are the classics.

SUSPECT: Khrushchev

THEORISTS

CIA counterintelligence chief James Jesus Angleton, Lyndon Johnson sometimes, Earl Warren, Edward Jo Epstein

SCENARIO

KGB recruited Oswald to make the hit

MOTIVE

Retaliation for Soviet setback in October Missile Crisis

STRONG POINT

Explains the official cover-up since discovery of a KGB hand in JFK could have meant nuclear war with USSR and 40 million U.S. casualties

DRAWBACK

Would the KGB trust Oswald? Would USSR risk war to promote LBJ?

SUSPECT: Castro

THEORISTS

Ambassador to Mexico Thomas Mann, columnist Jack Anderson, Mafia lieutenant John Roselli, Lyndon Johnson sometimes

---

SCENARIO

Castro recruited Oswald to hit JFK; in a variant, Castro captured and "turned" a CIA-Cuban hit squad sent by JFK to hit him

MOTIVE

Castro retaliation for JFK-CIA-Mafia attempts on his own life

STRONG POINT

Castro called JFK a "ruffian," threatened that CIA attacks on his life might "boomerang"

DRAWBACK

Castro liked JFK, disliked LBJ, had no access to Oswald, faced destruction if caught

SUSPECT: The Mafia

THEORISTS

Assassinations Committee, G. Robert Blakey, John H. Davis, David Scheim

SCENARIO

Mafia recruited Oswald, maybe also a second "nut"

MOTIVE

Stop JFK's anti-crime campaign

STRONG POINT

Many Mafia threats against JFK are on record; LBJ was softer on crime

DRAWBACK

Mafia had more expert hitmen than Oswald; could not have insured cover-up

SUSPECT: The Mongoose Team

THEORISTS

Jim Garrison, Fletcher Prouty, Mark Lane,

Robert Grodon, David Lifton, Jim Marrs, Philip Melanson, Peter Dale Scott

SCENARIO

Disaffected CIA and MI vets of Operation Mongoose formed "Enterprise"-type cabal, set up Oswald as patsy, planted false clues pointing to Cuba, USSR, Mafia

MOTIVE

JFK was soft on communism, was losing the Cold War, had lost Cuba, was losing Vietnam

STRONG POINT

Explains failure of official investigation, frame-up of Oswald

DRAWBACK

Cannot be officially proved until government is willing to risk its own legitimacy

SUSPECT: The Nazi "Odessa" Underground

THEORIST

Pseudonymous "William Torbitt"

SCENARIO

Post-war Nazi underground, "the Odessa," operated through U.S. intelligence assets

MOTIVE

JFK was losing the war against world Bolshevism

STRONG POINT

Explains link between Clay Shaw and Permindex, the latter being considered by some researchers a front for the Odessa

DRAWBACK

No conceivable proof or disproof; theory appeals to paranoia, which may be a plus

21

What to Do Now on the JFK Case

One hard fact about the great JFK assassination debate is that only about ten percent of the American people agree with the Warren Commission that Oswald was JFK's lone assassin. For over a quarter century, well over half of us have believed that JFK was killed by a conspiracy. The most recent poll, taken for Time/CNN in December 1991 (*before* the opening of Oliver Stone's movie, *JFK)*, showed that about three out of four of us reject the lone-gunman theory and indeed that over half of us believe that the CIA itself was somehow involved.

Whatever the merits of this view, it may not be healthy for so large a majority of us to be so deeply and for such a long time at odds with our government on a matter of such concern. No one profits from this situation, and the government should do what it can to resolve it. Several steps to move the debate ahead can be taken immediately and without undue expense.

1. Release all government JFK files.

As it closed down in early 1979, the House Select Committee on Assassinations did just what it began by promising not to do—and just what the Warren Commission before it had done—and deliberately sealed its files until the year 2029.

These files are in 848 boxes. Since each of these boxes may contain as many as 3,000 pages, we may be dealing here with two and half million pages.

A strong movement for the release of these documents has sprung up in the wake of the Stone film, supported (among many others) by Representative Louis Stokes (Ohio Democrat), who chaired the Assassinations Committee (and sealed its files in the first place) and by Senator Edward Kennedy.

This is to be welcomed, but the public should know that release of these files will almost certainly not reveal a smoking gun even if they contain one. This is because any legislation mandating their release is certain to contain restrictions protecting confidential sources, personal privacy, and national security. The CIA and the FBI will have the final say on what is released.

At least one particular segment of these files, however, is of particular and perhaps sensational interest—namely, a 265-page investigative report on Oswald's curious trip to Mexico City two months before the assassination. Known as the Lopez report (after its principal author, attorney Edwin Lopez), this document was immediately classified secret by the Assassinations Committee, and it was mentioned neither in the committee's 1979 final report nor in the 1981 book *The Plot to Kill the President*, by G. Robert Blakey, (the committee's chief counsel) and Richard N. Billings (its chief writer). Lopez has risked violation of his secrecy agreement to say publicly that his investigation did not support the Warren Commission's conclusion that Oswald had visited the Cuban consulate and the Soviet embassy in Mexico City demanding entrance to Cuba and a visa for return to the USSR. Lopez has said, in fact, that the conclusion he and his investigative team reached—and presumably documented in their secret report—was that Oswald had in fact been impersonated in Mexico City. This conclusion is supported by the facts (1) that a CIA photo of an "Oswald" at the Cuban consulate is clearly not Oswald and (2) that a CIA phone tap of an "Oswald" calling the Soviet embassy (according to two FBI men who heard the tape before destroying it) did not have Oswald's voice on it. Proof that Oswald was being impersonated at such a time and place would at least demand a radical reassessment of his alleged role in the events of Dallas.

The public should also be aware that even more interesting collections of secret documents exist under the control of the executive branch. These include the remaining unreleased records of the Warren Commission (1964) and the Rockefeller Commission (1975), as well as FBI, CIA, and other federal agency records which were never turned over to any other body. Of particular importance is the CIA's file on Oswald. Also fascinating was the discovery late in 1991 of some twenty boxes of Warren Commission documents that had not been previously catalogued. President Bush should direct that all these records be made public.

2. Declassify CIA files on the CIA-Mafia assassination program (Operation Mongoose, JM/Wave, and Task Force W).

Except for member Allen Dulles, who kept mum, the Warren Commission had no idea that the CIA had contracted with Mafia leaders to murder Castro. The project, code-named Task Force W and led by William Harvey, was organized under the canopy of a larger CIA anti-Castro program code-named JM/Wave, which itself was part of a government-wide program known as Operation Mongoose. If the JFK conspiracy encompassed rogue agents, Mafia godfathers and anti-Castro Cubans, Task Force W is a logical place to search.

3. Immunize and publicly depose Frank Ragano.

Jimmy Hoffa lawyer Frank Ragano has recently claimed to have been privy to certain sectors of organized crime in the 1950s, '60s, and '70s and to have knowledge that Hoffa, Carlos Marcello, and Santos Trafficante plotted the JFK hit. The FBI should immunize and interrogate Ragano. If his story holds up, a congressional committee should examine him publicly.

4. Complete the analysis of the acoustics evidence.

The single most important piece of evidence developed by the HSCA in 1978 was a Dallas police recording of the shots fired in Dealey Plaza. Laboratory analysis of this recording revealed that at least four shots were fired, three from behind the President and one from ahead. But after the HSCA was dissolved, the National Academy of Sciences rejected this analysis when a voice transmission known to have occurred about a minute after the shooting was discovered in the background of the putative shots. The committee's two teams of scientific experts, however, informally rebutted the NAS finding and reaffirmed their original finding of four shots and two gunmen. Congress should seek new expert opinion and further testing on this point.

5. Conduct ballistics-lab tests of the single-bullet theory.

The heart of the lone-assassin theory is the controversial claim that a single bullet caused all the nonfatal wounds to the President and to Governor John Connally. If this conclusion falls, then the lone-assassin theory falls.

In view of its central importance to the Warren Commission's reconstruction of the crime, this theory ought long since have been subjected to ballistics-lab analysis. Congress should at last remedy this striking omission.

6. Analyze the Bronson film.

An 8mm movie of the Dallas motorcade taken by Charles L. Bronson reached the Assassinations Committee too late for computer-assisted analysis by its photographic panel, but preliminary examination indicated that it may reveal two and possibly three people in the area of the Book Depository known as the "sniper's nest"—that is, the area on the southeast corner of the sixth floor from which the Warren Commission said all shots were fired. The discovery of a second person in the sniper's nest only seconds before the shooting would have obvious implications for the lone-assassin theory.

* * *

These six steps can be taken quickly without undue expense or the creation of a special legal apparatus. If document releases and new tests fail to support the lone-assassin theory, Congress should launch a new full-scale investigation. In view of the public's dissatisfying experience to date with presidential commission and congressional committees, any new investigative body should include civilian members.

Selected Bibliography

There are now about 600 titles on the JFK case. The following are recommended, though not uniformly endorsed.

Blakey, G. Robert, and Richard Billings. *The Plot to Kill the President: Organized Crime Assassinated JFK.* New York: Times Books, 1981.

Davis, John H. *Mafia Kingfish: Carlos Marcello and the Assassination of John F. Kennedy.* New York: McGraw-Hill, 1989; NAL Signet, 1990.

Garrison, Jim. *On the Trail of the Assassins: My Investigation and Prosecution of the Murder of President Kennedy.* New York: Sheridan Square Press, 1988.

Groden, Robert J., and Harrison Edward Livingstone. *High Treason, The Assassination of President John F. Kennedy: What Really Happened.* New York: The Conservatory Press, 1989.

Kantor, Seth. *Who Was Jack Ruby?* New York: Everest House, 1978.

Lane, Mark. *Rush to Judgment.* New York: Holt Rinehart Winston, 1966.

Lifton, David S. *Best Evidence: Disguise and Deception in the Assassination of John F. Kennedy.* New York: Macmillan Publishing Co., 1980; Carroll & Graff, 1988.

Marrs, Jim. *Crossfire: The Plot that Killed Kennedy.* New York: Carrol & Graff, 1989.

Meagher, Sylvia. *Accessories After the Fact: The Warren Commission, the Authorities and the Report.* New York: Random House, 1967; republished with preface by Sen.

Richard S. Schweiker (R-Pa) and intro. by Peter Dale Scott, Vintage Books, 1976.

Melanson, Philip. *Spy Saga.* Praeger, 1990.

Miller, Tom. *The Assassination Please Almanac.* Chicago: Regnery, 1977.

Moldea, Dan. *The Hoffa Wars.* New York: Paddington Press, 1978.

Morrow, Robert D. *Betrayal: A Reconstruction of Certain Clandestine Events from the Bay of Pigs to the Assassination of John F. Kennedy.* Chicago: Regnery, 1976.

North, Mark. *Act of Treason: The Role of J. Edgar Hoover in the Assassination of President Kennedy.* New York: Carroll & Graff, 1991.

Oglesby, Carl. *The Yankee and Cowboy War.* New York: Berkley, 1977.

Oglesby, Carl. *Who Killed JFK?* Berkeley: Odonian Press, 1992.

Prouty, L. Fletcher. *The Secret Team.* New York: Prentice Hall, 1973.

Ranalegh, John. *The Agency: The Rise and Decline of the CIA.* New York: Simon and Schuster, 1987.

Reeves, Thomas C. *A Question of Character, A Life of John F. Kennedy.* New York: Free Press, 1991.

Scheim, David E. *Contract on America: The Mafia Murder of President John F. Kennedy.* New York: Shapolsky Publishers, 1988.

Scott, Peter Dale. *Crime and Cover-Up: The CIA, the Mafia, and the Dallas-Watergate Connection.* Berkeley: Westworks, 1977.

House Select Committee on Assassinations: Report and Vols. I–XI. Washington, D.C.: Government Printing Office, 1979.

Senate Select Committee to Study Governmental Operations with Respect to Intelligence Activities, Final Report (The Church Report). Washington, D.C.: Government Printing Office, April 23, 1976.

Shaw, Gray. *Cover-Up.* Self-published, 1976.

Summers, Anthony. *Conspiracy.* New York: McGraw-Hill, 1980; expanded edition, Paragon House, 1989.

Taylor, Maxwell, Board of Inquiry. *Operation Zapata, The "Ultrasensitive" Report and Testimony of the Board of*

Inquiry on the Bay of Pigs. Frederick, Md.: University Publications of America, 1981.

Thompson, Josiah. *Six Seconds in Dallas: A Micro-Study of the Kennedy Assassination.* New York: Bernard Geis Associations, 1967.